THE **COMPLETE IDIOT'S GUIDE** TO

Barefoot Running

by Dr. Craig Richards and
Thomas Hollowell

ALPHA

A member of Penguin Group (USA) Inc.

ALPHA BOOKS

Published by the Penguin Group

Penguin Group (USA) Inc., 375 Hudson Street, New York, New York 10014, USA

Penguin Group (Canada), 90 Eglinton Avenue East, Suite 700, Toronto, Ontario M4P 2Y3, Canada (a division of Pearson Penguin Canada Inc.)

Penguin Books Ltd., 80 Strand, London WC2R 0RL, England

Penguin Ireland, 25 St. Stephen's Green, Dublin 2, Ireland (a division of Penguin Books Ltd.)

Penguin Group (Australia), 250 Camberwell Road, Camberwell, Victoria 3124, Australia (a division of Pearson Australia Group Pty. Ltd.)

Penguin Books India Pvt. Ltd., 11 Community Centre, Panchsheel Park, New Delhi—110 017, India

Penguin Group (NZ), 67 Apollo Drive, Rosedale, North Shore, Auckland 1311, New Zealand (a division of Pearson New Zealand Ltd.)

Penguin Books (South Africa) (Pty.) Ltd., 24 Sturdee Avenue, Rosebank, Johannesburg 2196, South Africa

Penguin Books Ltd., Registered Offices: 80 Strand, London WC2R 0RL, England

Copyright © 2011 by Craig Richards and Thomas Hollowell

International Standard Book Number: 978-1-61564-062-1
Library of Congress Catalog Card Number: 2010910371

13   12   11   8   7   6   5   4   3   2   1

Interpretation of the printing code: The rightmost number of the first series of numbers is the year of the book's printing; the rightmost number of the second series of numbers is the number of the book's printing. For example, a printing code of 11-1 shows that the first printing occurred in 2011.

Printed in the United States of America

Note: This publication contains the opinions and ideas of its authors. It is intended to provide helpful and informative material on the subject matter covered. It is sold with the understanding that the authors and publisher are not engaged in rendering professional services in the book. If the reader requires personal assistance or advice, a competent professional should be consulted.

The authors and publisher specifically disclaim any responsibility for any liability, loss, or risk, personal or otherwise, which is incurred as a consequence, directly or indirectly, of the use and application of any of the contents of this book.

Most Alpha books are available at special quantity discounts for bulk purchases for sales promotions, premiums, fundraising, or educational use. Special books, or book excerpts, can also be created to fit specific needs.

For details, write: Special Markets, Alpha Books, 375 Hudson Street, New York, NY 10014.

Publisher: *Marie Butler-Knight*

Associate Publisher: *Mike Sanders*

Senior Managing Editor: *Billy Fields*

Acquisitions Editor: *Tom Stevens*

Senior Development Editor: *Phil Kitchel*

Production Editor: *Kayla Dugger*

Copy Editor: *Tricia Liebig*

Cover Designer: *Rebecca Batchelor*

Book Designers: *William Thomas, Rebecca Batchelor*

Indexer: *Celia McCoy*

Layout: *Ayanna Lacey*

Proofreader: *John Etchison*

Contents

Appendixes

Introduction

Every so often an innovation comes along and surprises us by transforming the way we think about, play, and enjoy sports. Bikes have gotten lighter, swimsuits more aerodynamic, and golf clubs more precise. We know more about our own bodies, ways of training, and how to prepare for events than ever. We can all thank science, ingenuity, thinking outside of the box, and dedicated athletes for allowing sports to evolve to higher levels.

Running is no exception. The sport has also undergone transformations that have taken it to heights once thought unreachable. Somewhere along our recent path of discovery, however, we forgot about the crucial role our feet play in helping us respond to the world around us. In essence, we have taken them out of the running equation entirely by developing shoes that control every aspect of how we run.

That's where barefoot running comes in. Taking a step forward involves taking one step back. Barefoot running is a new way to think about how we were meant to run: more naturally, efficiently, and without injury.

By allowing your feet to feel, flex, and respond to the ground, you will build strengths that you never even knew you possessed, from more robust feet to stronger legs and proficient form. Barefoot running will teach you much about your own body and its abilities. It will help you build strength and improve your form. It will help you take your running to the next level.

Because it is paramount that you take it slowly while your body builds itself stronger, we have put this guide together to help you easily navigate your way through all the essential stages. We give you an overview of barefoot running, reasons to let your feet lead the way, a history of the modern running shoe, and what medical conditions might limit your barefoot running ambitions. We become your personal coach, teaching you how to get your feet used to feeling the ground, how to plan ahead, how to overcome barriers, and how to perfect your form along the way. We let you decide if minimal footwear (barefoot running shoes) is really an option for you, then head off-road into the wild outdoors to get your feet accustomed to all kinds of terrain. You'll also learn about managing weather, dealing with injury, and avoiding possible perils along the way. Lastly, we assist you in taking your own running further. Learn how to run both faster and longer, whether barefoot or in minimalist shoes. We also talk about the importance of nutrition with a natural, "bare" perspective.

When it comes to barefoot running, the sky is the limit. Enjoy both the journey and the destination. It is all a part of the barefoot fun!

How This Book Is Organized

We have divided the contents of this book into four parts to make the information easy to digest. Inside, you'll find information that appeals to both the novice and well-established runner wanting to learn more about the various ways barefoot running might benefit them.

Part 1, An Overview of Barefoot Running, gives you a thorough overview of the world of barefoot running. From the benefits to the arguments against it, we help you make your own informed decision about barefoot running. We take you on a historical adventure to learn why shoe design has changed so much over the years. We also help you through the tricky steps of assessing whether you should seek medical advice before running without shoes.

Part 2, Getting Started on the Right Foot, helps you get started with the art of barefoot running. From strengthening and stretching the feet to walking and eventually running shoeless, you will learn how to make a full barefoot transition. Learn about the fundamentals of technique to make yourself an efficient, forward-motion machine.

Part 3, Surviving the Elements, talks about the new world your feet will experience without shoes. Decide for yourself if minimal footwear might be right for you. Learn how to handle all the facets of barefoot trail running like a pro. Become proficient in running all year long, no matter the weather or temperature. And when accidents happen, know how to take care of your feet, legs, and body to not only assess but prevent injury.

Part 4, In the Long Run, discusses how you can take your barefoot running to new levels by gradually focusing more on distance and speed. Train smarter than ever by listening to your body, and learn to compete barefoot or in minimal footwear during your favorite events or races. Finally, find out the secrets of barefoot nutrition and the importance of fueling while training your body to run more naturally.

To make things both fun and easy, we have included several sidebars of helpful information:

DEFINITION

These are explanations of key words and phrases that will help you better understand the human body and barefoot running.

FROM THE SOLE

Here, we detail other dimensions of barefoot running of which you might not be aware, including fun facts and helpful tidbits of information.

ON YOUR TOES

Pay attention to these particularly important warnings about potential perils in your path.

TIP TOES

Here you will find helpful tips and sound advice about various facets of barefoot running.

Acknowledgments

I would like to thank my beautiful wife and daughter for all their love and support whilst I was writing this book. I would also like to thank the intellectuals who paved the road to the barefoot revolution: Steven Robbins, Benno Nigg, Joseph Froncioni, and Daniel Lieberman—we owe it all to you. And lastly, I am grateful to the running shoe manufacturers who made this book possible by creating an entire generation who have forgotten how to run naturally.

—Dr. Craig Richards

I would like to thank Fazia for her continued love and support as I pursue my writing and barefoot running dreams. I would like to express gratefulness to my agent, Mr. Bob Diforio, for his receptive and friendly modus operandi. Thank you also Mr. Tom Stevens at Alpha/Penguin for his belief in this book. I am indebted to Abbie Mood, the managing editor of www.Barefoot-Running.us, and JoAnna Haugen for their insight and editorial prowess. Terry, my eternal equal (a.k.a. loving twin brother), this was your brainchild as we ran shoeless that summer evening—I hope you enjoy! And Craig, thanks for all your hard work!

—Thomas Hollowell

Trademarks

All terms mentioned in this book that are known to be or are suspected of being trademarks or service marks have been appropriately capitalized. Alpha Books and Penguin Group (USA) Inc. cannot attest to the accuracy of this information. Use of a term in this book should not be regarded as affecting the validity of any trademark or service mark.

An Overview of Barefoot Running

Barefoot running is a whole new approach to the world of running. Research done thus far reveals its numerous advantages in regard to the lessened impact on and increased strengthening of the entire body. The goal in this part is to help you understand what barefoot running is all about, highlight your "smart feet," reveal the truths behind modern running shoe design, and help you decipher if any medical conditions might inhibit your barefoot running aspirations.

By understanding all of these facets, you will have a solid base of information to decide how you might like to use barefoot running in your training program. You might choose to run barefoot full time. Or you may wish to use it for warming up or cooling down. What we hope to show you is that increased barefoot activity will only help you achieve more no matter your running or fitness goals.

Learning About Barefoot Running

Chapter

1

In This Chapter

- What you should know about barefoot running
- When you should begin barefoot running
- Why running without shoes is healthy
- What the pros and cons are of barefoot running

Runners are starting a revolution by taking their awareness, skills, and proficiency to the next level. Their chosen mode of transport? Bare feet.

Barefoot running is not just about asking runners to toss aside their shoes. Rather, the goal of barefoot running is to help teach the minds and bodies of both novice and expert runners to perform more naturally and efficiently with less chance of injury. It can also teach runners worldwide how to connect with their surroundings and run more mindfully and joyfully.

A New Start on Running

Aristotle was one of the first philosophers to come up with the idea that the human mind is a *tabula rasa* at birth—a blank slate that is written upon throughout life. For many recreational runners, their slates have most likely been filled with a hodgepodge of training methods, some helpful and some potentially harmful. Runners who have had coaches showing them the ropes might have a better grasp on how to train, but they may not be conscious of the finer points of strengthening or form promoted by barefoot running.

The best feature of a slate is that it can be erased; however, wiping it clean and starting fresh takes time, dedication, persistence, and a clear path.

Barefoot running offers recreational joggers, runners, and even accomplished athletes an opportunity to approach their sport from a different perspective. It helps them develop innovative methods of training that will eventually overwrite old lessons. If you've been tying up your running shoes every afternoon for as long as you can remember, it may be difficult to change your body's habits, but with mental fortitude and a commitment to a new running style, even you can become a barefoot runner.

Learning the fundamentals of running barefoot is just one step. The practice requires that you think about running differently, plan for the long term, and develop new skills that will benefit your body, mind, and overall running life in countless ways. One of the most appealing characteristics of barefoot running is that just about any runner, at any point in his or her career, can start doing it by following a careful plan.

Fledgling joggers and experienced runners may not share the same athletic abilities, but anyone who has not completed a barefoot training program is considered a *tenderfoot*. Both amateur and professional runners alike must ...

- Set aside time for the transition period.
- Have tangible goals to ensure a gradual progression.
- Get their bodies and minds used to the experience.
- Focus on both strengths and weaknesses.
- Develop foot padding.
- Concentrate on efficient barefoot running form.
- Work on distance before speed.
- Increase skill and ability according to their goals.

DEFINITION

A **tenderfoot** in the barefoot running world is someone who is still getting used to running without shoes. Both amateur and professional runners are tenderfoots when they first start using barefoot techniques. Some barefooters believe that one remains a tenderfoot until the joy of running barefoot has been passed to another.

Individuals and coaches around the world have used barefoot running techniques in an attempt to build new strengths, develop technical know-how, enhance performance, and lower injury rates. At the amateur level, barefoot running has given numerous joggers and runners new hope for their running lives. Those with incessant injuries have run again without a reoccurrence of old traumas. Runners whose training has become stale, tiresome, and monotonous have breathed new life into their routines.

Natural Running

The Complete Idiot's Guide to Barefoot Running goes in depth about how barefoot running helps you develop a natural running style. Natural or barefoot running form is a way to describe runners who have developed biomechanically sound techniques, allowing them to run more fluidly whether on a paved street, back road, or forest trail. As you progress, the characteristics of an adept runner will become more apparent, showing you how to hone your own running skills and progress at your own pace.

If you are a regular runner, you have potentially taken millions of steps over the years. Each and every time your feet touched the ground, you developed a personal style of running. You could say this is "natural," as you have developed the way you run, but it doesn't necessarily mean that it is beneficial. Specific to you and your body, the manner in which you run is etched deeply on your brain. This happened, most likely, through constant repetition rather than a conscious focus on technique.

Barefoot running can be much more than a handy tool in your running kit. Depending upon your personal running goals, it can be the manner by which you make yourself stronger, lighter, less prone to injury, and more connected with the Earth.

No Shoes? No Way!

Barefoot running is exactly what it sounds like and much more. Although barefoot running includes the use of certain types of *minimal footwear*, which attempts to go against the grain of *mainstream footwear*, reaping the true benefits comes purely from redeveloping everything you know about running with nothing on your feet. It all comes down to the sense of feel. From simply getting used to walking without shoes to running with enhanced technique to eventually navigating nearly any terrain you choose, barefoot running requires a carefully planned transition period specific to you. It also requires you to toss aside your presumptions and naturally broaden your running knowledge one step at a time.

DEFINITION

Any shoe that eliminates unnecessary cushioning and weight while allowing your feet to feel the ground underfoot is **minimal footwear,** also referred to as minimalist footwear, minimal shoes, minimalist shoes, and even barefoot running shoes. Cushioned, high-tech shoes that control the way your foot lands and feels the ground are **mainstream footwear.**

Getting your feet used to the new sensations will take time. Learning how the body moves differently when shoeless and how gravity, gait, cadence, stride, and posture all work in your favor will help to make you an efficient forward-motion machine. You will undergo an entire preparation phase to get your feet, mind, and body ready to take advantage of the benefits of barefoot running. Once learned, you should continue to use the skills you have worked so hard to develop as a part of your regular running program, so that your feet remain strong, your body robust, and your form top-notch.

Minimalist shoes do have their place in the barefoot running world, but they should never overtake your barefoot sessions completely, especially during the initial transition period. After you have put your heart, soul, and soles into making yourself a better runner, hopefully you will never desire to return to any type of overly cushioned shoe again.

The Best Time to Start Barefoot Running

Mainstream shoes do little to work the foot in a natural way. Made up of a complex amalgamation of bones, muscles, tendons, and joints all working together, your feet will adjust well to the new demands placed upon them given a balanced plan combined with sufficient time. This is repeated more than once because it is a crucial part of transitioning carefully: take it slow!

Ideally, you would begin transitioning before or after the running season. Barefoot running requires repetition and a keen awareness to reroute the hard-wired methods you (and your brain) have developed. Not worrying about maintaining high mileage, hard training, or racing means less pressure for you to push yourself too far (or fast) too soon. Dedicated athletes can keep in shape by practicing another athletic pastime, such as swimming or biking. Your body will enjoy the break! All of this will help you accomplish your barefoot goals while preventing you from falling back on old running habits.

Think about barefoot running as an entirely different sport, one in which you must first focus on fundamentals. Approach it as if you are starting to run for the very first time. This will ultimately allow you to begin filling your slate with fresh ideas, enabling you to develop new skills carefully, intuitively, and flawlessly.

The Emotional Benefits

Numerous tenderfoots begin integrating barefoot running into their workouts because of positive anecdotes from fellow runners, barefoot running groups, magazines, or website forums, among other outlets. The idea of strengthening the body in new ways, being closer to nature, and running more naturally are all appealing reasons to give it a try. Runners who have made a careful transition are most often persuaded to keep up the practice because of their own physical gains and personal satisfaction. For barefoot enthusiasts, the pros of going shoeless tend to fall within the emotional/spiritual, mental, and physical spheres.

As was scientifically demonstrated in the mid-1990s in *The Journal of Sports Medicine and Physical Fitness*, running can brighten one's mood. For runners, it is no secret that running not only improves your day, but adds immensely to your overall well-being, and that it is one heck of a good way to relieve the stress of daily life.

In much the same way, barefoot running has an emotional appeal. Reflecting back on childhood moments of being barefoot in the grass, on the beach, or at the park brings back nostalgia with which plenty of people can relate. The emotional satisfaction that occurs when you feel the sand between your toes or the grass underfoot is undeniable.

Barefoot running is also a great way to connect with fellow running communities, make new friends, and share ideas. Whether running in a group through a forest trail or a refreshing creek, doing so in a group (whether in shoes or while in bare feet) only heightens this already delightful experience. In this way, barefoot running has the potential to bring people together in new and fun ways—something great for the mind, body, and world!

The Mental Benefits

Because of the interconnected relationship of the mind and body, runners can also benefit mentally from barefoot running. As described by Michael Warburton in his article "Barefoot Running" that appeared in *Sportscience,* when shoes are taken out of the picture, proprioception (or "one's own perception") is maximized. This enables the runner to more readily control balance, coordination, and overall mindfulness no matter the terrain.

When the foot is bare on the ground, even the smallest muscles in the foot and ankle are triggered to react, helping to maintain steady footing. Without shoes, the foot is able to spread completely over the terrain, allowing it to collect information. After the input has traveled up the spine, it is transmitted throughout the body, allowing it to make any necessary and immediate adjustments.

Besides input entering the body through feeling the ground, the body also dispels electric charges that have accumulated throughout daily movement. Dr. Nicholas Romanov of www.posetech.com suggests that this internal electric buildup can reach a point where your body can no longer deal with it sufficiently, which can lead to psychological and physical illness. Barefoot running helps break the rubber barrier between your body and the ground, eliminating the buildup of electrical particles and returning you to balance.

Barefoot Zen is reached through the physical aspect of being barefoot. You are better connected with the environment and your body's position within it. Ultimately, the mental stimulation brought about through foot-to-brain communication helps keep the mind assured, calm, and more aware.

The Physical Benefits

Barefoot running is full of benefits for your body. The following are the top five.

1. Strengthens the Lower Legs

Besides toughening the skin on the underside of the feet to handle a variety of surfaces, barefoot running aids in the overall conditioning of the lower legs. For example, the arches of the feet have been found to flatten if left unexercised, as reported by Headlee and Fiolkowski at www.sportsci.org. When you add barefoot workouts to your exercise routine, your lower legs are strengthened from the calf to the ankle to the arch. Barefoot activity increases the overall vigor of the entire musculature of the lower body.

FROM THE SOLE

The arch, or underside of the foot between the front pads and the heel, is composed of 18 muscles connected to other muscles, tendons, and ligaments. One study by S. E. Robbins revealed that, following prolonged barefoot activity, the arch of the foot actually shortens. It is therefore surmised that when the arch is strengthened, it tightens, shortens, and rises back into a natural and supportive location, providing a type of undergird for the body's weight.

2. Develops Natural Stride

People often believe that those with longer legs (and a potentially larger gait) make better runners. This, however, does not seem to be the case if one looks at the world's long-distance elites. Runners such as Abebe Bikila from Ethiopia, who not only trained barefoot but won Olympic gold (and set a new world record) in the 1960 Olympic marathon while running without shoes, take relatively short steps.

Barefoot running promotes a natural stride because overextending one's gait while shoeless feels unnatural and can cause discomfort or pain. Stride, gait, strike patterns, and cadence are talked about in more depth in the chapters on running form.

3. Furthers Running Economy

In other words, it saves you energy! A recent study by C. Divert and fellow researchers published in the *International Journal of Sports Medicine* reveals that training barefoot can actually help you save energy.

Several factors contributed to these findings, including the weight of the shoe, the change in running style when barefoot, and the loss of elastic energy with shoes. This is significant because even a small savings in running economy adds up exponentially over long runs, such as in an ultra-marathon when every bit of energy matters. The result is a better running metabolism, which means that you will go farther, easier, as the body breaks down stored energy at a slower rate.

4. Saves Your Legs

More than 75 percent of runners in the United States who run in mainstream shoes land with their heels first. Heel striking is counterproductive to forward motion in that landing heel first is like applying the brakes with each step. A landmark study published in *Nature* by Dr. Daniel Lieberman, a renowned professor of human evolutionary biology, and his team at Harvard, revealed that running shoeless promotes a forefoot landing.

Lieberman's analysis shows that habitual barefoot runners who land on the front or middle part of their feet suffer less impact force. Heel-strikers, on the other hand, suffer a great impact force with each and every step. Barefoot running allows the foot to land in such a way that the impact force is spread evenly underfoot and through different muscle pathways, allowing the natural absorption power of the feet and the springy elasticity of the legs to aid with each step.

5. Potentially Reduces Injury

Besides benefiting the overall health of the legs and feet, barefoot running has been shown to significantly reduce the stress placed on the joints. Using motion analysis software, researchers found that, when compared to barefoot running, running in typical athletic shoes significantly increased joint torque, or the amount of misaligned twisting. They concluded that this twisting was harmful to the hips, knees, and ankles (even more than wearing high-heeled shoes).

The researchers emphasized that footwear designers should construct products following the barefoot model that would reduce such joint torque. Their findings were published in *PM&R: The journal of injury, function, and rehabilitation.*

FROM THE SOLE

A handful of champion runners have abandoned their shoes in some of the world's biggest events, but not always on purpose. One of the most memorable stories is that of Jack Holden, a four-time AAA national marathon champion who ran barefoot for the last 9 miles of the 1950 Empire Games marathon held in Auckland, New Zealand, when his wet, sodden shoes ruptured. Not being used to running barefoot, his feet bled. He won the race by more than four minutes, adding another impressive championship to his career.

Advantages of a Little Barefoot Activity

For those out there who might not take a leap of faith into barefoot running right away, doing a little barefoot activity is better than none at all. After you've consulted your doctor or podiatrist about your decision to go barefoot, you can do yoga, walk around the neighborhood, or carefully increase your barefoot running sessions to take advantage of the many benefits. Exercising without shoes will help promote an overall healthy frame, especially in the muscles and joints of the lower body.

The benefits of barefoot running will become even more apparent as you immerse yourself into the transition. The real benefit of barefoot running is both mental *and* physical because, as a barefoot runner, you can rest assured that you have made a genuine effort to be the best runner possible. You have given your body a chance to become stronger, perform more naturally, and become highly efficient. The trait of a true champion is not who ran the fastest, per se, but the one who is able to keep on running for years to come.

A Balanced View of Barefoot Running

Barefoot running has ballooned into a movement ahead of any scientific studies that successfully prove (or disprove) whether the benefits claimed are in accordance with the facts. Having a balanced view of barefoot running is essential.

With all the hype, a majority of runners will give it a thought, while others will shrug off the idea as ludicrous. Those giving it a try might stick with it for some time or use it as a part of their running program even though they still wear shoes most of the time. Mixing training styles is an excellent way to ensure the parts of the body that might not be their strongest receive at least some attention. Additionally, those who practice mixed training might make the full transition one day after they experience the rewards of barefoot running.

No matter who decides to embrace barefoot running, fervent barefooters work hard to convince other runners to give it a try before denouncing it. With the joy, strength, and enhanced running skills that can result from running barefoot, it is hard to blame them. Runners tend to look at anything that might help them perform better. If you find barefoot running helps you, you'll be surprised how many runners will listen if you share your story.

The Three P's of Barefoot Runners

Barefoot runners who have made a successful transition share some common characteristics, which are called the Three P's of barefoot runners. Keep these in mind throughout your training to develop these esteemed qualities.

1. Patience

As you begin to plan and implement a barefoot running plan, be exceedingly patient with yourself. The transition to running well without shoes can take several weeks and even several months. Increasing your ability to run a significant distance without shoes takes time. Walking barefoot is the first step, followed by strengthening exercises, and increased barefoot outings. The old mantra, "Patience is a virtue," really holds true in barefoot running.

2. Persistence

Having steadfast persistence in this day and age is one of the major keys to success, whether at work, home, or play. Fitting your barefoot activity into your pre-planned schedule is going to require the same dedication as any of your other running goals, or even more.

Barefoot running requires a rewiring that will reteach the body how to run well. You might not be able to run the distance you once did (at first). You might have to do other types of aerobic activity to compensate. You might have to miss a few races that you really enjoy. All of this takes a commitment akin to any training you have done before.

3. Pride

For many of us, thinking about being barefoot invokes certain nostalgia of being a kid again. The idea sounds great! Actually going barefoot, however, might make you feel apprehensive. Tossing aside your shoes to expose your feet to the elements (or the public) might require convincing.

In fact, going barefoot is such a taboo that it permeates deep into the social conscience. Showing off your feet (except for when they are in sandals) is believed to be unsanitary, unhealthy, and uncouth. Many wonder what others will think: *What if people stare? What if people laugh? Won't even barefoot or minimal shoes draw attention? Would the police stop me?*

Facing the initial anxiety about being barefoot is a helpful (and perhaps healthy) starting point. Recognize that being uneasy or uncomfortable, apprehensive, or even anxious is a normal part of going barefoot. But barefoot runners are a warm, open, and proud bunch. There are new groups forming online (see the resources in Appendix B for a list) and meeting up to teach, train, and learn from each other. Just as shoes originally brought more people into the sport of running, barefoot running also has the potential to bring people together. A healthy communal activity almost anyone can do, barefoot running should make you proud, too!

Arguments Against Barefoot Running

Critics of barefoot running have worthwhile arguments and concerns. Shoes are not necessarily bad. Leonardo da Vinci claimed, "The human foot is a masterpiece of engineering and a work of art." Although the human foot is one magnum opus of design, so are some running shoes in what they do for runners.

Shoes have brought many people into running by supplying them with protection and stability that their doctor has recommended or that they feel helps them perform more safely. Runners should be happy to have other runners sharing the experience, whether they are barefoot or not. For those with medical conditions, shoes are a lifesaver. The following are the strongest arguments against barefoot running, with counter observations where necessary.

1. "If it ain't broke, don't fix it."

One of the strongest arguments against barefoot running deals with the fact that runners should probably not worry about fixing what is not broken. If you have a pair of shoes (or a brand) that you enjoy using, that cause you no pain and make you feel comfortable and secure, then why make the switch?

For many, this rationalization makes sense. It falls short of offering the benefits of barefoot activity, but some runners have other obligations in their lives, careers, and athletic pursuits that don't allow them to devote the time, energy, or effort required to change their overall running lifestyle. Some simply may not feel they need anything different in their running life, which is perfectly acceptable.

Moreover, no evidence exists that shoes either cause or prevent injury. Despite all the bells and whistles of modern shoe design, no scientific data proves that running shoes keep you injury free, and even though some barefoot runners claim that shoes do not treat them well, there is no conclusive evidence that shoes are to blame. In fact, some runners do very well in orthotics or custom-designed shoes. However, no proof exists that barefoot running causes injury or is any more dangerous than running with shoes.

2. "Look, Mom!"

If you go barefoot in a public place, some onlookers will stare, comment, question, or worse. Most barefooters will state that people rarely point and laugh, but people do take notice of someone walking or running in bare feet. The minimalist shoe designers have a wonderful stake in the market because many people agree that you should wear something to cover those unsightly feet! Realistically, though, running barefoot is becoming a more accepted activity. In all our years running barefoot, we have only had questions from observers (or other runners) intrigued by the practice.

3. "Yeah, I stepped in that."

Shoelubbers across the nation are rightly concerned about stepping in or on something that will soil, puncture, or damage their feet. As with any activity, you have the potential to injure a part of the body that is not protected. But the feet adapt to the environment in amazing ways, learning to handle nearly any terrain.

You will need to develop certain skills to quickly ascertain whether the ground before you is safe and free of debris. Stepping on glass, thorns, rocks, sticks, bottle caps, or even woodland creatures is always a possibility. However, you will be surprised how aware you become while running barefoot. This book shows you how to prepare and avoid such misfortunes, and how to deal with any setbacks in these pages. For certain conditions (or even some events and races), minimalist footwear can provide you with all the safety and security you need to run your best.

4. "I'll hurt myself!"

When people begin to think about going barefoot, they often consider the hazards involved, and rightly so. Exposing your feet to your surroundings is something that you have been taught to avoid at all costs; you are made to believe your feet are always in need of protection. Some questions you might ask are: *Is going barefoot dangerous? What if I step on something sharp? What if my feet get dirty?*

It may not be convincing enough that experienced barefooters claim that running without shoes is not dangerous (if you have properly conditioned your feet), you can easily avoid perils (with your eyes), and being barefoot is actually sanitary (more so than wearing sweaty shoes). Most evidence is anecdotal, and going barefoot is a journey of self-discovery where you learn about your own body's abilities, how to build upon learned skills, and how you can slowly extend your personal limits.

Most injuries from barefoot running are labeled as overuse injuries, which are usually stress traumas in the lower extremities caused by doing an activity too soon, too fast, too long, or too hard. This is one of the main reasons we feel so strongly about putting a book on the shelves for people to learn about barefoot running.

Athletes making the switch can increase the risk for Achilles tendonitis, severe calf strain, and plantar fasciitis by neglecting the need to plan ahead and implement carefully. Taking the transition slowly, allowing plenty of time (even several months) to adapt, and slowly increasing barefoot activity will allow the body to adjust. Don't think that minimal footwear will protect you from overuse trauma. The main objective of barefoot running without any type of footwear is to allow the feet and legs to build up slowly. Minimalist shoes might give you a sense of false support or protection early on, which allows you to push yourself beyond your real limits.

The Least You Need to Know

- Barefoot running has given many runners a new start on their running lives.
- Both novice and elite runners who want to begin barefoot running must start slowly and carefully.
- A major benefit of barefoot running is the development of a more natural and efficient way of running.
- The benefits of barefoot running are emotional, mental, and physical.
- One major argument against barefoot running is that doing too much too soon can cause overuse injuries.

Your Barefoot Potential

In This Chapter

- How barefoot endurance running shaped the evolution of the human body
- Why your "natural springs" are valuable assets to distance running
- How your feet provide both protection and stability
- The best way to learn how to run barefoot

As humans, we love to run. The masses of people participating in events such as the Boston Marathon and Sydney City to Surf are testament enough. Humans evolved as long-distance machines, so running is a way to connect with who you are, where you have come from, and where you are going. Your body provides you with all that you need to run well. Read on to learn about why you have great barefoot potential!

Humans: Built for Distance

Biologically, humans are not very good sprinters. Of all the world's species, humans rank around twenty-fifth. Even Usain Bolt—one of the fastest men alive—is only slightly faster than an elephant. But when it comes to *distance running*, we have our place on the champion's podium.

As a species, humans are only capable of a top speed of 27 miles per hour (mph), or about 44 kilometers per hour (kph). Nonetheless, we can sustain nearly 14 mph (22 kph) for 13 miles (21 km), or a half-marathon. Double the distance to 26 miles (42 km), a full marathon, and we only slow down by 1 kph. As we move into the ultra-endurance range, our speed continues to be remarkably sustainable. The 62-mile (100 km) world record for both men and women was run at nearly 10 mph

(16 kph). The 24-hour world record of 188 miles (303 km) was set by Australian ultra-runner Yiannis Kouros. He averaged a steady (and amazing) 8 mph (12.6 kph) pace.

Two species are comparable to humans in regard to *endurance running*. Both dogs and horses, which were domesticated by our ancestors, have undeniably impressive endurance capabilities. Champion endurance horses have carried both themselves and a rider more than 100 miles (160 km) at 15 mph (25 kph) and just more than 60 miles (100 km) at faster than 16 mph (26 kph), respectively. Sled dogs are reported to be able to run while pulling a sled more than 60 miles (100 km) at faster than 12 mph (20 kph) and distances up to 250 miles (400 km) at 7.5 mph (12 kph).

DEFINITION

Distance and **endurance running** are two related but distinct concepts. Distance running involves running distances of 5 km or more. Endurance running, however, involves running at a pace that is sustainable over a longer period of time. This depends upon various factors, such as running efficiency and oxygen delivery to the muscles, both of which you can improve over time.

So humans currently rank number three, or a bronze medal. This spot, however, is at risk to the wildebeest and hyenas, which are capable of maintaining speeds of approximately 11 mph (18 kph), slower than many runners. The distance performance of other species drops off considerably.

Dogs, horses, wildebeest, and hyenas derive their speed from being able to canter sustainably, but most other four-legged species such as zebra and antelope can only travel over long distances by reverting to a slower, more economical trot. Ponies, for example, would be at the back of the pack of runners in endurance-related events. They cannot trot faster than 9 mph (15.8 kph) and preferably trot at 6 mph (10 kph).

Evolution of the Human Distance Machine

Distance running isn't only a modern recreation dreamed up after industrialization made our lives easier. Somewhere in our distant past, our ancestors relied on their ability to run long distances to survive.

Humans possess a skeleton with highly developed structures that serve no other purpose than to support our frame when running over long distances. The development of our current form would not have occurred had it not served a key purpose in our survival. We are very good at walking, but the shape, function, and makeup of our bodies does not lead scientists to believe that we evolved solely as walkers.

Originally our ancestors may have used distance running to scavenge kills made by other predators, competing with hyenas in the process. However, as our capacity to make tools evolved, we began to use our strengths as runners to hunt.

Persistence Hunting: Endurance and Efficiency

Although sprinting is crucial if you are trying to escape from a speedy predator, as a hunter, the role of speed versus distance changes dramatically. The faster your prey is over a short distance, the more likely they are to tire quickly. Most species will attempt to use this burst of speed to escape to a burrow or tree, or to rejoin the herd. The endurance hunter, however, forces the prey to keep running. Known as persistence hunting, the long-distance hunter only has to pursue until the animal tires to kill it for food.

Elderly Aboriginal women in central Australia still use this technique to hunt feral cats. The women slowly trot along in pursuit of the cat, which responds by repeatedly sprinting a short distance at high speed to escape. Eventually the cat fatigues. It is then easily caught and killed.

In Africa, the Kalahari bushmen are known to hunt antelope using a more extreme version of this same method. These hunts are deliberately undertaken in the heat of the day to leverage not only our ability to gradually run down antelope over long distances, but also our superior ability to ward off overheating through perspiration.

This hunting method involves both pursuing the antelope and preventing it from finding sources of water or taking a break in the shade. In contrast, the Kalahari carry water and use sweat to their advantage. The pursuit ends when the antelope becomes so disorientated with heat stress and dehydration that it collapses. Any athlete who has seen a runner stumbling and confused at the end of an event can imagine what the antelope's final moments must feel like.

TIP TOES

A persistence hunt is captured in all its horrific beauty in Episode 10, "Food for Thought," of David Attenborough's documentary *Life of Mammals*. Note that, despite running in sneakers, the Kalahari bushman has retained a forefoot strike on one side while having converted to a heel strike in the other foot.

Most of us would never consider hunting animals this way, out-enduring other species in the animal kingdom. Persistence hunting is a testament to our potential as runners. Clearly such hunting methods come at a significant energy cost. Success with these hunting methods is determined not by whether you catch your prey, but whether the nutrition you garner from your catch outweighs the energy cost of the chase. As runners we know this includes not only the energy expended during the run, but also during the recovery period afterward.

In this sense, our capacity to run efficiently is just as crucial as speed and endurance. Efficiency means less energy wasted in the chase, and also means that you recover quickly to hunt again. Distance running, therefore, should not place undue mechanical stress on the body leading to injury, or hunting would no longer be possible. It is this evolutionary triad of speed, endurance, and efficiency (both energy and mechanical) that has shaped our natural running abilities. One question remains: can we take full advantage of these abilities while still wearing shoes?

Understanding Natural Mechanics

To make the most of our natural strengths as distance runners, we must first understand what running is and how humans are designed to do it. By definition, running involves flight. It sounds strangely simple, but this is a crucial point: if you never leave the ground you are not running, you're walking.

Therefore, running occurs in two distinct directions. The first is horizontal: to go anywhere, you have to move. You usually do so in a forward direction. The second is vertical, or the flight stage of running. To run any direction, you must oscillate up and down with each step.

The flight phase of running requires you to repeatedly throw your body into the air and then slow your descent as you land. Working against gravity in this way requires significant forces to be generated. If you were to achieve these movements by muscle contraction alone, you would very quickly become exhausted.

To overcome this problem you have, quite simply, evolved to bounce. When you start running, an initial burst of energy is required to push you into the air. As you land, the arch of the foot lengthens, then the ankle, knee, and hips all flex. The spine bends slightly. The opposite movement then occurs as you launch yourself back into the air again. Some of the force that drives you back into the air is due to muscle contraction, but a significant proportion is simple elastic recoiling. When underway, little effort is required to keep you bouncing or running.

Our bodies are able to bounce thanks to the way we are built. Our bodies are basically a series of levers. We have rigid levers, such as the thigh (femur) and lower leg (tibia and fibula), and we have flexible levers, such as the foot, with its arches, and the spine, with its ability to flex. Joining the levers together to help us run are our major joints, namely the ankle, knee, and hip.

The role of the *tendons*, *ligaments*, and muscles that support these joints is crucial. As a complete structure, this series of levers makes us much like a spring. The elastic recoiling occurs, for example, when you jump into the air, move forward, and land. The body responds like any spring by shortening and then lengthening again through the cycle.

DEFINITION

Tendons and **ligaments** are both fibrous connective tissues, which connect bones together. Tendons attach each end of a muscle to the point where it inserts into a bone. They also allow contracting muscles to move two bones closer together. A single ligament will connect two bones together directly. Tendons and ligaments therefore limit how far bones can separate when you move. Then they elastically return the bones to their resting position after the tension is removed.

Magically, Elastically Built

Elasticity for bouncing while running is provided by the arch of the foot, its muscles and tendons, as well as the calf muscles. At the ankle, the highly elastic Achilles tendon provides substantial recoil. At the knee, springy action comes from three of the four quadricep muscles and a large tendon that attaches to the kneecap and then the tibia. The gluteal muscle can function as the spring at the hip, but it does not do so when we run.

The main objective in using your natural springs is to optimize efficiency when running by using as much of the body's natural recoiling as possible. Using your springs rather than pure muscle contraction helps you to conserve large amounts of energy when you run. The goal of barefoot running is to help you move more efficiently, using your legs' natural ability to move you efficiently forward. Learning how to use your arches, ankles, and knees to achieve the best recoil possible is a part of the journey in running more naturally, efficiently, and lightly.

What Long Legs You Have

As humans we have remarkably long legs compared to our bodies. The advantage of having such lengthy levers is that we can cover a lot of ground with each step. However, the length of these levers also means that our muscles are at a significant mechanical disadvantage; therefore, we can only move ourselves forward rapidly by using this long stride if there is little resistance to forward motion.

Fortunately, Newton's First Law of Motion states that when a body is in motion, it will continue to move at a constant speed unless acted on by an equal or opposite force. In other words, your long legs may make it hard for you to accelerate, but after you are running at a constant speed on flat ground, you shouldn't slow down unless a force pushes or pulls you in the opposite direction.

ON YOUR TOES

Newton's Second Law of Motion can equally be applied to running. His Second Law describes how the force required to accelerate your body is proportional both to its mass and how fast you want to accelerate. If you are a bigger runner, you have to generate more force to bounce and to accelerate forward. But it's not all bad. When you are moving at speed, the bigger you are, the harder it is to slow you down!

Clearly this is not our general experience as runners. Running is hard work! As soon as we stop expending energy, we come to a screeching halt. The weight of our legs plays a significant role in this, as does air resistance. However, these forces are not enough to explain the amount of effort that is required to keep us moving forward at a constant pace.

It would seem that there is an invisible force keeping us from adhering to the laws of motion. However cruel it may seem, the force holding us back is our own bodies. As most of us run, we continuously create braking forces that slow us down.

The first of these braking forces results from the footstrike itself. Unless your foot is moving backward at the same speed that you are moving forward when it touches the ground, it will slow you down. And if that foot lands and those muscles are even partially contracted, they will also slow you down. In particular, the quadriceps and calf muscles should be relaxed as you land (until your body has passed over the foot), and the hamstrings and shin muscles should be relaxed as you bounce upward.

These movements require precise split-second timing. You need a precise monitoring system to let you know if any unwanted braking forces are being created, either during the footstrike or while your foot is planted. It shouldn't be a surprise that the most precise sensors are at the interface between your body and the ground: the soles of your feet!

We Wear Smart Feet

If you think back to being barefoot when you were younger, you might remember a time when you jumped off of a picnic table, chair, or swing-set onto the grass. Your feet helped you not only control the way you landed, but also to absorb the impact when you hit the ground. The muscles of your body actually adjusted to what you were about to do, what you did, and the pending result. Your body prepared itself before, during, and after the motion.

The foot is an intricate system of nerves, tendons, ligaments, joints, and muscles, and contains more than 25 percent of the total number of bones in the entire body! The human foot has the ability to react and adjust itself with each step you take. Without shoes, the body better predicts and prepares itself accordingly to the expectant impact of each step. A person walking or running barefoot makes these adjustments automatically. It is the role of the feet to help protect your body from harmful muscle and bone vibrations shooting up the legs, into the back, and even up the spinal column. Because shoes block the way you feel the ground, they can cause you to land differently than you would without them.

Searching for the Right Step

The body employs a system of precise monitoring and control systems that allow you to run. Thankfully, you do not need to be in control or even really conscious of this complex process. Your nervous system is already hardwired with the capacity to learn how to get the best out of your legs.

This self-educating control system includes receptors in the soles of the feet, in muscles, joints, and tendons. The information gathered by these receptors is sent into parts of the brain, namely the cerebellum, the motor cortex, and basal ganglia. When you take off your shoes, these parts all work together to develop and refine new motor control patterns.

FROM THE SOLE

The motor cortex sits on the outside surface of the brain and is responsible for planning and executing movements. When a complex new movement has been successfully developed, the motor cortex sends this information to be stored in the basal ganglia, deep in the brain. The next time this movement is required, the motor cortex will request these instructions from the basal ganglia and request advice from the cerebellum on the speed and timing of the muscle contractions. The cerebellum sits behind the brain stem and not only assists in planning the movement, it also monitors the movement as it occurs and in real time adjusts the muscle contractions to ensure that the desired movement is performed.

Particularly crucial to running is the feedback from the nerves, or sensory receptors, in the soles of the feet. One reason we erroneously think the skin on our feet is so fragile is because they contain so many nerve endings! There are two major types: nociceptors, which fire to tell us when something is painful, and mechanical receptors that tell us about forces acting on the foot.

The mechanical receptors tell your brain precisely what position your foot is in and how hard it is pushing and pulling on the ground. They tell you when you are pushing downward on the ground too hard, indicating excessive impact; your springs and bounce can be adjusted accordingly. They tell you if your feet are pushing forward or backward on the ground, indicating whether you are slowing yourself down or speeding up, allowing you to adjust your stride appropriately. And they tell you whether your foot is stable on the ground, or if you are unstable and need to activate other stabilizing mechanisms.

Abrasion Resistance

The mechanical receptors in your feet need to be both protected and yet able to detect changes in pressure. The skin on your feet thus needs to be soft enough to allow these sensations to occur, while not interfering with the way the foot moves. This skin also needs to provide significant abrasion resistance and protection from penetrating injury.

Having skin on your feet rather than hooves or pads clearly has its advantages in allowing you to carefully feel the ground, but to most of us this seems to come at a cost in terms of protection. That humans have not evolved a more rigorous foot covering suggests that what we already have is more than adequate. Perhaps your soles are not as fragile as they might seem.

This is supported by the observation that the use of footwear varied among indigenous cultures. Indigenous Australians, for example, don't seem to have used any type of foot protection despite the broad range of challenging environments underfoot. The famous running tribe of Mexico—the Tarahumara—ran (and continue to do so) in leather sandals. The first nations of North America used leather moccasins. In Africa, many runners are still barefoot.

The skin on your feet is in fact very different from that on the rest of your body. It is naturally thicker, it is stronger, it provides better grip, and it is more water-resistant. It is at least six times more abrasion-resistant than other parts of the body. Perhaps, most importantly, is that it can adjust in strength and thickness in response to the environment in which it is exposed.

FROM THE SOLE

The hairless thick skin on the soles of your feet is the same as the skin on your hands. In contrast to the hairy skin on the rest of your body, it contains encapsulated sensory nerve endings, which makes it suitable for directing movements requiring precise control, such as running and writing. It also lacks sebaceous glands, which is why you don't get pimples on your feet. On its surface are a series of ridges that are unique between individuals, meaning that your footprints can get you in trouble just as easily as your fingerprints!

Having grown up in a shoe-wearing culture, most of us have lost perspective of the incredible capacity of the soles of our feet to adapt. Until the early 1900s, shoes were too expensive for everyday use in many countries, and children in particular were barefoot most of the time. Some of you will remember fondly kicking your shoes off when school ended for the summer and how after the first two weeks your soles toughened up in response to grass, dirt, gravel, and even sun-baked asphalt.

Footstrike and Barefoot Running

Given the mechanical and neurological complexity involved in running, it is little wonder that feet are also incredibly complex structures. At the point at which we make contact with the ground, they allow us to form a stable connection with the earth. This is achieved even though the terrain is constantly changing underfoot and you must balance on one foot with each step as you run forward.

Your feet function as a flexible tripod formed by the ball of the foot, the heel, and the outside edge of the forefoot (known as the lateral forefoot). These three tips are connected by a series of flexible arches. The first runs from the heel to the ball, the second from the heel to the lateral forefoot, while the third stretches across the foot to connect the middle of the first two arches. These three legs of the tripod meet at the talus bone, which, in turn, articulates with the tibia and fibula to form the ankle joint.

Each point of the tripod is specialized to support a different gait pattern. In bare feet, sprinters land on the ball of their foot, walkers land on their heel, and distance runners land initially on the outside edge of their forefoot. This lateral forefoot strike is sometimes mistakenly referred to as a *mid-foot strike*, which in fact refers to landing with the foot flat on the ground.

> **DEFINITION**
>
> **Mid-foot strike** is a term coined to describe landing flat on the foot in a shoe with a contoured footbed. Because of the lateral arch of the foot, it is actually impossible to land on the mid-foot in bare feet unless the lateral forefoot has already touched down. The mid-foot does not come into contact with the ground until the arch flattens. In most regular running shoes, the contour of the footbed allows a runner to simultaneously bear weight on the forefoot, mid-foot, and heel, thereby allowing a mid-foot strike.

This lateral forefoot strike is followed by the landing of the ball of the foot and the heel so that all three points of the tripod are in contact with the ground, forming a stable base. Touching down with the lateral forefoot first allows the foot to flex and conform to the ground and the talus to be positioned before the vertical forces acting on the foot peak and bounce you back into the air.

By way of comparison, four-legged distance-running species run only on their forefoot. Their heels are actually higher up their leg and never come in contact with the ground. Four-legged runners always have two legs in contact with the ground. This means that they remain stable despite having one less point of contact on each foot.

Changing the Way We Run

Modern running shoes are essentially an angled wedge of foam with rubber on the base and laces on top. When compared to the size, weight, and function of your legs and feet, they seem rather insignificant. Shoes, however, alter the mechanical and sensory functions of your feet to the extent that they profoundly change the way you run. Modern, mainstream running shoes …

- Impair your bounce.

- Promote heel striking.

- Alter your natural levers.

- Create an unstable base.

- Cause loss of sensory input.

- Cause skin atrophy.

- Create unhelpful movement memory.

Impair Your Bounce

Wearing modern running shoes seriously impairs your natural ability to bounce. The cushioning in these shoes means energy that could have been stored as elastic energy by your tendons and muscles and then returned as bounce is now being less-effectively stored and released by the cushioning in the shoe.

To illustrate, try bouncing a tennis ball on a mattress. The energy returned to the ball does not allow it to bounce very well. When bounced on a hard surface, however, very little effort is required to keep the ball going up and down because it loses very little energy with each bounce.

The same principle applies to cushioned running shoes. When wearing shoes, you have to drive your feet into the ground harder in order to continue bouncing.

Promote Heel Striking

The vast majority of runners—around 80 percent—start landing on their heel when they put on shoes. It is not known whether this is a more efficient way to run in shoes, or if it is a maladaptive response resulting from an inability of the feet to feel the ground. Regardless, when you wear shoes, the powerful calf muscles and Achilles tendon are no longer the spring for the ankle joint. Instead, the smaller, weaker muscles of the shin replace them. Not only does this have the potential to overload your shin muscles, it also wastes the energy stored—it cannot be used to propel you back into the air.

Moreover, a heel strike results in the loss of the arches of the foot functioning as springs. In most shoes, artificial arch support combined with the lack of room for the foot to spread out completely upon contact with the ground further limits the arch's elasticity and capacity to function as a spring.

With the arches and the ankle no longer functioning as springs, increased pressure is placed on the knee. This increased workload is exacerbated by the fact that heel-strikers land with their knee extended. This means that as you land, the line of force travels up the leg compressing the knee joint, rather than acting perpendicular to the leg and causing the knee to bend.

To add insult to injury, because your foot is in front of your body while this is occurring, these same forces will also act to slow you down. Putting the heel first is essentially putting the brakes on the forward motion of the body.

Alter Your Natural Levers

When you wear modern running shoes, the shoe becomes a significant lever, altering the weight and length of the leg in regard to how the foot comes into contact with the ground. Attempting to modify your natural levers changes the way you run and land dramatically.

One might argue that there are also potential benefits from wearing a shoe with a thick heel because of the increase in leg length. However, it seems unlikely that increasing the length of a single lever in a complex mechanical system without proportional increases in both the length of the other levers and the capacity of the muscles that drive it would be a way to improve the way you run.

The weight of the shoe should also not be underestimated. When wearing shoes the energy cost of running increases by approximately 4 percent. Clearly some of this increased workload is carried by the muscles that lift your foot off the ground, fling it out in front of the body, and accelerate it backward ready for footstrike.

TIP TOES

If you are interested in participating in research into the effects of running barefoot on injury rates or running performance, keep your eyes open. Researchers recruit both locally via running clubs and online via running forums. Alternatively, you can approach universities directly to register your interest in participating in existing or future work.

Create an Unstable Base

The foot is designed to provide a stable base with each step, but modern running shoes seriously impair this capacity. The heel is the least compliant part of the foot, with the worst capacity to conform to the ground. This most often results in over-pronation—allowing the foot to roll too much inward.

Cushioning makes this even worse. Shoes for runners with normal (or neutral) feet contain features designed to oppose pronation. The foot and ankle are intrinsically stable but shoes impair this stability. So shoes must be designed to prevent the problem they are causing.

Additional instability comes from having your heel elevated, which interferes with your body's ability to monitor the angle of your ankle. This makes it more difficult for you to identify when your ankle is rolling and to activate the stabilizing muscles to prevent injury. The width of the heel (called lateral flaring) of most shoe heels is designed to keep this from happening. In reality, they further increase the rolling forces acting on the ankle when you do land on the outside edge of the sole.

Cause Loss of Sensory Input

For the sensory receptors in the sole of your foot to function efficiently, you must be running on an irregular surface. That is to say, if no alterations to the terrain are felt when you run, the body's ability to regulate bounce and stability is disabled.

The loss of input from these receptors also means that you have lost one of your primary means of knowing when you are slowing yourself down. Only the receptors in the sole of your foot can detect the forces that occur when the foot is landing.

When the foot is placed in a shoe, your body responds by increasing its sensitivity in an attempt to compensate for the loss, which is most obvious when you try to walk in bare feet after a lifetime of wearing shoes. Doing so can be painful at first. Most people wrongly interpret this as a request from the feet to be protected. Your feet are reacting much as your eyes would if exposed to light after being locked in darkness for many years. When left unstimulated, the nerves of the body can become hypersensitive until they readjust to changes.

Cause Skin Atrophy

Without use, the skin on the foot can become de-conditioned, making it prone to blistering, lacerations, and penetrating injuries. It can also result in a predisposition to fungal infections. Going in bare feet helps to keep this skin strong, elastic, and more resistant to the elements.

Create Unhelpful Movement Memory

Perhaps the most insidious change to your body caused by running in shoes actually occurs in your brain. Every time you run in shoes, it further embeds the complex movement pattern required to run in shoes—making it more of a habit. This can make the first few months attempting to change the way you run very challenging.

This might be one reason why African runners, who may not use shoes until they are accomplished runners, have come to dominate the world distance-running scene. It is thought that these athletes have so heavily imprinted an efficient barefoot gait into their brains from a very young age that they respond less to shoes when they do acquire them. This gives them a competitive edge by allowing them to maintain a gait pattern closer to barefoot despite training and racing in shoes.

Unfortunately, you are attempting to make the opposite transition and will probably always carry remnants of your shod running stride. The good news is, the sooner you stop wearing shoes, the sooner you will begin to reverse this process and overwrite it with your new barefoot form.

Rediscover Your Barefoot Self

If you have worn shoes your whole life to run, then, to some degree, you have already learned how to get the most out of your body in them. A new challenge awaits. It is time to rediscover a natural skill that has been lost in modern times, buried beneath the weight of your shoes. The challenges are colossal. From strengthening the feet and learning to run with improved form, you are going to have to listen more than ever to your body, allowing your brain to make the gradual connections to reteach the body a more natural, efficient, and fluid way to enjoy running while connecting with your surroundings like never before.

Footstrike, Bounce, and Spring

One of the major tasks your body must achieve is relearning how to bounce. Your first task is to relearn how a natural footstrike feels. This requires you to relax the shin muscles so that the outside edge (or lateral part) of the forefoot comes into contact with the ground first. This will in turn activate the muscles in the foot and deep calf to support the arches of the foot as weight is applied. You will also have to learn when to activate spring muscles in the calf and thigh, the soleus and quadriceps, so that you extract maximum bounce from your tendons while simultaneously relaxing the shin and hamstring muscles so that your bounce is not damped. For most people this actually requires a significant decrease in muscle tension.

When you've made the transition, you'll find that your legs like to bounce you up and down approximately 180 times per minute. You won't bounce as high or as forcefully as you do in shoes, but your feet will feel light and snappy when in contact with the ground. Your stride will be shorter. As your legs get used to bouncing at this speed, you'll be able to gradually lengthen your stride again without reverting to a higher, slower bounce.

ON YOUR TOES

As your calves and feet adapt with time, make sure that you do not get trapped running too slowly because you are focusing on running softly. When you are able to run slightly faster without shoes, your increased stride length will actually decrease your bounce. This will lessen the amount of work your springs need to do.

These changes will occur in response to information sent from your feet telling your brain how hard you are landing and then pushing on the ground. The goal is not a high bounce, but simply an efficient bounce that requires little muscular effort.

Structural Modifications

When you begin going barefoot, the first changes happen to the soles of your feet. The skin not only has to increase resistance to the elements, but the nerves must also adjust to the new sensations.

The mechanical changes that need to occur to support these changes in movement relate to your natural springs. Muscles adapt rapidly, but tendons and ligaments (such as the Achilles tendon) are less metabolically active, are slow to adapt, and therefore more susceptible to injury if you push yourself too much, too early. So you will have to take it slow so your entire body will adapt to the changes you are making. The levers themselves, your bones, will also need time to remodel. The new stresses that barefoot running brings will put a new load upon them.

In reality, these processes occur simultaneously. The skin on your feet toughens up and desensitizes rapidly in the first two weeks of barefoot activity. This gradually improves as you begin spending more time barefoot while attempting new terrains.

The feet actually adapt rather quickly when compared to the broader changes that will take place in the legs, which take much longer to occur. The most dramatic changes can take place during the first six months, but full adaptation of the springs, bones, and other leg structures can take nearly two years to adapt with regular barefoot running.

FROM THE SOLE

Keratin is the key protein that gives skin its strength. Skin cells progressively form keratin as they move from deeper layers within the skin toward the surface, where they will be exposed. Keratin acts as scaffolding within the skin cells, giving individual cells their strength while another structure binds the skin cells together. Stimulating the skin with barefoot activity will result in both more keratin within cells and stronger linkages between them.

The Brain

As we have described, learning to run barefoot requires you to develop an entirely new running style. This requires your brain to develop a new set of complex instructions to control muscle contraction and relaxation from your toes to your hips. Trying to consciously change the way you run to achieve this is difficult, inefficient, and potentially injurious. Although you can hone aspects of your technique, the real changes take place at the subconscious level through practice.

To allow this subconscious learning to occur, it is important not to overthink your running. *Trying* to run the way we have described is a poor substitute for allowing your body to identify the barefoot running style that is most efficient for you. Your existing subconscious running controls can also be a problem. The more ingrained it is from years of running in shoes, the harder it is to change. For this reason, novice runners may well find learning to run barefoot easier than seasoned distance runners.

If you are finding it difficult to make the transition, you may need to reboot your existing motor control pattern. Marathoners traditionally use long, slow runs to achieve this. A series of shorter, fast-paced intervals will achieve the same purpose. Just remember, the session has not begun until you are tired!

Continuing to run once you are fatigued forces your brain to stop relying on its existing way of doing things and find new and more efficient ways of running. Gradually trying to increase your speed while running at a barely sustainable pace will prevent you from recovering and thus letting your brain off the hook. You have achieved your objective once you are running fluidly and easily. Make sure you run again in the next day or two, or your new running style will not be consolidated into movement memory and you may have to start the process over again.

The Least You Need to Know

- Humans evolved as accomplished and efficient endurance hunters.
- Running barefoot relies on using your legs as elastic springs so you bounce efficiently with little muscular effort.
- Your feet are designed to withstand abrasion and to provide a stable base on varying terrain.
- Modern running shoes dramatically change the way you run, preventing you from using your natural strengths.
- Learning to run barefoot requires you to change the way you run and to strengthen the structures in your legs.
- Your body will teach itself to run barefoot efficiently if you allow it to do so.

Evolution of the Running Shoe

In This Chapter

- Possible reasons as to why runners become injured
- How modern shoe design left science behind
- The factors that have contributed to the look, feel, and function of the modern running shoe
- Why science has not proven or disproven whether shoes (or barefoot running) prevent or cause injury

Only one thing is more frustrating than getting an injury—having recurrent injuries. Back in 1998, co-author Dr. Richards was the quintessential injured runner. After spending money on the best shoes he could buy, he spent more time in physical therapy than running. His desire to escape repeated injury is where his barefoot running journey began. Essential reading for anyone who wants to understand the modern running shoe, this chapter outlines what we're trying to achieve and at what point we might have gone wrong.

Running Shoe Philosophers

In a recent study, D'Aout, et al. questioned Western society's use of footwear, with a central focus on whether the use of shoes changed our feet. The research operated under two presumptions:

1. The structure of the human foot has not changed (or evolved considerably) for nearly 1.5 million years.

2. The invention and wearing of shoes as we know them is a relatively modern occurrence.

Like many studies before, the authors drew the obvious conclusion: that wearing shoes alters the natural shape and function of the foot.

Clearly all shoes provide protection, but this comes at a cost. Similar to wearing a cast on a broken arm, a foot in a shoe undergoes atrophy. By inhibiting the foot's natural movement and contact with the ground, shoes lead to misshapen, weakened, and softened feet. But modern running shoes go much further. Rather than merely trying to protect the skin on your feet, the whole intent of these shoes is to change the way you run. If simply covering the foot can cause problems, what potential injuries could a shoe cause that deliberately changes your basic mechanics?

Surely shoe manufacturers had a clear reason to develop such a revolutionary design? And surely they carefully tested and retested their shoes to ensure there were no negative effects on their loyal customers? Let's find out!

The Fun-Running Revolution

In the 1970s, the distance-running craze began to spread like wildfire. Everyone from the milkman to the accountant realized that they were marathoners at heart. The latest evolutionary biology studies strongly suggest that they were right—humans were made to run, and run far.

But when this new wave of hundreds of thousands of distance runners began hitting the pavement, they also began to pound on the doors of sports medicine practitioners with *overuse injuries.* They came primarily with aches and pains in their feet, Achilles tendons, shins, and knees, and left with exotic diagnoses such as plantar fasciitis, stress fractures, Achilles tendonitis, shin splints, and runners knee.

DEFINITION

Between 37 and 56 percent of average recreational distance runners become injured at least once each year. The vast majority of running injuries are **overuse injuries,** which result from the accumulation of repeated micro-trauma to your bones, tendons, muscles, or joints. In regular and barefoot running, overuse injuries can be prevented by increasing mileage gradually, developing an efficient running style, recovering adequately, and listening carefully to your body.

No one really knows whether the rate at which these injuries occurred actually increased or whether it was a reflection of the sheer volume of people taking up running. Sports medicine practitioners and researchers began to theorize about why runners might be so susceptible to injury. It was at this point that some researchers began to wonder if humans were simply not meant to run.

A Shoe Savior to the Rescue

Even in the early days of the running boom, it was clearly understood that repeatedly overloading a structure would cause it to weaken and eventually crack or tear. This basic engineering knowledge can be applied to the human body, in our case to the feet and legs of runners.

The injuries runners were presenting almost always started out with a minor ache that gradually worsened over time. This was consistent with the notion that these injuries were caused by chronic overloading. These runners were therefore viewed as continually causing slightly more damage to their body while running than could be fully repaired before their next session.

Understanding that most running injuries were due to chronic overuse meant that sport practitioners could now advise runners to reduce their mileage or training intensity and increase recovery time. Runners now understood that they were directly responsible for preventing their running injuries, and coaches understood that improved training methodologies were required. This meant challenging attitudes that pain and fatigue were demons that needed to be conquered and ignored rather than signals that needed to be heard and responded to. This led to concepts such as training periodization and recommendations on maximum increases in weekly mileage.

At the same time, researchers were trying to identify how running causes overload in the first place. They hypothesized that the major source of micro-trauma was vertical impact with the ground, particularly when running on hard surfaces. Some researchers went as far as suggesting that our skeletons are completely ill-suited to running, while others hypothesized that we had evolved only to run on soft, sandy surfaces.

More Than a Shoeful

While all of this theorizing was going on, runners continued to do what they set out to do—to simply enjoy running. Essentially, early running shoes provided protection from the elements but provided little or no cushioning. Runners were already wearing shoes suitable to various terrains, made of leather, canvas, and thin rubber bottoms.

Once hard surfaces and high-impact forces began to be blamed for running injuries, cushioning was proposed to be the ultimate solution. Advances in industrial chemistry made ethylene vinyl acetate (EVA) foam available, which was strong, weather-resistant, did not absorb water, and did absorb impact. It was cheap, suitable for mass manufacture, and offered a different feel to the user—a cushioning that encased the foot and provided a sensation of walking on clouds.

This led to the invention of the mid-sole, a sheet of die-cut EVA foam glued between the outer sole and the interior of the shoe. Inserts of EVA were rapidly incorporated into all distance-running shoes.

Runners loved the softness and shoe companies loved the profits. The idea of the running shoe as an overuse- and injury-prevention device was born. Sports-medicine practitioners and running magazines alike promoted these cushioned running shoes as the new frontier of injury prevention. Impact forces were the problem. Cushioning was the solution. It all just made sense.

Rock and Role of the Foot

Strangely enough, and to everyone's dismay, runners were still getting injured. Cushioning was of obvious benefit, so additional theories were sought. Perhaps things were worse than suspected? What if the problem was the human foot itself?

Researchers wondered if, after four million years, evolution had not gotten the design of the human foot quite right. They were particularly suspicious of the alignment between the heel bone and the *talus bone*. It was thought, similar to a marble column, that a vertical alignment should be maintained in this joint to allow efficient load bearing. A majority of runners displayed a sloppy collapsing of this joint, where the heel rolled inward slightly, called *pronation*.

DEFINITION

Weight is supported and transferred at the end of your leg bones (tibia and fibula) onto the **talus bone.** The talus in turn distributes this weight onto the calcaneus (heel-bone) posteriorly, as well as the calcaneus and the navicular bones anteriorly. This complex joint allows your heel to roll inward (pronation) and outward (supination). The joint between the talus and the calcaneus is known as the sub-talar joint.

Because the talus bone is connected by ligaments to the bones of the foot and the shinbone (which connects to the knee joint), abnormal movement at the sub-talar joint has the capacity to cause abnormal movements both up the leg and down into the foot. Pronation was the new enemy and had to be stopped before it wreaked havoc on runners worldwide.

As with cushioning, a simple mechanical solution was proposed. If heels were rolling in too much, then either alignment of the sub-talar joint had to be restored or pronation itself should be minimized. Improved alignment was achieved by building up the inner edge of the shoe by a few millimeters. Placing more foam along the inner edge of the heel promptly stopped any such rolling.

FROM THE SOLE

There are a number of common methods used in distance-running shoe construction to try to control pronation. The most common is the use of a medial post, where the foam in the medial (inner) portion of the heel is higher in density than the foam used in the rest of the shoe. The more pronation control is being sought, the higher the density of the foam and the further it extends down the side of the shoe from the heel and under the arch.

Such innovations were again great for business. Not only did it mean that more features could be incorporated into shoes, feeding consumer demand for new running shoe technologies, it also meant that runners now needed to seek specialist advice to determine what sort of deformity they had to find out which shoe they should wear to correct it.

A warm, fuzzy glow emerged as running magazines promoted this new theory to runners, sports professionals diagnosed pronation, and shoe manufacturers designed and sold the remedy. Even injured runners felt confident and better cared for.

The Arch Enemy Appears

Manufacturers figured out that more technology (or foam) and world-famous athletes professing their newfound love would mean even more profits for shareholders. Of course runners kept getting injured, so shoe manufacturers pressed on. Perhaps something was missed in all the research and advancement. The shoe had already undergone so many changes, what else was left?

Of particular interest to shoe makers was the height and flexibility of the arch of the foot. It was found that feet could be classified into three broad groups: those with high, inflexible arches with a tendency of the heel to supinate; those with flat, very flexible arches and a tendency to over-pronate; and finally those with medium arches with no or mild pronation, who were considered normal.

It was believed that these differences in foot types better explained the different rates and types of injuries in runners. It was thought that those with high, inflexible arches, for example, had feet that absorbed impact poorly, predisposing them to injuries such as stress fractures. The solution was of course more cushioning to absorb impact and give a little more flexibility to the resulting pronation.

Runners with floppy arches and a high degree of pronation were thought to have feet that absorbed too much shock and were excessively mobile, causing injuries such as shin splints. It was believed that these runners would be best served by wearing a less-cushioned shoe with significant arch support and a high degree of pronation control. Finally, those with normal arches and pronation were given a more neutral shoe design. However, even these shoes had pronation control features to counterbalance the pronation caused by the shoe itself.

Heeling the Masses

Of all the defining features of the modern running shoe, it is the prominently raised heel that continues to stand out most. For 30 years it has been the visual statement declaring your love of going the extra mile, of being smart, protected, and, above all, serious about running.

As with many such ancient and powerful symbols, you seem almost willfully ignorant as to its origins. Shoe manufacturers themselves seem to have almost forgotten why the heel is so pronounced. The modification of the heel has no preventive rationale or scientific literature behind its construction.

One might theorize that it is simply another way to offer cushioning. Surely modern gel pads could achieve the same purpose without such a hefty design. One might also theorize that building a higher heel is an attempt to take strain off the Achilles tendon by allowing the heel to decelerate over longer distances. This might work if one lands on the forefoot in certain models, but 80 percent of people do not. Most modern running shoes, in fact, are specifically designed to ensure you land heel first, even though your natural distance-running gait has always utilized a forefoot and mid-foot strike pattern.

So where did this design originate from? Christopher McDougall's groundbreaking book, *Born to Run: A Hidden Tribe, Superathletes, and the Greatest Race the World Has Never Seen*, sparked many people's awareness of the shoe industry's tactics and idea of barefoot running. McDougall credits Bill Bowerman, co-founder of Nike, with theorizing that an increase in stride length and thus speed could be achieved by landing with the foot extended out in front of the body. This style of running contradicts what naturally occurs when in bare feet or in uncushioned running shoes.

Although Bowerman may well have advocated for an evolution of running gait to heel strike, Nike cannot take credit for the innovation of adding a foam wedge to the heels of running shoes. Nike was originally an importer of Onitsuka Tiger running shoes. In 1966, well before Nike came into existence, Onitsuka Tiger released the Mexico, which featured an EVA wedge, albeit without an accompanying full-length EVA midsole.

By the 1980s, all running shoes featured a significant heel wedge, and the heel became the hot spot of the shoe. When you went to buy a shoe, the first thing you did was pick it up and look at the heel. If it was wide, prominent, and looked like a piece of equipment developed by NASA, then that was your shoe.

TIP TOES

Running shoes typically feature a built-up backend in the range of 8 to 12 mm (and up to 15 mm) higher than the thickness of the sole under the ball of the foot. When the insole is added, the foot can be 2.5 cm or more off the ground. By way of comparison, women's shoes are not considered high heels until they are at least 8.5 cm off the ground.

The heel officially made the shoe an iconic statement of human progress. The running shoe emphatically demonstrated that you would not be limited by evolution, that you understood biomechanics, and that you could fix your flaws. For the right amount of cash, you could super-engineer your foot right off the shelf.

The Facts

Let's get this straight: there is no evidence that modern running shoes prevent running injuries or make you a faster runner, nor is there any direct evidence that they increase injury rates or slow you down. Why? Because the studies simply have not been done.

After 30 years and billions of dollars in sales, no one ever bothered to ask whether or not these shoes actually work. That said, modern running shoes have been heavily studied. Hundreds of *biomechanical* studies have been published, examining how these shoes change the way we run.

DEFINITION

Biomechanics is the study of the mechanics of living things. It examines what movements occur and the forces that make them happen. Biomechanists study both normal (running) and abnormal (during car crashes) movements and forces. Footwear biomechanists study how shoes alter the way we walk and run.

This is all very interesting, but unfortunately we have no way of knowing what the results of these studies mean. We have no way of knowing whether the changes observed during 30 minutes on a treadmill are sustained over time as the runner fully adapts to their new shoes, and we certainly don't know whether they translate into changes in rates or types of injury or changes in real world performance.

Hard or Soft

Perhaps more surprising than the lack of efforts to test whether running shoes prevent injuries is the lack of testing even the basic assumptions on which they are based. For 30 years, we have been fearful of running on hard surfaces. But did anyone bother to check whether or not they do in fact cause running injuries?

ON YOUR TOES

One of the few pieces of evidence cited to support the excessive surface hardness hypothesis actually involved sheep, not humans, and walking, not running. Sheep were kept in a pen with an asphalt floor and walked on concrete daily for two and a half years. The knees of these sheep were then examined and found to have changes suggestive of early osteoarthritis when compared to sheep kept in paddocks.

Three studies have paid some attention to the relationship between surface hardness and injury rates. Although they weren't properly designed to specifically examine whether harder running surfaces cause more injuries, these studies suggest that there is no clear relationship between surface hardness and injury rates.

One study found that more time spent running on concrete actually decreased the risk of back and thigh injuries in runners training for a marathon. Another showed that running over 40 miles a week, having had an injury in the past 12 months, and having been running for less than three years were strong predictors of injury, but running on concrete and asphalt was not. (Remember this three-year figure—no doubt a similar figure exists for novice barefoot and minimalist shoe runners.)

So if there is no clear evidence that hard surfaces are the problem, then why have we all been wearing cushioned running shoes? Is there clear evidence that cushioning prevents injuries irrespective of how hard the ground is?

The answer is no. No one has ever tested whether putting cushioning in running shoes decreases injury rates. However, as early as 1987, Dr. Steven Robbins was questioning whether putting cushioning in running shoes might actually cause injuries rather than prevent them. He elegantly demonstrated that putting cushioning in footwear not only impaired balance but also caused his study subjects to strike the ground harder.

FROM THE SOLE

Since the 1980s, Dr. Steve Robbins (www.stevenrobbinsmd.com), a Montreal-based physician who has published numerous papers investigating the effect of shoes on natural foot function, has been busily making enemies with nearly everyone who has a vested interest in running shoes. It is his belief that modern running shoes are the cause of rather than the solution to running injuries. Twenty years ahead of his time, he began questioning the widely accepted but completely unproven notion that cushioned running shoes decrease injury rates.

At the heart of a 1997 study by Dr. Robbins & Waked, a group of runners were told they were going to run in state-of-the-art shoes with the latest in injury-prevention technology. Another group was given what they believed were low-end shoes offering no real protection. In actuality, both groups received the same type of shoe.

Those runners who believed their shoes offered more protection and motion control had a greater amount of impact force with each step; those who thought their shoes were of lower quality hit the ground with much less impact. The study revealed a distinct relationship between the belief in what a shoe can do for you and the resulting impact. What came later was even more unexpected: runners in the supposed lesser-quality shoes reduced their impact as they continued running. These runners adapted their steps to land lighter based on the belief that their shoes were not going to protect them.

Robbins interpreted his findings to mean that our legs are wired to protect themselves from instability and will increase impact forces to achieve this. In effect, he felt that his study subjects were striking the ground harder, so they compressed the cushioning more quickly and spent less time wobbling on a piece of foam.

An equally valid alternate explanation would be that your legs stiffen automatically when running on soft surfaces so that impact forces are maintained and you still bounce efficiently. Alternately, the cushioning can be viewed as blindfolding the foot, causing you to misjudge when the impact will occur and strike the ground harder than you intend.

Whatever the actual driver, by impairing stability and causing us to strike the ground harder, cushioned running shoes clearly have the potential to cause the problems they were designed to prevent. Robbins had good cause to be concerned and so did shoe companies, who firmed up their cushioning materials to try and avoid the unexpected responses Robbins had observed.

Unfortunately, neither Robbins nor the shoe manufacturers ever addressed the core issue of whether or not putting cushioning in running shoes increases or decreases your chance of injury. Has anyone bothered to close this significant gap in our understanding in the meantime? Sadly, no.

Deformed but Corrected?

From military trials we have learned that soldiers with high arches are at increased risk of overuse injuries of the knee and foot, and that both flat feet and high arches are associated with an increased risk of stress fractures. For runners, the picture is less clear. One study showed no association between arch height and injury. In a second, there was no clear association between either arch type or rolling in of the heel and injuries.

However, in a recent study of female runners, runners classified as supinators and over-pronators did in fact miss three times as many training sessions as a result of running-related pain than those classified as having normal feet. Unfortunately, the authors didn't perform statistical analysis on this data, so we don't know if this difference was real or just a quirk of the sample size. Because they were wearing shoes, we also don't know whether these foot types only put you at risk if you are wearing traditional running shoes.

We don't yet clearly understand how differences in pronation and arch type relate to injury risk, but we do know that wearing shoes specifically designed for runners with these foot types are at best ineffective and at worst injurious.

FROM THE SOLE

Militaries around the world have been particularly interested in whether foot types are predictors of injury and whether shoe modifications can decrease the risks. Clearly soldiers need to be resilient when pushed beyond their limits, and injured soldiers can endanger the lives of others. If anyone has an interest in understanding the causes of lower-limb injuries, it is the military.

From a scientific perspective, soldiers are a perfect population to study. Soldiers do what they are told, when they are told. Militaries maintain databases of injuries suffered and analyze them to make training more effective. Unfortunately, soldiers do more in their combat boots than run, so studies may tell us about general leg injuries, but not those specifically related to running.

Militaries are particularly interested in stress fractures of the metatarsal bones. This injury was originally known as march fractures due to their frequent occurrence in soldiers, particularly during basic training. They most commonly occur in the second metatarsal.

The U.S. military has recently conducted three massive trials that examined whether recruits were better off wearing running shoes designed for their foot type, or wearing a stability running shoe designed only to overcome the over-pronation caused by the shoe itself. Again, we need to remember that military recruits don't just run and they also wear boots. However, the results were clear. There was no difference in injury rates between the groups.

Even more surprising is that preliminary civilian data exists for this question. In women training for a half marathon, those fitted to a shoe designed for their foot type missed twice as many days of training as a result of running-related pain than those wearing shoes not designed for their foot type.

Overall the results mirrored those of the military trials, with those wearing the stability shoe irrespective of foot type having the lowest number of missed training days. Sadly, the authors didn't perform the statistical analysis required for us to know whether this was a meaningful difference or whether it could have been due to chance.

What does this mean? It means that shoe companies currently don't have a leg to stand on and are probably consulting carefully with their lawyers. Unless a larger trial shows results to the contrary, the pronation-control experiment is simply dead.

Heel Elevation

No one has ever conducted a study looking at how building up the heel of a running shoe affects injury rates or distance-running performance. We do know that Achilles tendon injuries appear to have actually increased over the past 20 years, but don't have the data to know whether running shoes are responsible.

Who Is to Blame?

It is easy to lay the blame for the failings of mainstream running shoe design squarely at the feet of the shoe manufacturers. Clearly these companies have built empires based on these designs and continue to profit from them despite legitimate questions about their safety.

There is no question that running shoe manufacturers should have tested their products at some point in the last 25 years. But to lay the blame at their feet alone is overly simplistic and prevents us from learning from the broader failings that allowed this to occur.

Why weren't sports physicians, podiatrists, and physical therapists asking shoe manufacturers to produce the evidence that their product did indeed prevent running injuries? Why were these health professionals prescribing and recommending these shoes without knowing whether they were truly helpful or whether they could in fact be harmful to the athletes they were seeking to help?

Runners also have to stand up and take responsibility. We are the ones who bought these shoes because they were featured in glossy magazines and worn by athletes being paid to wear them. We picked shoes because of their color or—worse still— because they were the most expensive on the shelf. We trusted brands; we trusted running magazines; we trusted shoe shops.

Why? Because as runners, we wanted to believe that a shoe would allow us to disrespect our bodies by running too hard, too far, and too often and not pay the consequences.

The Least You Need to Know

- Common running injuries are due to chronic overloading of bones and soft tissues in our legs.
- Cushioning and pronation control was added to running shoes in an attempt to decrease running injuries.
- Heel elevation was added to shoes to try to improve distance-running performance.
- No scientific proof exists that determines whether running shoes decrease or increase injury rates—the same for barefoot running.

Perceived Barriers to Running Barefoot

In This Chapter

- Injuries that might prevent barefoot running
- Rare medical conditions that are genuine barriers to running barefoot
- Is barefoot running suitable for runners of all ages, body types, and levels of experience?
- Sensible ways to manage your barefoot transition

The reality is that the vast majority of people can learn to run barefoot safely and enjoyably. Running barefoot is all about developing and utilizing your body's natural strengths. Any healthy runner can learn to run without shoes thanks to the adaptability of the thick skin on the bottom of the foot; the elastic tendons; the muscles, joints, and bones; and the nervous system.

That said, a lot of runners feel anxious when first starting out. You might have had injuries in the past or might need to consider particular medical conditions. You might be concerned about your weight, your age, or your inexperience as a runner.

This chapter discusses some of these common concerns and gives general advice about how these concerns can be sensibly managed. For specific advice, make sure you talk to your health professional.

Injury to Your Springs

Running barefoot is all about learning to use your body's natural springs to bounce rather than relying on a shoe to do it for you. This requires the elastic plantar fascia, arch, and Achilles tendon to work closely with the muscles of foot, calf, and thigh.

Clearly barefoot running puts substantial strain on these natural springs. Your job is to rehabilitate them to their intended strength. If you give them time over several months to gradually adapt, strengthen, and increase elasticity, they are more than capable of adapting.

That said, these springs are common sources of injury in shod runners. You may need to resolve existing injuries before starting your barefoot journey, or modify your expectations about how quickly you should progress. Do not rush—patience is the key!

Achilles Tendon Issues

The Achilles tendon is particularly impressive in this function. It acts like a bungee cord, lengthening and recoiling with every step to absorb and release energy. Achilles tendons do occasionally rupture, which requires surgery and a well-planned rehabilitation program. If you have had a ruptured Achilles tendon, speak to your physical therapist about the appropriate time to incorporate barefoot walking and then running into your program.

Achilles tendonitis is felt as pain between the base of the calf muscle and the back of the heel bone. The Achilles is made to naturally react and stretch—a motion that is limited when a built-up heel and motion control elements are added to shoes. It is an insidious injury that has driven a significant number of shod runners to go barefoot. Converting to barefoot running may very well resolve the cause of your existing Achilles tendonitis if done carefully and gradually. If not, then existing Achilles strain can worsen or new pain can arise.

TIP TOES

Increasingly, Achilles tendonosis (rather than tendonitis) is being diagnosed in shod runners. Tendonosis of the Achilles tendon is a degenerative condition where the tendon is not inflamed but has lost its powerful elasticity. It's often identified in runners with overuse injuries, but treatment actually requires increased loading of the tendon, not rest.

If you currently have Achilles tendonitis, the most sensible approach is to stop running and replace it with other aerobic workouts until the tendonitis is resolved. When you are fully recovered, you can then gradually return to walking and eventually running. Starting in bare feet should help ensure that you go slowly and take your time.

You may experience an initial flare of your Achilles tendonitis, as the tendon remains somewhat inflamed and hypersensitive. Reduce training and build yourself up even more slowly. Take the long-term view—you are attempting to resolve the injury forever.

Plantar Fasciitis

Inflammation of the plantar fascia, or the extended ligament running along the bottom part of the foot, is called plantar fasciitis. It is another common cause of foot and heel pain in both athletes and nonathletes alike. Pain from the region most generally arises from the development of small tears in the tissue that cause inflammation. Pain might feel like it is rooted in the heel bone because the plantar fascia connects tightly to it. Plantar fasciitis can cause heel spurs, although these are not themselves a source of pain.

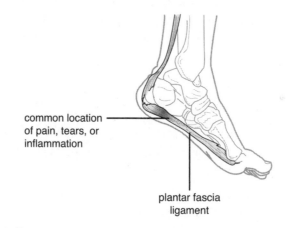

common location
of pain, tears, or
inflammation

plantar fascia
ligament

Plantar fascia ligament.

The cause of plantar fasciitis is poorly understood. One theory is that it results from pressure caused by a weak arch, which relies on the plantar fascia for support. A sudden increase in activity, arthritis, or even nonuse can cause pain in the region. A common culprit cited in plantar fascia pain is an incorrectly fitted shoe. Some podiatrists will suggest that more cushioning might be required, although others disagree. Barefoot activity will initially increase the stress on the plantar fascia, as your shoes are no longer preventing the arches from flattening and the plantar fascia from stretching. However, as stimuli underfoot begin to reactivate the underdeveloped muscles of the foot, your foot muscles rather than the plantar fascia will increasingly support your arches. The plantar fascia will then be protected and have a chance to heal and escape further trauma.

ON YOUR TOES

Barefoot running is not a quick fix to any injury, and you should not view it as an alternative method of healing without first consulting your doctor or physical therapist. The inevitable reality is that only time and careful rehabilitation will allow you to fully recover and prevent a reoccurrence of trauma.

If you have plantar fasciitis, it is recommended that you focus on developing your barefoot walking capacity before starting to run barefoot. Walking barefoot stimulates the muscles without putting significantly increased stress on the plantar fascia. This will give the foot muscles a chance to build up and begin doing their intended job of supporting the arches. When you can comfortably walk barefoot for several miles on uneven ground without stirring up your plantar fascia pain, then you are ready to start introducing barefoot running a few minutes at a time over the course of several weeks.

Bones and Joints

As a runner, your joints and bones are crucial. They must be able to compress, twist, and stretch with every step without breaking. Your joints transfer your weight from one bone to the next while in motion.

Bones have an impressive capacity to remodel, strengthening themselves slowly over time at exactly those points where more strength is required. That said, a number of runners suffer stress fractures, and older runners may be at increased risk of *stress fracture* due to osteoporosis.

DEFINITION

Stress fractures are also known as "fatigue" or "overuse" fractures, occurring over a period of time. Stress fractures do not result from sudden impact traumas, such as spraining an ankle or falling on the ice. Stress fractures result from too much repetitive pressure on a part of the frame causing hairline cracking on a particular bone in the body.

Your joints are less capable of remodeling, particularly once damaged. Distance running does not cause osteoarthritis, except perhaps in elite marathoners, but many older runners are faced with various forms of arthritis and are keen not to let it get in the way of their running.

Osteoporosis

Usually you think of your bones like the stone columns of Athens and Rome. These columns successfully hold up buildings because of the compressive strength of the pillars. When the supportive column is slanted, it will snap in two under its own weight.

The bones of the human body tend to act more as levers than as rigid balusters. When you run, your ankles, knees, and hips are bent as you cycle between each foot hitting the ground. By acting as levers, your leg bones allow your muscles and tendons to transmit force to the ground. Your leg bones are exposed to significant bending, twisting, and compression forces that act upon your frame while running.

When a bone is bent or twisted, it relies on its compressive, tensile, and stretching ability to withstand breaking. When a bone is exposed to extreme bending forces, such as when falling, it can potentially fracture, splinter, or even break completely. For runners, most bone-related ailments that occur are stress fractures.

Some people have weakened bones, a condition called osteopaenia. In more severe cases, it becomes osteoporosis. Runners with such a bone condition are obviously more likely to develop stress fractures than runners with healthy frames. Learning to run barefoot requires the bones of the feet to become used to the new stresses.

Don't underestimate the magnitude of this change. A rise in the potential risk of stress fractures is probable for runners who do too much, too soon in their transition. Even with strong, healthy bones and strengthened feet, the initial transition could take several months to a year or more. The full rebuilding, strengthening, and eventual remodeling of the feet to withstand higher levels of barefoot activity will vary greatly with each individual.

Especially for persons with osteopaenia or osteoporosis, weight-bearing exercise can prevent further weakening of the bones and help to maintain bone mineral density. For those with compromised skeletal conditions of the foot, you will need to be particularly conservative when starting out.

A gradual transition to more barefoot activity can strengthen the bones of the feet. When beginning to do more barefoot exercise, ensure that you make only one change at a time, whether it is to types of footwear, running style, surface, mileage, or speed. Discuss these changes with your doctor or therapist in order to develop a plan that works well with your individual needs.

Arthritis

Arthritis simply describes the presence of inflammation in a joint. It should be differentiated from arthralgia, which describes a painful joint that may or may not be inflamed. When talking generally about arthritis, you are most often referring to chronic arthritic conditions where the joint is being progressively damaged in some way. Inflammation may be a side effect of the damage or the cause. In auto-immune diseases, including rheumatoid arthritis and systemic lupus erythematosis (SLE), the inflammatory process is the source of damage. Joints that are acutely inflamed from sprains and strains do not fit under this category.

ON YOUR TOES

Rheumatoid arthritis and SLE are complex, multi-system diseases that result from poorly understood malfunctions of the immune system. Although joint pain is a factor, sufferers who wish to begin barefoot running need to consider whether they are also susceptible to infections. Drugs used to treat arthritic conditions can also be immunosuppressants. If your immune system is compromised in any way, make certain to talk with your doctor about your susceptibility to infections from barefoot activity.

Having arthritis doesn't necessarily rule out barefoot running. However, if your condition has resulted in heavily damaged or deformed joints in the toes, foot, ankle, or leg, then running—with or without shoes—may not be possible.

That said, if you have significant arthritis in your ankles, knees, or hips that affects your desire to run pain-free, then slowly adding barefoot activity to your exercise program may lead to a reduction in pain and swelling. This depends on the distribution of your arthritis both between and within certain joints. In some individuals, the dramatic change to a barefoot gait may allow you to begin using less-damaged regions of your joint surfaces, which will help alleviate pain in more worn-out areas. The strengthening of the muscles supporting the joints will also be of benefit.

If you do have arthritis and are unsure what effect running barefoot is likely to have on your joints, it is not unreasonable to attempt a very slow, graded trial of barefoot walking first. Sufferers of arthritis need to be mindful that ligaments, muscles, and tissue surrounding affected areas can also be impacted, which means that damaged joints are less supported and prone to even further damage. If you have arthritis in your feet or legs, give yourself a lot more time to strengthen your barefoot running muscles and tissue.

Foot and Leg Irregularities

Foot and leg irregularities are actually quite common. Many athletes may not even be aware that it is an issue. One of the most common types is leg-length discrepancy, which, unless severe, will not pose a problem for barefoot runners who will naturally compensate for the slight difference. Runners with more pronounced distortions might be more aware of their limitations. In and out of shoes, severe differences in leg length might cause problems in regard to running performance.

At the fundamental level, runners with foot and leg irregularities can still take part in barefoot running if certain features of stride, gait, and landing are not unduly affected by the condition. These include the ability to land on the forefoot, a functional arch and ankle, as well as knee and hip joints that can move through the required range of motion.

Nerves and Immunity

When running barefoot, you are intimately dependent upon the feedback from the nerves in your feet to protect you from injury and to run efficiently. If you suffer a cut, you are completely reliant on your immune system to clean up afterward and kill any bacteria before they can cause infection. Significant impairment of either the nerves in the foot or the immune system are generally uncommon, but these rare conditions dictate extreme caution running barefoot.

Loss of Foot Sensation

If you cannot feel your feet (or your feet cannot feel the ground), then barefoot running is not for you. In fact, if you have issues at all with sensory feedback from your feet, then you should discuss with your doctor if running (even with shoes) is safe. Any condition involving damage to or failure of the nerves of the legs, feet, or hands is called peripheral neuropathy. Signs of such a condition might include weakness, fatigue, numbness, a burning sensation, or a loss of reflexes in the feet. The condition can arise from a number of medical conditions including stroke, spinal cord damage, or diabetes.

If the foot's sensory nerves are not functioning, then someone running barefoot would not be able to quickly ascertain when a sharp object, for example, is stepped upon. The ability to react quickly—in this scenario by taking the weight off the foot—minimizes potential damage to the area; the inability to react can mean a greater amount of damage. Those who cannot feel their feet may be unaware that a cut or blister has even occurred. Continuing to run on a damaged area will make the injury significantly worse.

Just as important is the role of the nerves to relay precise information about impact forces and foot positioning with each and every step. If the foot cannot determine how, when, and where to land, then one's risk of injury is multiplied greatly. With a loss of foot feeling, a barefoot runner might attempt to strike the ground harder to obtain some amount of feedback. This can lead to higher impact rates causing trauma, overuse injuries, or instability leading to tripping or rolling an ankle.

> **FROM THE SOLE**
>
> In a number of experiments, scientists have simulated how losing sensitivity in the foot as a result of applying ice to the sole of the foot changes how people walk. Applying ice to only one part of the foot caused people to transfer their weight onto the part of the foot where sensation was preserved. When the whole foot was iced, people walked much more hesitantly.

A number of conditions, from vitamin deficiencies to syphilis, can cause damage to peripheral nerves and pathways. One of the most common today is damage due to diabetes. Diabetes hinders blood circulation to and from the feet in such a way that nerve endings are potentially damaged. For people with diabetes who have developed peripheral neuropathy, the lack of feeling in the feet means that they won't relay information readily enough to help them should discomfort, pain, or injury arise. People with poorly controlled diabetes have to pay careful attention to their feet by visually examining them daily for any swelling, redness, or sores.

Susceptibility to Infection

A reasonable fear that many people have about running barefoot is the risk of cuts, bruises, or punctures that can lead to infection. Such a level of risk, however, needs to be evaluated based on where you plan to be running.

In some countries, serious parasites are potentially picked up through the skin of the foot. If this is the case in your region, then running barefoot may pose a risk to your health. Perhaps choosing a minimalist shoe would be the best option. Equally, if you reside in an area where the risk of stepping on foreign objects is a potential risk, such as a nail, syringe, or glass, then barefoot running will not be worth the risk.

However, the potential for foot damage is lower than what you might believe. In most areas, no serious parasites are of concern, and sharp objects can also break through most shoe bottoms. The real daily risk comes from breaks in the skin due to blisters, abrasions from scuffing, and thorns from various plants or trees.

The first and most important barrier against infection is the skin. If you have a skin condition that makes you susceptible to developing broken skin easily, then you should be very wary about running in bare feet. If you have broken skin, wait until the area is fully healed before running without shoes. If the area is bandaged, then running in minimal footwear might be an option. In bare feet or footwear, avoid places where the area might be exposed to dirt, debris, or dirty water.

The second defense against infection is your immune system. If your immune system is not functioning properly—meaning you are immunosuppressed—then you should carefully consider whether running barefoot is for you. Even though you will be able to feel the ground, people with any sort of immunosuppression should take precautions to ensure they are not risking infection. For those with milder forms of immunosuppression, restricting your barefoot running to clean surfaces where you can clearly see the ground might be an acceptable compromise. Either way, this might be another circumstance where minimalist shoes can take you halfway.

Immunosuppression can be genetic, the result of disease, or a consequence of treatment for a disease. People with normal immune systems can become immuno-suppressed because of treatment with *corticosteroid* tablets or injections (such as for asthma, arthritis, or auto-immune disease), treatment for cancer, poorly controlled diabetes, poor circulation, or reduced *lymphatic* drainage from the legs.

DEFINITION

Corticosteroids are a group of medications that simulate the actions of cortisol, a naturally occurring hormone in the body. In contrast to the muscle-building anabolic steroids, corticosteroids are primarily used for their anti-inflammatory effects.

Lymphatics are small vessels that drain excess fluid in the tissues and return it to the bloodstream. These lymph vessels pass through lymph nodes where large clusters of white blood cells examine the fluid to determine whether any infection is present.

Deformed, Dysfunctional Feet

Two generations of runners have now been indoctrinated to believe that our feet are effectively dysfunctional. We have been taught that it is possible to determine exactly what abnormal features our feet possess by examining the height of the arch, or how much we pronate or supinate. Structural and functional differences do tell us something about one's risk or predisposition to injury, but no current evidence suggests that wearing shoes can help prevent injury. It is even suggested that wearing shoes designed to prevent natural motion might have a detrimental effect upon the lower extremities.

Listed next are some of the current conditions that medical professionals might label as abnormalities. None of these conditions means you shouldn't run barefoot.

High Arches

High arches are most often described as rigid or less-compliant regions of the foot that result in less flexibility and shock absorption. When vertical pressure is placed upon the foot, the arch would normally spread outward to handle the pressure. However, because of the increased angle in high-arched persons, the arch tends to move downward when pressure is applied. This means that the bones of the arch are exposed to more force while the soft tissues supporting it absorb less force than they should.

Having high arches does not mean that you should not try barefoot running. As you have seen in the previous chapter, the strongest data drawing an association between high arches and injury rates has been gathered in military recruits, and not runners. Data from recreational runners is less clear and presumably was derived from runners wearing modern running shoes with the vast majority landing on their heels. Thus it is not known whether having high arches is even a risk factor for injury when you land on your mid-foot or forefoot in bare feet.

Even if a high, rigid arch is someday found to increase the risk of injury for barefoot runners, no current evidence shows that shoes decrease this risk. Therefore, individual runners may simply manage potential risks by learning to run well, keeping in mind potential limitations.

FROM THE SOLE

Although the arguments regarding the effects of foot structure and function on injury rates continue, one group of runners has sidestepped the issue completely. Amputee runners continue to run very successfully without their natural feet, instead using metal or carbon-fiber prostheses. The performance of South African runner Oscar Pistorius, known as the "fastest man on no legs," raised the uncomfortable question as to whether middle-distance runners might be better served by prostheses in place of their natural legs.

Runners with high arches may actually have something to gain from running barefoot because it engages the arches in beneficial ways. The mid-sole support provided by most shoes disengages the arch until after the heel has struck the ground, which might prove detrimental to foot, ankle, and leg health over time. When running in minimalist shoes or in bare feet, using a mid-foot or forefoot strike means that the Achilles region and calf muscles help to absorb shock and control landing naturally.

The increased sensory feedback from running in bare feet will also allow you to judge impact more accurately and soften your stride as required. By way of contrast, runners with high arches are traditionally placed in the softest shoes. You saw in the last chapter that more cushioning between a runner and the ground can result in striking the ground harder. Therefore, well-cushioned shoes may be more harmful than good for runners with high arches.

Flat Feet

On the other side of the coin are those with "flat feet," with low, often flexible arches. Flat-footed runners do not always develop pain in their arches. Most often, flat feet are blamed for injuries that should be attributed to other factors. Even when flat-footed runners are injury-free, many are told they should wear a specialized shoe for the condition.

The theory that flat feet cause injury is based on limited studies of Western runners wearing mainstream shoes. The arches of many habitually barefoot populations, including Kenyans, would be considered very flat even though they are, of course, well developed and strong. With that in mind, flat-footed persons should not be discouraged from barefoot running. As with people with high arches, they might actually benefit from it in the long run.

With virtually every other hyper-mobile joint of the body, the best method of treatment is to improve the strength of the tissues that support it. Stronger muscles mean better support. With the feet, however, humans have taken a different path altogether. Flat feet are often treated with orthotics or arch supports. Even if you are a runner with pathologically flat, flexible arches and find yourself dependent on orthotics, slowly introducing at least some barefoot activity will strengthen the arch to support itself.

In Western countries, orthotics have artificially replaced the need to strengthen one's feet. Rather than continue the trend of giving weak muscles and joints false support, slowly strengthening the area may actually improve its function.

Over-Pronators and Supinators

Classifying runners into certain categories, such as over-pronators and supinators, is firmly rooted in the heel-strike paradigm. If you land on your heel when you run, you will see all sorts of abnormal movements take place. The heel is designed as an instrument for walking, not running, so when a heel-strike is used in running, the resulting impact causes the area to move awkwardly, which is where the notion of over-pronators and supinators evolved.

Running in bare feet (or minimal footwear) with a forefoot strike pre-positions the foot properly before heel contact occurs. This braces the foot naturally, which markedly decreases the forces acting upon the heel. Whether you have been classified as an over-pronator or supinator in the past, this bears little relevance to your stride after you convert to a mid-foot and forefoot strike.

Concerns About Weight

When you're overweight, the body has to work much harder when you run. Heavier weight puts increased stress on the muscular-skeletal systems, and the effects of small biomechanical inefficiencies can be magnified. Thus, for heavier individuals, it is crucial that you make sure you are using your legs as efficiently as possible. Running barefoot is beneficial as it gives you the necessary sensory feedback to run as lightly as possible. It also ensures that you increase your activity gradually as the lower body adapts slowly.

If you are severely overweight, be mindful of the increased stress placed upon your body and springs when running. Give yourself extra time to adapt by adjusting your expectations for how quickly you can progress.

TIP TOES

Contrary to popular belief, people who are obese are often malnourished. A diet that only focuses on calories can make this situation worse. Overweight individuals tend to consume an excess of high-energy foods. These types of foods are often poor sources of vitamins and other essential nutrients. If you are taking up running to try to lose weight, your first priority should be to eat a balanced diet that meets your daily requirements of vitamins, minerals, and essential fats and proteins. Eating lots of nonstarchy fresh fruits and vegetables will allow you to achieve this without filling up on empty calories.

Being a lightweight decreases the strain on your body, but just because the workload is decreased does not mean you lessen the chance of injury. Being underweight increases the chance of weakened muscles and bones. If the body is malnourished, it is stressed. A stressed body does not have the full capacity to quickly repair damaged areas. This is particularly the case with bone. Underweight individuals put themselves at an increased risk of stress fractures. Underweight female runners in particular should monitor themselves carefully. If your period has stopped because of the physical (and mental) stress your sport places on your body, be diligent about monitoring the health of your feet and legs. Maintain a healthy weight with a nutritious diet.

Underweight or malnourished individuals may need to be even more careful, conservative, and cautious when transitioning to barefoot running than overweight persons. If you develop foot pain in the toes or toe bones (metatarsals), be particularly wary of possible stress fractures to the region. Those who suffer bulimia or anorexia nervosa should seek help from a specialist. Eating disorders are very common in elite runners and, if left untreated, will prevent you from achieving your true potential.

Age and Experience

Lots of runners worry about whether their age or their level of experience as a runner precludes them from running barefoot. The reality is that neither age nor experience is a significant barrier.

Novice vs. Experienced Runners

Novice and experienced runners each stand to benefit from running barefoot, but will face differing challenges along the way. For novices, running barefoot is the best way to learn how to run. The precise feedback from your feet will drive the development of your form, rapidly moving you past that initial slow and often awkward phase.

The difficulty for a novice is that he or she may not have the experience to know when to stop pushing themselves. Going too far, too fast, is the number one cause of overuse injuries. Additionally, because beginning barefooters have a limited running background to compare with barefoot running, they may be easily swayed by peer pressure to return to mainstream running shoes. They may not give their bodies the time to fully transition and get used to the activity.

Experienced runners, on the other hand, are challenged first by their physical fitness. When learning to run barefoot, their fitness and mental discipline enables them to continue running through a certain amount of pain. Such runners need to be even more diligent about listening to what their feet and legs are telling them, rather than paying attention to distance, time, or even heart rate.

Experienced runners who are accomplished athletes also face the psychological challenge of having to revert some (or all) aspects of their training back for a period of time. This loss of time away from a regular training program might prove too much. If you don't have the confidence or discipline to slow down for 3, 6, or 12 months (even to the point of allowing inferior athletes to outperform you), then you are unlikely to make the full transition to barefoot running.

Although dedicating a block of time to only barefoot training is the best approach, later in the book ways to transition while continuing aspects of your current training program are discussed. If you have the patience and perseverance, the transformation to more efficient, stronger running is worth the sacrifice.

Barefoot Running for Children and Older Athletes

It is an interesting and important question to ask whether running barefoot is beneficial or harmful for children or older runners. Children are growing and developing. Older runners are attempting to maintain their health while staving off their natural physical decline.

Children's feet should be allowed to develop fully without being impeded by restrictive, motion-controlling shoes. Going without shoes may not be possible all the time, but choosing shoes that do not cause the *molding* of a child's feet is essential to the overall health of their lower bodies.

Barefoot or not, children will naturally run as part of play. Doing so while barefoot will not only eliminate the unnecessary weight of shoes on their legs, but also potentially hone their *motor skills* with improved sensory feedback of the world around. Running in large, heavy shoes can disrupt a child's overall foot and leg development. If your child is healthy, allow them to play in bare feet whenever possible.

DEFINITION

Molding is the process whereby the feet slowly change their shape over many years. They will often take on the shape of footwear. It is unknown to what extent this process is reversible in habitually shod populations who then return to barefoot.

Motor skills require co-coordinated movement. Running is an advanced motor skill that is not achieved until crawling and then walking have been progressively achieved. Doing so while barefoot allows the nerves of the child's feet to begin sensing the world without hindrance.

One vexing question is whether children should be barefoot when running on the road or other hard surfaces. On one hand, there are children in famous running communities such as east Africa and Mexico who run long distances to school on a daily basis either barefoot, in sandals, or in uncushioned shoes. These children spend more time on natural surfaces (dirt trails, for example) without shoes; the surface does not seem to matter after the feet have been toughened.

As a parent, you have an inherent duty to protect your children, so such a decision should be made carefully. The evidence allows you to encourage adults to attempt barefoot running (even beginning on hard, smooth surfaces), but it may not be the same for children. Barefoot play, activity, and even running in children should be promoted, but caretakers should restrict their children's barefoot activity to clean, debris-free, natural surfaces such as grass and trails. If there is any risk of cuts, bites, thorns, or temperature extremes, then consider purchasing them a pair of shoes that at least meet the minimalist-footwear criteria described later in this book. As children become adults, they will then be able to make their own decision about which surfaces they prefer to run on in bare feet.

For older runners, age is not necessarily a barrier to barefoot activity. Older runners do not have as much strength or elasticity in their feet, ankles, or legs as younger ones, but making a transition to barefoot walking and even running is possible at any age. Mature individuals will adapt more slowly to barefoot activity, but the benefits might prove worthwhile.

Stimulating and exercising any part of the body is beneficial no matter one's age. So doing so in your later years is no different. Going barefoot is a way to maintain, build, and enhance the coordination and balance of the body. Additionally, going barefoot strengthens the body's tissues, but also the bones of the lower extremities. As discussed, bone density is maintained through weight-bearing activity. Putting one's weight on the shoeless feet, even for a few minutes a day, will help keep the bones of the foot, ankle, and leg in optimum shape. Finally, because going barefoot reconnects us with that which is around us, it enhances our mood, stimulates our brains, and gives us another way to enjoy the world.

Older runners need to be very patient if making a transition to any barefoot activity. If the transition is not a success, then returning back to shoes should not be a problem. Certain types of minimalist shoes might also be good for older individuals to attempt. If exploring the world barefoot appeals to your sense of adventure, offers a new challenge, and brings you joy, then do not let age limit your desire.

The Least You Need to Know

- Most injuries and medical conditions will not prevent you from running barefoot, but they may require a more conservative transition program.
- Children should be encouraged to go barefoot, but only on safe, natural surfaces.
- Increasing age and weight problems require a more gradual transition to barefoot running.
- Experienced and inexperienced runners face different challenges when learning to run barefoot.
- If you have a medical condition that you think might prevent you from running barefoot, or will require special precautions, seek specific advice from your doctor.

Getting Started on the Right Foot

Jumping into barefoot running with both feet first is a common mistake. However, you need to take it one step at a time. Here in Part 2, you see how to properly transition into barefoot running before you toss out your trainers. This part spends a little time helping you learn how to strengthen your feet and legs and develop a more natural way of running to lessen impact, increase energy, and maximize each and every run you do.

You will undoubtedly have a handful (or footful!) of questions along the way. We will do our best to answer them as you begin increasing the amount of barefoot running you do.

Barefoot Running 101

In This Chapter

- How to get started with barefoot running
- The best methods to prepare your feet and legs
- Why walking and hiking barefoot will help you transition
- A carefully outlined plan of action to follow
- Understanding any aches or pains you might experience
- Answers to frequently asked questions

Many runners become so enthralled with the idea of barefoot running that they literally leap into it without giving themselves enough time to transition. Whether you are new to running or are a seasoned marathoner, a well-planned period of adjustment is essential to ensure that your running will not come to a startling halt after the first day out.

Everyone has a unique experience transitioning to this more natural way of running, because each person's body is different. Those who have run for years in traditional running shoes and who take part in no barefoot activity will take longer to adjust than someone who walks on the beach regularly or who practices yoga without shoes. Taking the preliminary steps to properly transition will allow you to hit the ground running without aches, pains, or injury.

Laying the Groundwork

To begin training without shoes, you need to take a step back to your running infancy. Before learning to jog or run, you learned to walk. Learning to walk again is an important step in transitioning to barefoot running.

Today, most feet are clad in shoes, inhibiting movement, strength, and full development. To start barefoot running, you have to become used to walking without shoes to allow your feet to become accustomed to the ground, to allow the foot's padding to thicken, and to give time for all the muscles and tissues in the feet and lower legs to gain new strength. Many people's feet are simply not ready to support their bodies during prolonged physical activity without shoes; this is a major reason why you must take it slowly.

Developing Super Feet

Just as important as the strength of your foot is the way it feels and responds to the ground. The rubber of most modern footwear separates you from the ground and has blinded most of your feet's *sensory perceptions*. Nerves, like unused muscles, become stagnant when not used or stimulated. Nerve endings need time to become accustomed to the new world underfoot. When you take off your shoes and begin walking barefoot, it feels good simply because the nerves are becoming active and alive, feeling the ground without impediment, just as they were designed to do.

DEFINITION

Sensory perception is the body's ability to understand the world around it using the sense of touch. This information is collected by nerves, sent with neurons, and processed by the brain. The process is how you "feel" what's around you.

Waking up those nerve endings is an essential first step to barefoot running. Allowing your feet to adjust slowly will help you later when you have to immediately react to the ground on which you are running.

Having a fine-tuned sensory perception of the world from the ground up makes happy and healthy feet, which contributes to having a happy and healthy body. Those who spent a portion of their childhood playing without shoes, ballet dancers, and even yoga practitioners might have an advantage over the rest of us in regard to their foot strength and their sensory perception.

Step I: Toss Those Trainers

Time: Weeks 1 through 3

Duration: 10 to 20 minutes, 3 times per week

Surface: Indoors (wooden floors, linoleum, and even carpet)

Goal: Stimulate, enliven, and awaken the feet

Barefoot Extras: Find surfaces other than concrete to walk on indoors; set a timer to ensure you do not overdo it

Start out by walking around your house barefoot. This might sound simple enough, but you will be surprised at how sensitive your feet are to their surroundings. Spending some time barefoot in your own abode is the best way to ensure a safe environment for your sensitive feet. Try doing a few household chores while going barefoot—but be sure to watch out for the vacuum cleaner! You don't have to do it every day, but aim for 10 to 20 minutes at least three times per week. You can increase this to four times per week during the last week if you feel up to it.

For some people, getting the feet used to walking around without shoes indoors could take longer than two to three weeks. For those runners who wear shoes indoors, and especially those who wear orthotics, you need to give yourself plenty of extra time to adjust. At first, walking barefoot may not feel natural. Your feet might ache in places you have never experienced. Your legs might ache a little at night. Stretching, along with leg and foot massages, will help immensely through the initial stages.

TIP TOES

Throughout the stages of barefoot walking, remember that, contrary to popular belief, the human foot does not need any additional support for it to function properly and to feel good. The feet only need time to develop various muscles, ligaments, tendons, and nerve endings.

As you continue walking around indoors barefoot, take a few minutes to pay attention to how you walk. If you land heavily, try landing a little lighter. If you scuff or shuffle along, try lifting each foot slightly higher off the ground with each step. You might also take note of how your feet sound as they land and come up off the floor. If one of your feet rubs with the surface (perhaps causing a squeak), you might be putting extra pressure on (or slightly twisting) the foot as you walk. These finely tuned skills of feeling, listening, and observation will help you perfect your technique later as you begin doing more barefoot activity.

Beyond the home, consider going barefoot in your office. Even if you have to wear flat, flexible slippers, this might give you the time you need to awaken your feet. Be careful if you wear socks, which can be slippery on smooth floors. If you work at home, even better.

Step II: Barefoot Alfresco

Time: Weeks 4 through 8

Duration: 5 to 10 minutes, then 15 to 30 minutes, 3 to 4 times per week

Surface: Outdoors: Smooth sidewalk and track; after two weeks, mix it up with grass, sand, dirt, and pebbles or gravel

Goal: Begin building foot resistance, padding, flexibility, and strength

Barefoot Extras: At this point, begin lightly stretching and warming up the feet before longer barefoot bouts; see the next chapter for warm-ups and stretches

After the initial two to three weeks getting the nerves of your feet used to their freedom indoors, take your bare feet into the great outdoors. Start out on a hard, smooth, and debris-free surface. Whenever you find a few moments, take off your shoes and start out walking 5 to 10 minutes three times per week. Build this time up slowly to 15 to 30 minutes by adding an extra few minutes with each session. Take off a day between barefoot sessions to give your feet the rest needed to build up stronger.

Now that your feet are more used to being exposed, you will feel more confident (and better prepared) to step out into the elements. Take your time with this step. It might take you more than a month to begin toughening the foot's *ventral skin* to become used to different types of terrain.

DEFINITION

Barefoot walking (and barefoot hiking) will toughen the foot's **ventral skin,** or the skin located on the bottom of the foot. Over time, this skin will become used to the elements and will not be as tender. If any issues arise—such as dry skin, cracking, or corns—see the chapter on foot care, and be sure to visit your podiatrist.

If you can't get outside, consider going barefoot while at the gym or on the treadmill. Walking on an indoor gym track (or even on Astro Turf) can make a good alternative. If regulations will only permit you to wear minimal footwear while doing so, take advantage of the opportunity to get your feet used to flexing, splaying, and moving more naturally as you continue to build overall foot strength.

After the initial two to three weeks, begin experimenting with various terrains for a few minutes at a time. Once you are sure that no hidden obstacles are underfoot, begin walking on grass, then sand, if possible. Sand will aid greatly in the toughening of the ventral skin, as well as working the foot's arch, ankle, and toes in new ways. (Get creative if you must. Sometimes you can even use the long-jump pit at your local track.)

Try to resist the temptation to run just yet! Once you can walk on sand for 20 minutes or more without issue, try walking on a dirt path or pebbled (or gravel) surface. Work yourself up to 10 or more minutes on these rougher types of terrain. Don't worry about getting your feet dirty; you can always wash them! Notice how all the different terrains feel. How do they make you feel physically? Mentally? Emotionally? Do you feel more aware? If such surfaces cause you great sensitivity or irritation, then walk slower and spend less time on them until you are fully ready. If your feet are still hypersensitive on such ground, consider returning to easier surfaces for another two weeks while coming at such terrains even more gradually.

TIP TOES

One beneficial exercise is the Blindfolded Barefooter. To start, examine a surface you wish to walk on to ensure it is free of debris. (You can leave rocks and small sticks on the path, however.) Return to a predetermined starting point and walk 5 to 10 steps with your eyes shut. As you walk, try to avoid stepping on any objects that you remember being in your path. If you do step on something unfamiliar, stop and try to guess what it might be. Do you feel a pebble? Blades of grass? A crack in the sidewalk? This exercise helps you develop awareness and also allows you to feel the adjustments your body makes when encountering even the smallest of surface changes.

While walking on pebbles or gravel, you might notice how you change the way you step when compared to walking on a flat surface. The feet tend to shuffle more directly under your body as the weight is shifted to the forefoot region. This type of landing allows your feet to react more readily to the ground underneath, absorb shock over a greater surface area, and help you balance. Each foot will naturally be kept in line with your center of gravity, located at the hips. If done properly, your knees should never fully extend. If in doubt, try to walk with your leg extended out in front of you, landing with the heel first while walking on gravel. You will immediately understand the difference!

As you progress, attempt walking with a forefoot landing no matter the type of terrain you find yourself on. Lift your leg straight up off of the ground and do not push off as you step forward. It will take more concentration and patience, but keep working at it. This exercise will aid greatly in the acclimation of the muscles and ligaments on the top of your foot.

After you can walk comfortably outdoors for 30 minutes on any one terrain, start switching up the areas where you walk, even in the same barefoot session. Do this at least three times a week for two to three weeks. Throughout, don't forget to treat your feet with some tender loving care. Stretch them lightly, massage them gently, and give them some extra attention. Avoid soaking your feet or using lotion on them, however, as this will cause them to soften up and hold moisture.

With time, weak tootsies will undergo a metamorphosis into super feet, and having super feet means that you will be able to handle nearly any man-made or natural surface you encounter! It can take several weeks or even months for the ventral skin and padding of the feet to thicken. The foot pad becomes more durable with time as new layers of skin grow. As new skin grows, moisture in each foot is replaced by fat deposits that add to your foot's overall padding. As the foot solidifies, you will begin handling once-difficult surfaces with greater ease. In fact, your feet will continue to thicken up even more as you continue spending more time without shoes. During this time, your feet might feel tingly, irritated, or hot. Consider massaging them with foot balm. Be sure to give yourself a day off or more between each barefoot session to allow this new skin to develop fully.

Step III: Hiking Barefoot

Time: Week 8 onward

Duration: 20 minutes, then 30 to 60 minutes, 2 to 3 times per week

Surface: Outdoors

Goal: Build foot padding, muscle strength, and tissue resilience

Barefoot Extras: Continue warming up and stretching your feet; spend as much time barefoot as possible, whether indoors or out

More than walking down your driveway or on the grassy field at your child's school, barefoot hiking can enrich any outdoor lover's experience even more. It should be a part of your barefoot running transition, but you must graduate to it carefully after your foot's padding has adapted to the landscape outside.

After your feet are used to various terrains, kick off your shoes for a few minutes during a weekend jaunt on a forest trail. Many trails are actually easier to walk on than the harder man-made surfaces. When all the elements (dirt, pebbles, and rocks) are combined, your feet will discover a cornucopia of sensations. This will give you an even greater appreciation for the ground and help fine-tune your foot's muscle groups and nerve endings. Remember to concentrate on form and keep your eyes solidly on the terrain in front of your body, watching carefully for sticks, glass, sharp stones, and random animal droppings.

Proponents of barefoot hiking will walk on nearly all terrains in all sorts of weather because of how much it adds to their overall experience. Similar to barefoot running, some barefoot hikers will use minimal footwear to protect the foot in certain conditions. Even with minimal shoes, however, you will enjoy the way your feet respond naturally to the conditions around you.

For the first week, start out doing one barefoot hike on your favorite trail for 20 minutes. Bring shoes to throw on if you want to keep walking afterward. Resist the urge to push yourself, as trails pose new risks for your feet and legs. Add 10 minutes each week while working yourself up to doing 30 minutes. Then, work your way up slowly to walking 45 to 60 minutes on trails. Back off if your feet tire or begin hurting. Give yourself an extra day or two off from barefoot activity if you feel any pain inside the feet or legs. Pain is common in the calves, ankles, and top and inside of the foot. A day or two off should help those areas heal up, which makes them stronger.

More natural terrains, such as a trail—with all the miniscule variances of the surface, dirt, mud, sticks, and even rocks—will truly help you develop strong super feet. Walking or hiking barefoot is also a wonderful way to spend time with a loved one or pet and is a great way to meditate with nature rather than feel separated from it. Remember not to push yourself too much and to carry a pair of shoes if you are unsure of the terrain you might encounter.

Plan in advance to maintain barefoot walking and hiking, even when you become an adept barefoot runner. Go out at least once per week on a barefoot walk or hike. This will help you to maintain foot strength and allow you to use the foot in a slightly different way than when running. Plus, walking puts less pressure on your feet and legs, so you will more easily assess how your barefoot running transition is coming along.

Your main objective through all of this is to take your time while you build your feet's resistance to the elements. It will all really take shape once you begin alternating surfaces. You will be able to feel the difference as the foot's skin becomes tougher and smoother. You might even begin noticing the thickening of the foot pads as your body naturally begins depositing fat there. Remember, however, that even if your feet feel tough, it will take much longer for the internal tissues—including the muscles, ligaments, and tendons of both the feet and legs—to strengthen and adjust. Taking your time throughout these stages will ensure that both externally and internally, your body is ready to begin barefoot running.

Beginning Barefoot Running

Now that you have been walking barefoot and building up the strength in the feet and lower legs (along with paying attention to your landing style), it's time to take your first barefoot run. Just like when you were learning to walk barefoot, this stage of the program continues to carefully and cautiously prepare you for the road ahead.

The following is a precisely outlined program that you can alter to fit your needs. It is broken down into a workable model that will take you from running only a few minutes to running for longer periods of time sans shoes. If you decide to outline your own plan, try to include written goals as well as some fun barefoot extras that give your feet something different to enjoy. The goal of the five-step plan is to allow you to continue building foot strength, dexterity, and flexibility while still increasing the development of your feet's padding to their full potential.

ON YOUR TOES

Judge your ability to move to later stages not on your ego (or mental fortitude), but on what your body and feet are telling you. If you experience any foot or leg pain, slow down, take an extra day off, and massage the area. If you become injured, do not attempt to run through the pain. When you're completely healed, resume your running program with caution. When you begin going barefoot again, work yourself back up to the point where you left off, and only move on to later stages when your body is truly ready.

Step I: Run in Place

Time: Weeks 1 through 2

Duration: 5 to 10 minutes, 3 times per week

Surface: Hard, flat, and smooth

Goal: Practice landing as lightly as possible

Barefoot Extras: Be sure to warm up and lightly stretch the feet before and after each session and throughout each step; continue doing one barefoot hike of 30 to 45 minutes each week

To begin proper barefoot running, you have to search for a hard, smooth, and flat surface on which to begin, such as your basement floor, concrete garage, or nicely paved driveway. Begin running in place for 5 to 10 minutes. Running in place ensures that you will not extend your knees or overstride. Your heels should not hit the ground, nor should you try to land on the tips of your toes. Instead, focus on landing ever so lightly on the forefoot region of the foot, allowing the lateral area of the foot and big pads beneath your toes to tap the ground with each step. Try to land as lightly as possible. One thing that might help is to think or say out loud "land" and "lightly" as you alternate steps. The less sound you hear from the foot landing, the better.

If your feet are hitting the ground extremely flat (with the forefoot and heel landing at the same time), you will feel a greater amount of shock than if you are landing on the front region of the foot, where landing lightly is made easier.

Avoid sprinting in place or bringing your knees too high. Make certain that each time your foot touches the ground, it does so instantaneously before your other foot meets the ground. Refrain from pushing off the ground with your toes.

As you get used to letting your foot lightly absorb each step, attempt to maintain a straight posture, always keeping your knees bent with your feet landing at your center of gravity under your hips.

Add two minutes to each session after the first week to help increase your barefoot stamina. Many barefoot runners do this drill before certain runs, which serves as a nice warm-up and also as a reminder to land lightly. The key is to be light, efficient, and focused.

Step II: On Your Mark

Time: Weeks 3 through 4

Duration: 10 to 20 minutes, 3 times per week

Surface: Hard, flat, and smooth

Goal: Practice landing as lightly as possible while maintaining good posture

Barefoot Extras: Continue barefoot strengthening as described in the next chapter; do one long or two short barefoot hikes each week

Now that you have walked barefoot for longer periods of time; begun developing super feet; and warmed up, stretched, and strengthened the foot, it is time to build upon the work you have done.

For this step, commence running without shoes for 10 to 20 minutes outside on a nice hard, smooth surface, such as a sidewalk. Go very slowly while finding a comfortable rhythm. Wear a watch to ensure you don't go over your predetermined time. Avoid using the watch to go faster. If you notice any soreness or stiffness, consider taking an extra day off.

TIP TOES

When you first begin barefoot running, try not to overthink it too much. Stay relaxed, because being nervous about being barefoot or about form could lead to muscle tightness. Rest assured you will accomplish your goals because you are following a careful plan. The finer technical points of form will come with time.

Step III: Begin Alternating Terrains

Time: Weeks 5 through 6

Duration: 20 to 30 minutes, 3 times per week

Surface: Road, trail, dirt, and sand

Goal: Continue all previous goals and continue developing foot padding

Barefoot Extras: Continue barefoot strengthening; do one long barefoot hike each week for up to one hour

Now you can finally get off the pavement! At this point, feel free to rotate the surfaces on which you run barefoot. If you choose a dirt trail or a grassy field, be sure that you have walked it before so that you are aware of all the hidden risks (or treasures) before taking off. Take it very slowly.

For one day each week, dedicate 10 to 20 minutes or more to running on sand, which will help push pad development. If you extend this step past two weeks, take one of your running days and add an extra 5 to 10 minutes to it. Throwing in some longer days slightly past your comfort zone will help you determine if you need more time developing your barefoot base. Also, during this time, it is imperative that you alternate terrains from one session to the next. If you spend one day on a rocky trail, spend your next scheduled running day on something smooth. Once you are ready to spend more time on trails, see Chapter 10, which will help you take your barefoot adventures offroad.

Step IV: Extending Your Ability

Time: Weeks 7 through 8

Duration: 30 to 40 minutes, 3 to 4 times per week

Surface: Road, trail, dirt, and sand

Goal: Continue all previous goals and foot padding development; begin focusing more on overall form

Barefoot Extras: Continue previous extras; do one long (and more challenging) barefoot hike; explore new territory and terrains

For the first week, continue doing only three sessions. For the second week, add one extra session on the weekend that allows you to vary terrains, such as a trail and road combination. Try to avoid running in the hottest part of the day if your feet aren't used to hotter surfaces (see Chapter 11 for information on running in various types of weather). Also, begin focusing on developing natural running form (see Chapters 7 and 8). Continue to land lightly, and do not push yourself beyond your limit. As you run, imagine your legs turning as if pedaling a bicycle—a circular motion where the foot taps the ground with each rotation, the knees remain bent, and you land lightly. Avoid pushing off the ground with each step. This is a good stage to really pamper your feet.

Step V: The Final Countdown

Time: Weeks 9 through 10

Duration: 40 to 60 minutes, 2 to 3 times per week

Surface: Road and trail

Goal: Focus on form and run for up to one hour barefoot

Barefoot Extras: Continue previous extras; back off hiking during the week you plan a longer barefoot run

If you are experiencing substantial discomfort after a 40-minute run, even with a day off in between sessions, consider taking off for a few days. Then, give yourself two or more weeks to continue slowly increasing your barefoot distance. Only when you feel up to it, plan on running your longest barefoot run yet. Give yourself plenty of time, and do a fun loop that alternates terrain and is one you really look forward to completing. Avoid wearing a watch, as you should avoid pushing yourself beyond your comfort zone. When you reach your goal, stretch lightly, massage your feet, and reward yourself!

Barefoot Fundamentals

Your transitional stages will make or break your barefoot running experience. There is no "one size fits all" transition process for every type of runner, but knowledge from current barefoot experts can help you avoid mistakes, injuries, and setbacks.

Many novice barefooters have questions about training plans and how they should tackle certain aspects of barefoot running. Let's get some answers to these common questions.

Barefoot Running on Grass, Sand, and Trail

Because grass is one of the most splendid terrains underfoot, one would be led to believe that running on it might be the best way to begin barefoot activity. However, when you first start barefoot running, you should avoid too many soft surfaces. Just like running in cushioned shoes, running on a soft surface could result in the foot landing heel first or not landing as lightly as possible.

When you first start out running without shoes, begin on a hard, flat, smooth surface. This ensures that you don't step on any foreign objects, that your feet are landing lightly, and that you are relaxed with good posture. Moreover, running on a smooth surface will help to toughen your ventral skin beyond the point of easily getting blisters. Most likely, even after you have spent a good deal of time walking without shoes on a variety of surfaces, your feet will blister when you begin barefoot running. Technique does play a part in this, but there's no real way around it. Nearly 90 percent all of the barefoot runners experience blisters during the beginning stages. After they heal, your feet will be stronger and able to handle rougher terrain without any hint of blisters forming.

That is one major reason you should avoid grass until at least week 5 or 6 of your barefoot running transition—not because of the grass, but because of what can hide in it. If you step on a stick, thorn, bottle cap, or piece of glass without having strong skin, your feet can puncture. Believe it or not, tougher skin underfoot can withstand such objects from puncturing, tearing, or even bothering you as you run over them.

Running on shorter grass, such as on a golf course, might mean that you can better see the ground underneath you. However, running on such a soft surface will still not allow you to feel the ground as well or focus on the reaction of your legs with each step. Moreover, golf courses often treat their greenery with chemicals, which can cause irritation. Stronger skin can resist such treatments, but you should be careful to not have any breaks, cuts, or scrapes on the feet before you head out to run on any type of surface without shoes.

Walking and running on grass certainly has its place; it's simply too fun to resist! If you cannot resist the urge to begin on grass, be sure that the area is clear of debris. Begin walking for a few minutes before jogging.

If you are following a barefoot running plan, try to rotate workout surfaces with each day's run. If the conditions outdoors are good for barefoot activity, get outside as often as you can. After you actually begin running barefoot, you can rotate from a smooth sidewalk to a local track, and then to a well-padded dirt path. Starting on a hard surface ensures that you will pay closer attention to proper landing rather than how the ground feels.

Similarly, starting off too early on trail or sand can result in problems for the under-prepared. Sand is great for building up the foot's muscles and padding, but it should be reserved until the plantar region of each foot has become stronger. On trails, even the most minute nooks, crannies, cracks, and uneven surfaces can cause foot maladies, as well as unneeded strain on the ankles, knees, and hips. Trails, one of the most fun places to run barefoot, can be a central focus of your barefoot adventures. In fact, walking barefoot on trails is an early component before actually running them.

The American Podiatric Medical Association, a proponent of proper fitting, stabilizing, and cushioned shoes for the masses, is confident that running shoes can aid greatly in necessary shock absorption for a variety of surfaces. The organization warns about running on soft and uneven surfaces until one becomes accustomed to the activity. When barefoot running, be sure that you have first developed your foot's padding, as well as worked on foot, ankle, and lower leg strength (see the next chapter) before setting out on any sole-seeking adventures.

Transitioning on a Treadmill

Running on a treadmill is not the same as having the earth under your feet, but it can be a great way to start, especially if outside conditions do not cooperate. If you are inspired to transition to barefoot running, but would like to do so on a treadmill because of time or weather, talk with the folks at your workout center if you do not own your own machine. There might be certain regulations about which you will need to be aware. Before running barefoot on a workout facility's equipment, explain the importance of barefoot strengthening for your running program. Present the idea at a meeting, if possible, showing the overall benefits. When you are a barefoot pro, you might even be asked to teach an introductory class or two!

Begin your barefoot running training on a treadmill just as you would if you were running outdoors. Follow the instructions for developing super feet earlier in this chapter before attempting to run on a treadmill. When you begin running, increase your time slowly, perhaps two minutes per week. Avoid going more than a few miles per hour or inclining the machine for the first month. Take this time to focus on the fundamentals of form. If you have the opportunity to run in front of a mirror to evaluate your technique, do so.

Though you cannot vary the surface on a treadmill, increasing distance and incline over time will help your feet, ankles, and legs become stronger and used to hills. And, just like beginning barefoot running outdoors, don't lace up any minimalist footwear until you have devoted a certain period to learning to run without shoes. Feeling the ground and paying attention to how your feet feel and land is as essential on a treadmill as it is outside. Finally, remember that distance comes before speed, so develop endurance and stamina before increasing your pace (see Chapter 14 to learn more about advanced barefoot training methods).

Starting out on a treadmill can help you prepare for outdoor barefoot running. As with running outdoors, take your time and opt for slow distance over speed.
(Photo by Yasmine Bennis)

Using Transitional Footwear

Imagine painting while blindfolded. The result would probably not turn out as well as if you been able to see the work in front of you. The blindfold (no matter how thin, flexible, or wonderfully designed) blocks your eyes from *seeing* what is actually before you. Similarly, something between your feet and the ground does not allow your feet to *see* what is underneath them. If the foot does not *see* (or feel) the ground, your body will not receive the full and precise feedback it needs to run your best.

The combination of cushioned or minimal shoes and improper form results in muscle vibration, which can lead to fatigue and injury. According to Nigg's, et al. Vibration Model, from the *Journal of Applied Physiology*, vibration is dealt with differently depending upon the landing style of the foot. Running incorrectly in shoes can increase muscle fatigue by providing a false sense of comfort via cushioning. Shod running causes the body to absorb shock differently than when you're barefoot and landing properly.

When you first start out as a barefoot runner, try to avoid being stupefied by all the wonderful products on the market. Without actually spending some time being barefoot, it is hard for fledgling barefoot runners to resist anything claiming to increase performance. Just as there is a myth that high-tech, mainstream shoes do more than protect your feet from the elements, such as helping to keep you injury-free, so there is a belief that you need a layer between you and the ground to help with the transition period.

The real benefits of using a minimalist shoe come later, not when you are first starting out. Don't use minimalist footwear to help you transition to barefoot running more quickly, to push yourself to new heights, or to help you maintain your current mileage. If you want to keep up with your current running program, it's better to keep running in regular shoes while you slowly increase barefoot activity. If you suddenly switch shoe types without adjusting your current training routine, you risk serious injury. Minimal shoes can mask pain that can tell you if you are going too fast, too far, or with improper landing.

For the barefoot runner, minimalist shoes can take the place of your regular shoes only when your legs and feet have gotten used to running without the support that regular or mainstream shoes provide. This can take anywhere from six months to two years. Only pure barefoot running can help you relearn form, landing, and technique. The foot-to-ground connection is simply too important to ignore.

Once you have devoted several months to barefoot running, minimalist shoes can help you take your natural running goals to new heights. For the beginning barefoot runner, minimal footwear should only be used to help you …

- Manage unyielding terrain.
- Get through inclement weather.
- Finish a run when your foot padding has had enough.

Running barefoot is not only about running without shoes; it is about fundamentally changing the way you run altogether. The discomfort you feel at first is quite normal. Because any type of shoe blocks the feelings associated with running, wearing a transitional shoe goes directly against your overall goal of becoming a more natural runner.

ON YOUR TOES

If you are considering running barefoot right away, give yourself plenty of time to transition. Barefoot running requires that you run without shoes for a certain length of time while you learn to develop natural form. Even if you have your eyes set on a great pair of minimalist shoes, wait until you are fully ready before buying any. For habitual barefoot runners who have undergone the stages outlined previously in this chapter, limit your minimal-footwear runs to less than 30 percent of your total running hours. In the winter or on certain terrains, this ratio will change accordingly.

Continuing to Run in Regular Shoes

Similar to learning another language, it is going to take dedicated effort to become fluent in barefoot running. And, as with learning a foreign tongue, if you dedicate a fair amount of time to it, practice it accordingly, and immerse yourself in it, you will have an easier time learning the finer points of the subject matter. However, runners often do seek out the endorphin rush, or "runner's high," so asking runners *not* to run their regular mileage can be next to impossible.

As a beginning barefoot runner, you have to design a strategy that matches your overall running goals. After you create a solid transitional plan, then you will feel more confident about what the future holds.

If you want to mix running barefoot with regular workouts in mainstream shoes, then prepare a plan around this goal. In the summer, do your barefoot walking and running routines before you run in shoes. This will ensure that your feet are not sensitive, soft, or damp as you take off in bare feet. Proper pad thickening and development depend on your feet being as dry as possible. In the winter, start out running indoors to get the feet nice and toasty before taking off outside. Your feet will more easily maintain their temperature once the blood begins to flow through them.

If you wish to mix and match your barefoot outings, carry one shoe in each hand to maintain balance, or throw them in an ultralight backpack so that you can explore new terrain without worry. In this case, having a pair of shoes to throw on when you need them is a good idea. This sort of mix-and-match transition might work well for you, but be sure that you carefully outline a plan, build yourself up slowly, and maintain good form.

Going Further, Farther, Faster

While running barefoot for five minutes on a treadmill (because it was winter), one triathlete in training exclaimed that he had never experienced "such a wonderful delight!" Later, without anyone watching, he snuck back to run 40 more minutes without shoes. The next day as he entered the pool for that morning's workout, he could barely walk. His calf muscles were in knots, his feet tender. Instead of a swim, he sat on the edge and soaked his legs and feet in the cool water.

When you first experience barefoot running, you might feel the urge to push yourself beyond your initial limits. You may not feel any pain even after several minutes of running, especially if you do so on a soft surface (such as grass, sand, or a treadmill), and you might keep going for a longer period of time. The next day, however, you could pay dearly for your previous day's bold endeavor—something as simple as walking out to the mailbox might prove painful!

Running through discomfort or pushing yourself past your limit while barefoot is risky and greatly increases your chance of injury. In an article on www.competitor. com, Matt Fitzgerald, an author of several books on running and fitness, says the barefoot running movement has created an "injury epidemic." This increased risk of injury from barefoot running does not stem from the movement itself, however. It originates from new barefoot runners doing too much, too soon. Darwin Fogt, a physical therapist interviewed in the piece, says heel injuries and plantar fasciitis are the main afflictions of those who visit his office.

To avoid joining the ranks of athletes who become injured when they first attempt barefoot running, you have to learn to listen to your body's response to barefoot activity and combine that with the knowledge you have about how the transition will go. Your body will not offer its feedback for nearly 24 hours following any workout. As you work to diligently develop foot padding, strengthen the lower body, and concentrate on form, you must learn to listen to the feedback from your body, but combine this with the knowledge you have now gained. Stick to your guns, even if you *want* to go farther than you intended. When you are fresh and have never run barefoot before, your assumptions are unreliable. Trust your brain over your body as you build yourself up.

As a basic rule of thumb, extend your barefoot runs by no more than 10 to 15 percent each week. Take at least one day off between barefoot sessions for the first three months. As you begin increasing your barefoot activity, you can begin trusting your body more, but always play it smart. More than ever before, you should think, plan ahead, and know that you will have to keep yourself from overextending. Doing so will mean a smooth, solid, and fun transition as you become a new, more natural runner.

A zealous passion for running barefoot is something that numerous tenderfoots experience when they first take off their shoes. Experienced barefoot runners will admit to a time when they pushed themselves past a limit because they did not feel any pain or did not want a particular run to end. Generally speaking, experienced barefoot runners can excel in distance and speed, but rookie barefoot runners should avoid pushing themselves *further* than they should, *farther* than they should, and *faster* than they should.

Pushing further than intended refers to the internal drive that runners feel to test their limits. After you have developed a barefoot training plan, do your best to stick to it. Believe in yourself and your plan enough to know that down the road, you will have the ability to push yourself further than you ever thought possible.

Running farther means the physical distance run. A golden rule of running applies to barefoot running as well: it is better to be undertrained (and take it slow) than to overtrain (and become injured). When you are out on that country back road or forest trail for the first time without shoes, avoid going farther than what you have planned. Pushing beyond your predetermined distance is asking for extra recovery time in a doctor's office or on the couch. Enjoy the 10 minutes you have now to revel in the hour you will have later.

Running faster is a big problem for tenderfoots. Though barefoot running has a wonderful way of slowing runners down so that they first learn proficient technique, some speed demons out there will try running faster than they should at first. This is a major issue in particular for those who start out in minimal footwear, which does not allow you to adapt your form as well as when entirely without shoes. Certain techniques discussed in Part 4 of this guide will help you with speed training, but those who go too fast when first starting out risk injury.

ON YOUR TOES

If speed is your middle name, then consider ways to slow down. Does music pump you up? It has been shown that some runners will push themselves 20 percent more when their favorite tunes are jamming. At first, it might be best to plan barefoot sessions without music. Do you like keeping up with the fast pack? Try running alone to avoid throwing yourself into barefoot running too quickly.

No Pain, No Problem—Not Really

Your feet have a wonderful way of telling you when you have done something wrong or have gone too far. One of the main reasons that runners might give up on barefoot running is that it hurts. This plain, simple fact deters many runners from ever enjoying the long-term advantages of barefoot running. These runners are not considering that pain is a regulator of your body's limits. In many ways, pain is a friend tapping you on the shoulder, telling you to take it easy or pay the consequences.

When barefoot running, your feet send your body all sorts of messages. Communication between the ground, your feet, and your body is especially crucial as you learn to run more naturally. If you're not clearly receiving these messages, the result is bad running habits that will take much longer to undo than they did to develop.

Too Much, Too Soon

Most injuries associated with barefoot running occur simply because the runner has done too much, too soon. These avoidable types of injuries can cause problems on the outer foot, such as blisters. They can also cause other, more detrimental problems, such as tearing of the tendons or ligaments, or stress fractures. You can avoid these types of injuries if you are in tune with the messages your body is sending you.

ON YOUR TOES

Blisters may form due to the elements of heat, moisture, and friction. Getting the foot used to these variables slowly is key. Blisters tell you a lot about your form; you might need to land lighter, more centered, or without pushing off, overstriding, or heel striking. Wearing a minimalist shoe could prevent you from noticing the elements of bad form.

Pain will subside, but if you are injured, you need to take ample time off from barefoot activities until you are completely healed. Those pesky sore calves or the slight tenderness of the top of the foot are quite normal and they should not keep you from running altogether, but they should tell you when a day off might be necessary. Similar to taking a day off between barefoot walking sessions, you will also want to take a day off between barefoot running sessions as you implement them into your barefoot training cycle.

What's Pain Got to Do with It?

After spending a good portion of your life in shoes, it will take a while for your feet to get used to the ground, no matter the surface. The slight pain of barefoot running will come in many forms as you progress. Of course, this is not the same pain you feel when injured. This is referring to mild soreness and tenderness or being stiff, achy, and slightly irritated due to the strengthening of your feet, legs, and body.

It is important for you to recognize the difference between a slightly nagging pain and an actual injury. As you continue to build your body up to barefoot running, it is important that you are able to discern between the two.

 ON YOUR TOES

The discomfort of barefoot running might be achy, stiff feet. With an injury, you might feel a shooting sensation through an area of the foot, ankle, or leg. Sometimes injuries do not show up right away. Grade your pain on a scale of 1 to 10 (10 meaning you have excruciating pain). If you judge it to be a 7 or higher, seek medical attention.

Especially in the beginning stages of barefoot running, your calves will be sore and tight. It happens to more than 90 percent of tenderfoots transitioning into the sport. As you progress, your calves are stretching, flexing, and building up more than ever. With barefoot runners, this can last anywhere from two weeks to two months. (As you increase your mileage, you will continue to experience tight or sore calves.) After a while, you might begin questioning whether this type of pain is actually normal or not. Keep up with your barefoot plan and if they are really sore, take two days off in between each barefoot session. It is important to stretch, massage, and work out your calves and Achilles tendons between barefoot running days (see the next chapter for ways to stretch and strengthen the calves).

Aches in the top foot or big toe are hard to judge. Pain in the top of the foot or the big toe is usually rooted in the connective tissue of the region, usually in the tendons connecting to the metatarsals. Stretching the foot and warming up before and after a barefoot session will help. If the pain is dull, take a day or two off. Ice the area and massage it lightly twice a day. If that does not help the pain subside (or swelling occurs), continue to ice the area and see a doctor. An injury here is entirely due to overuse and can be a precursor to more serious issues, including tendonitis.

Shin splints, an achy pain in the front of the lower leg, can occur in any running program as well as the transition to barefoot running. Avoid these by transitioning on various types of surfaces, including grass and dirt paths. Strangely enough, shin splints are thought to be associated with the building up of the arch of the foot; many who have "flat arches" claim to suffer from shin splints in some form.

As you transition, try not to lean too far forward as you walk (or begin running) barefoot; the pressure exerted on the front of the ankle and the connecting tissue to the tibia needs time to adjust. The strengthening of the shin and arch is one of the great benefits of going barefoot.

As you run barefoot, you will be paying a lot of attention to the ground ahead of you. Because you are running more carefully when in bare feet, your upper body might stiffen up as your neck stays in one position, watching the ground. As you run, try to relax your shoulders; shake your arms loose every few minutes. If your neck is really tight, walk for a few minutes and stretch it slowly. If your neck is loose, the rest of your body will be more relaxed.

Jumping into barefoot running too quickly or using transitional footwear too soon could cause you real pain down the road. Take your time and build your feet up slowly. Choose the barefoot path less traveled and reap the rewards that a careful transition will bring.

The Least You Need to Know

- Walking indoors and eventually outdoors without shoes will awaken the nerves of the feet and help you build up your foot padding to handle various terrains.
- Following a careful transition plan will ensure that you are giving your body ample time to adjust.
- Not overdoing it and paying attention to what your feet are telling your body are the best ways to succeed in barefoot running.
- Using minimal footwear as transitional shoes during the initial stages of barefoot running could lead to you pushing yourself too far, too soon.
- Learning to recognize and care for any initial pain will help ensure that you are ready to move ahead in your barefoot training.

Warm-Ups, Stretches, and Exercises

In This Chapter

- Understanding the foot-to-body connection
- The best ways to properly warm up before running barefoot
- Ways to carefully stretch the foot, ankle, and lower legs
- Exercises to strengthen the lower body for barefoot activity
- Drills to build calf strength and overall balance

As you learned in the previous chapter, following a careful plan will help you make a smooth transition to barefoot running. When you ran in regular running shoes, you probably stretched either before or after your activity. It is the same for barefoot running, but with more of a focus on the lower legs, ankles, and feet.

As you work your way through the stages of barefoot walking and running, continue warming up, stretching, and working the body so that your muscles and other tissues will be ready for each run. Cold or sleepy feet are less responsive to the ground, so thoroughly preparing them will mean a much safer and enjoyable experience as you build up your barefoot abilities.

Warming Up for Barefoot Activity

Before setting out on any barefoot walking, jogging, running, or drill session, it is imperative to "awaken" the feet by warming them up. Like other muscle groups that have been dormant for most of the day, the feet, too, need to be enlivened before setting out on any barefoot adventure.

Warming up before engaging in any barefoot activity allows the thousands of nerves to be stimulated, ready to fire any necessary information to your body throughout your activity. It also helps boost proprioception, one's ability to determine the position, location, and movement of the body relative to surroundings.

Your job may keep you stuck at a desk all day and not as active as your cave-dwelling ancestors. Waking your nerves up allows them to react more astutely to any changes you might encounter in the terrain. Warming up the feet also allows the toes to flex and stretch, which engages the bottom pads, plantar fascia, and Achilles tendon, which helps to loosen the regions of the calf and heel.

In reflexology, a manner of massage that focuses on reflex points (pressure points) to treat illness, it is thought that various points on the body (the hands, head, and feet) link to all other areas of the body. For the purposes here, stimulating and warming up one region of the foot ultimately helps your entire body enliven itself for the forthcoming workout. The following warm-up exercises will help you "awaken" your feet and body to the world.

It is especially crucial for beginning barefoot runners to undergo warm-up sessions before each outing just to make sure your feet are 100 percent ready for the activity. If your feet or lower legs feel sore, fatigued, or injured, lightly warming up and performing a few stretches will help you determine if you need an extra day (or more) off from any barefoot activity.

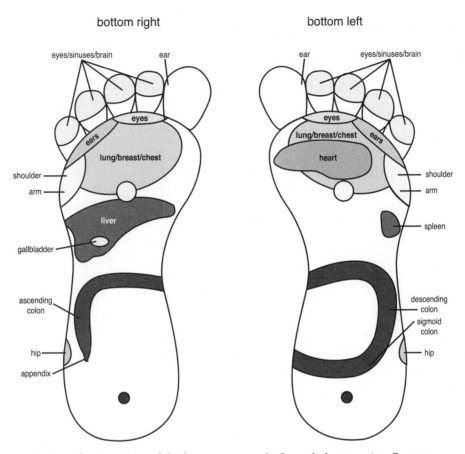

bottom right   bottom left

In this reflexology chart of the foot, one can see the foot to body connection. Because pressure points correspond to other areas of the body, reflexology is thought to improve circulation, relieve tension, and promote natural healing.

Jump It Up!

It is important to start every barefoot session by slightly warming up your body before performing any stretches or drills, so that the body wakes up before you narrow the focus to the feet. One way of doing this is to jump rope or perform jumping jacks, both described next. When done barefoot, such warm-up routines have the added benefit of helping you focus on proper foot landing, warming up the calf muscles, and getting fit while having fun!

Jumping Rope

Jumping rope not only warms you up, you learn how to land carefully when barefoot.
(Photos by Eric Lang)

If you are new to jumping rope, the idea is to swing the rope over the body while jumping each time it swings under the feet. Start out very slow, and try to land as lightly as possible.

Jumping rope helps to increase your heart rate, which helps to pump more blood through the limbs. It is the perfect way to get the whole body warmed up and working together.

If you already jump rope as a part of your exercise program, try it without shoes. If you do not have a jump rope, consider fashioning your own or simply jumping without one. Start out doing only 2 sets of 10 twice a week for the first two weeks. Only then should you increase to 3 sets of 15 for two weeks.

Jumping Jacks

Jumping jacks help to warm up all the parts of the foot.
(Photo by Eric Lang)

Jumping jacks are an exercise where the legs spread outward and the hands clap together above the head for one jump, followed by the feet returning to their position under the body with the arms at the sides. Start out doing two sets of 10 to 15 jumps. Increase this slowly over the next few weeks.

You should try to jump rope or do jumping jacks on a flat surface, such as in a gymnasium or on the sidewalk.

On the Ball

Now that you have warmed up with some light activity, your entire body will be more limber, and the focus can be moved to the feet. The exercises described here are best done with a small ball, such as a tennis ball or a small rubber ball. Buy two balls: one for home and another for the office.

When first attempting these routines, avoid pressing down too hard on the ball with the weight of your body. Also, avoid moving other parts of the leg too much; the focus is on the foot and ankle, not the knee or hip. The foot should be doing most of the work. Ball exercises stimulate, stretch, and strengthen the various underside regions of the foot.

Feel the Heel

Focusing the ball just underneath the heel will warm up this often-neglected region of the foot.
(Photo by Eric Lang)

Give the heel some attention to warm up the ankle and Achilles tendon regions. To start, keep the front pads of the feet on the ground while rolling the ball underneath the heel. You can move back and forth as well as side to side. Another variant is to move the ball under the heel in a circular motion, which increases ankle flexibility. As you practice this drill, you will become better at it. Do this 10 to 20 times per foot and increase over time.

Front Pad Focus

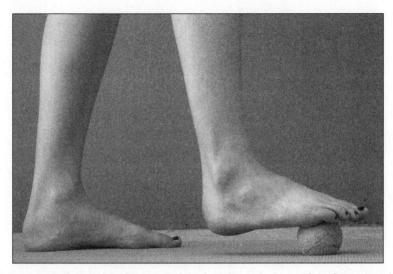

Rolling the ball under the front pad of the foot allows the bones of the feet to stretch, making them stronger and more nimble.
(Photo by Eric Lang)

Start out by rolling the ball forward and backward underneath the foot. The middle part of the foot, just underneath the arch, will bend slightly with increased pressure. Do this up to 20 times per foot before moving on.

With the heel on the ground, move the ball to the front part of the foot, just below the toes, to the forefoot pads. Move the ball back and forth, and then side to side 20 times per foot. Next, raise the heel off of the ground, allowing the toes to bend, while continuing to apply light pressure on the ball. With time, increase pressure slowly with both of these drills so that you feel the area stretch nicely. This part of the foot flexes most when running on trails and uneven terrain. The area flexes as if grabbing the ground to move you along.

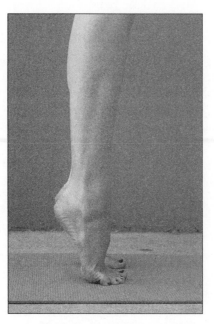

Coming up on the toes stretches the metatarsal bones and brings the toes to life!
(Photo by Eric Lang)

Pick Me Up Before You Go

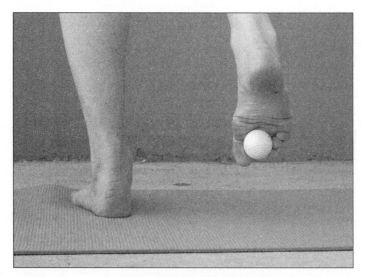

Picking up various sizes of balls (from golf balls to tennis balls) or other objects with the foot is one great way to build foot strength, adroitness, stamina, and agility.
(Photo by Eric Lang)

A ball is a versatile tool to help you gain total foot fitness. Start out by picking up a ball smaller than a tennis ball. A golf ball tends to work well. Hold the object for a count of five before lowering it to the ground. As an alternative, scrunching a towel with the toes is another good workout. As you progress, build yourself up to picking up larger (or smaller) objects. Coins, pens, pencils, erasers, and even sticks and leaves are all fair game!

ABCs and 123s

This drill is not for the faint of heart! The idea behind it is to write either the ABCs (or count to a certain number) by writing the letter or number in the air with each foot. This routine puts a lot of focus on the ankle in particular, as well as the Achilles tendon and calf muscles. As a bonus, the upper leg gets a nice isometric workout as well.

Writing the alphabet or counting to a certain number with the feet is one great way to loosen and build ankle fitness.
(Photo by Yasmine Bennis)

The best way to complete this routine is to sit flat on the ground with each leg extended out in front of your body. Place your arms behind you for added support. Lift your leg into the air to a comfortable height. Instead of completing the entire alphabet with each foot, start out by completing the whole alphabet with both feet (one foot does half, followed by the other). Or, better yet, count to 10 with each foot. After a few weeks, you'll be writing barefoot letters to all your fellow runners!

Keep 'Em Limber: Barefoot Stretches

On our website, while coaching, and while conducting clinics, the many advantages of regularly stretching not only the entire body, but especially the feet for barefoot activity, are highlighted. When warmed up, stretching the foot, ankle, and calves will help you substantially reduce any aches you might feel later. Additionally, carefully stretching the plantar fascia region has been shown to effectively treat 83 percent of patients who suffer from pain in the region. The ball exercises described previously will help, but here are a few other stretches to keep the lower extremities loose and limber.

ON YOUR TOES

Don't overstretch your feet. Perform all drills, exercises, and stretches carefully without straining. For those stretches that might require you to straighten your leg in front of the body, feel free to bend your knee if needed to avoid over-stressing the back part of the thigh, which is called the hamstring.

Toe-Back Stretch

While sitting on a flat surface, extend one leg in front of your body. The other leg can rest at your side. Place your hand behind your toes. Your fingertips should touch the upper part of the ball of your foot. Pull back gently. The toes will bend slightly back toward your body. Hold for a count of five before switching to the opposite foot. Do this two to three times per stretching session. If you're not quite flexible enough to reach your toes comfortably, use a towel, belt, or yoga mat strap to help.

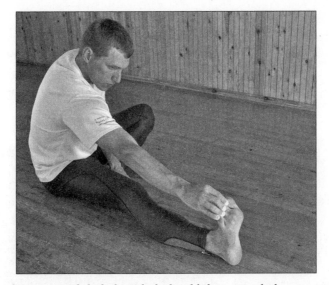

Bending the toes toward the body with the hand helps to stretch the toes antago-nistically. This is similar to how you must lift the toes when running over rugged terrain to prevent stubbing.
(Photo by Yasmine Bennis)

Upper-Foot Twist

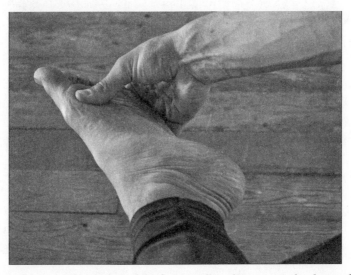

A wonderful stretch for the ball of the foot as well as the metatarsals, plantar fascia, and the lateral malleolus. The light twisting helps to quench any barefoot tightness.
(Photo by Yasmine Bennis)

This stretch is best completed while sitting on the edge of a chair. Place your foot on top of the opposite leg. If stretching your right foot, place the palm of your left hand underneath your foot while bending the four fingers to grip below the pinky toe, then place your left thumb on the underside padding beneath your big toe. Stretch the area by lightly pulling upward with your fingers and by pressing outward with your thumb.

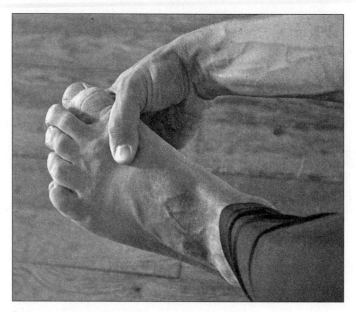

Upper-foot twist (opposite direction).
(Photo by Yasmine Bennis)

You can also do this stretch the opposite way, where you place your thumb on top (and slightly behind) your big toe while your four fingers press gently outward on the underside of the smallest toe. For beginners, both of these stretches should be held for 5 to 10 seconds with only two repetitions per foot.

Cool Feet: Toe Fan

Fanning your toes is one way to develop coordination between your toes and your mind. While sitting, place your heel on the ground and spread your toes out as wide as you are able. Hold for a few seconds before relaxing. Next, try wiggling your toes while spreading them.

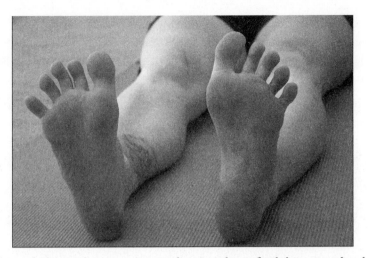

A stretch that teaches toes-to-eye coordination, the toe fan helps to spread and stretch the upper foot.
(Photo by Eric Lang)

Slant Stretch

Great for the Achilles tendon, plantar fascia, and calf muscle, the slant stretch culminates the stretching routine by bringing the foot and lower leg stretches together.
(Photo by Yasmine Bennis)

You can do the slant stretch while either sitting or standing. For beginners, it is best done while sitting down so that you can more readily control the pressure you place on your foot. If you already do this stretch while standing (which mostly benefits the calf muscles), try it sitting down to feel the difference while in bare feet.

Begin this stretch by placing your foot upward against a wall. Your heel remains on the ground as close to the wall as possible. Keep some space between the wall and the arch of your foot. Begin applying light pressure by moving your shin toward the wall, which will stretch your toes and plantar fascia. When done standing up, you can more easily focus on your calf muscles.

Ankle Stretches

Walking slowly with your feet pointed inward helps to stretch your outer ankle.
(Photo by Yasmine Bennis)

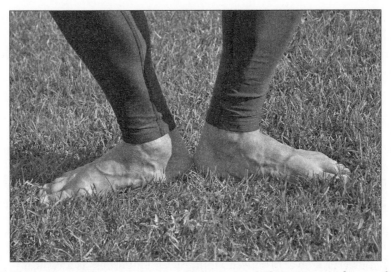

Walking with your feet pointed outward helps to stretch the inner part of your ankle.
(Photo by Yasmine Bennis)

Walking on the sides of your feet helps to stretch the top of your feet and helps with foot strengthening and flexibility.
(Photo by Yasmine Bennis)

Stretching your ankles helps to relax your foot and loosen the tissue connecting the calf and shin regions of your lower leg, so please note that such exercises should be done carefully. If you have suffered ankle pain (or injury) in the past, check with your doctor before performing these stretches.

Barefoot Strengthening

Throughout your barefoot transition (and beyond), building up the strength of your lower legs and feet is an endeavor that requires fortitude, resolve, and willpower. The drills outlined here are great for beginning barefoot runners as they help to strengthen those areas that are most vulnerable during the transitional stages.

Many runners who give up on their barefoot pursuits throw in the towel because of the initial aches or soreness in the foot, ankle, or calf. They might not have been aware that a certain level of muscle, foot, or leg tenderness is a typical part of the transitional process. Building up these areas of the lower legs results in less suffering, an easier transition, and faster recoveries.

Feel free to build these routines into your barefoot training plan, especially while you practice walking barefoot. Rotate barefoot walking days with drill days to give your body a break between each activity.

ON YOUR TOES

Ben Franklin's famous quote, "an ounce of prevention is worth a pound of cure," is undeniably true in the running world. When it comes to barefoot running, you'll want the muscles, ligaments, and tendons surrounding your foot and lower leg to become accustomed to stretching, flexing, and supporting you through various activities.

Do the following exercises without shoes (or socks) to ensure you have a full range of motion and feeling. Exercises described in later chapters will build upon these.

Ankle Pulls

For this exercise, you need a simple elastic resistance band (an exercise band or fitness band), which you can find at your local fitness store or online. You could also use a partner, but it's okay if you don't have one.

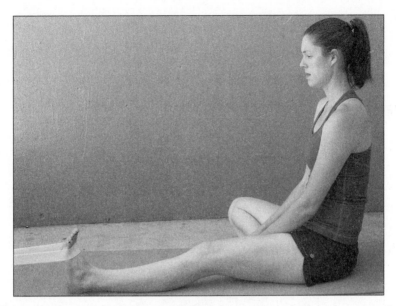

This ankle stretch should be done carefully. Be sure to count slowly and never strain your ankle too far in either direction.
(Photo by Eric Lang)

Sit flat on the floor (or on a yoga mat) and extend one leg out in front. The other leg can be in a rested position. Place the elastic band over the top of the extended foot. Now, have your partner slowly pull the elastic band away from your body so that it is partially taut. If you do not have a partner, tie the band around a solid object, such as a table or sofa leg.

Allow your foot to bend down so that your toes are pointed toward your partner, but not too far or the band will fly off of your foot! While counting in three-second intervals, move your foot upward toward your body until your foot becomes vertical again. Hold for a count of three. Then, lower it back down toward your partner while counting to three.

Start out doing only one set of five per foot, twice a week, for the first week. During the second and third weeks, do two sets of five per foot twice a week. As you continue, increase repetitions steadily by 10 percent, moving onto three sets a week by the two-month mark. You can also do this exercise in the opposite direction, where you hold the elastic band at your chest and provide resistance for your foot as you move it slowly downward.

Calf Raises: From the Floor

This exercise works the back of the lower legs. Rise as high as you can on the balls of your feet.
(Photo by Yasmine Bennis)

For this exercise, you will not necessarily need a partner, although having someone available to count or use as a stabilizer might prove useful. Best done on a yoga mat, place your feet about one foot-length apart. Slowly, counting in three-second segments, raise onto your toes. Hold for up to three seconds then count to three as you return your feet to their starting position. You can also do this routine by pointing the toes outward and inward.

Do five repetitions twice per week for the first two weeks. If you have no tenderness or pain, do it three times per week starting the third week, with 10 repetitions per set.

After a few weeks of doing calf raises with two feet, try one leg at a time. Remember to count slowly and take your time.
(Photo by Yasmine Bennis)

With one foot at a time, rise up onto the ball of your foot while counting to three, hold for one second, and lower slowly back down while counting to three. After doing five repetitions on one foot, move to the other. Do this exercise twice per week. After a few weeks, rotate between one- and two-foot calf raises.

Doing both ankle pulls and calf raises on a continual basis through the transition period and beyond will help ward off aches and pains later. Preliminary strengthening of these regions is vital before you ever take a running step without shoes.

Angled Balance Exercises

Doing the following routines on a raised, angled platform works nearly every part of the feet, calves, shins, and other lower-leg regions. Hold each pose for only five seconds at a time when you first begin. After two or three weeks, begin holding each stance for 15 to 20 seconds with two repetitions twice per week. Don't worry at first if you cannot raise up onto the balls of your feet. The skill will come with time. Don't forget to work each foot!

These balance routines help overall foot, ankle, and lower leg fitness isometrically. They are best done on a small, raised platform wide enough for one foot at a time. (Photo by Yasmine Bennis)

For the first exercise, the upward angle position, place one foot on the angled platform, toes pointing forward. Bring the opposite foot off the ground and slowly attempt to rise up on the toes of the foot on the platform. Focus your balance on the mid-section of your foot. As you hold, notice how your foot adjusts to the slight swaying of your body. This is similar to what your foot does as it adjusts to varying terrains.

Next, stand sideways on the platform to test your ability to maintain this slanted position. Try it with both feet at the same time and then with only the lower foot supporting your weight. Turn and face the opposite direction to work the other side.

Sideways angled balance.
(Photo by Yasmine Bennis)

Downward angled balance.
(Photo by Yasmine Bennis)

Finally, place one foot on the platform with your toes pointing downward. Bring the grounded foot up and try to balance on this slight downward slope. Do not lean backward or forward too far, just to the point where it feels like gravity might push you slightly forward. You will notice how much easier it is to come onto the mid-section of your foot.

This latter exercise allows you to focus (as if in slow motion) on what going down a hill with proper foot landing would be like. To run naturally downhill, your foot should carefully (and lightly) land below your center of gravity, while avoiding the heel-strike pattern that many runners use while flying down sloped terrain.

The Least You Need to Know

- Warming up before you run barefoot will increase bloodflow to the feet, which will prepare them for increased activity.
- Using a rubber ball or tennis ball before you run can help you warm up the nerves, muscles, and other tissues of the foot.
- Stretching and strengthening your feet will help them build resistance to the initial aches and pains of running without shoes.
- Stretching and strengthening the calf region of the legs will help immensely as you transition to barefoot running.

Natural Running

In This Chapter

- How modern innovations in running form affect you
- What to consider when thinking about running form
- How running barefoot promotes natural running form
- The fundamentals of running more naturally

The act of running is one of humanity's most astounding natural gifts. The human form in motion compares to that of any wild animal in its sheer beauty. Like any art, the skills that you learn over time can be improved with careful concentration, practice, and a dedicated desire to improve. Even if you have been running for decades without paying much attention to form, you can enhance the way you run to make the movement more natural, efficient, and energizing. It all starts with running barefoot.

The Philosophy of Form

Running form is a hot topic that has dominated the inner world of athleticism for some time. A variety of books and websites offer readers a variety of perspectives and other ways to think about human motion. Sports scientists in the field of biomechanics have studied the way humans move for decades. These experts are interested in a myriad of debates ranging from the evolution of human movement to the study of the most efficient way humans can run.

Understanding the mechanisms of how humans run can help you improve your performance, reach goals, push limits, and do what was once thought impossible. No one ever thought it humanly possible to run a mile in less than four minutes. Nor did they believe it feasible to run 100 miles without stopping, even for sleep. Both of these impossibilities became realities in the recent past, thanks to developments in human athletics and performance training. Knowing how to run more efficiently and naturally empowers runners to reach for the seemingly impossible.

FROM THE SOLE

The Guinness Book of World Records has Arulanantham Suresh Joachim as the world record holder for the longest treadmill run in 24 hours. On November 28–29, 2004, he completed 160.24 miles (257.88 km) in Ontario, Canada. For females, shoes off to Edit Berces who, on March 8–9, 2004, completed 153.6 miles (247.2 km) in Budapest, Hungary. Off the treadmill, the records are not as exact: ultra-marathon legend Dean Karnazes of the United States ran nearly 350 miles (560 km) without stopping, while Yiannis Kouros of Greece, known as the "Running God," owns several world records for ultra-distance running. He has even run 1,000 miles (1,600 km) in just over 10 days. He is rumored to have covered 456 miles (730 km) nonstop in four days in the late 1980s.

The *way* you run plays a crucial role in *how* you run. Simply fine-tuning your form will not necessarily mean that you will be able to conquer your first ultra-marathon, but perfecting your running style is central to making yourself a better all-around runner. Aspiring to perfect running technique is just one way to become a more fundamentally sound athlete.

An essential step in developing natural running form is to run barefoot. Simply taking off your shoes will not automatically result in better performance, but running barefoot promotes a more natural way of running that you can see and feel.

The top three benefits of taking off your shoes are that you will no longer …

1. Heel strike.

2. Overstride.

3. Rush your training.

If a coach is trying to teach proper form to athletes, simply having them take off their shoes eliminates several days (or weeks) of intensive sessions devoted to foot strike, stride, and habituating the body to change its old ways.

DIY Form

Some coaches rightly believe that each runner should discover his or her own form through careful experimentation. This is understandable, but runners must first be made aware of the fundamentals of the natural, relaxed technique that will assist them as they develop their gait, cadence, and stride.

Essentially, the philosophy of running form is identical to that of other sports: how you perform is heavily dependent upon the technique that you have learned, applied, and, of course, practiced. Humans possess a natural ability to run longer distances than any other species in the animal kingdom, so when it comes to reaching your distance-running goals, the Three D's of endurance running might help you out.

- **Devotion:** A devotion to the sport, bettering of your form, and sticking with your training program is easier said than done. Those who are devoted for the long term will enjoy many years of running.

- **Development:** The development of form is a crucial aspect of learning to run more naturally. When you develop the skills, you have to make sure that you do not develop bad habits that will hinder your ability later. Practicing form after an intense workout, especially when you are tired, will help you maintain solid technique on race day.

- **Distance:** You have to establish a training routine that allows you to increase your distance proportionally to the goals you have set. If you are not meeting your distance goals each week, reconsider your training plan or any events you have scheduled.

This is an exciting time to be a runner. Cutting-edge innovations such as barefoot running are giving athletes the opportunity to experience revolutionary ways to run like never before.

One Size Does Not Fit All

Just like the foam-and-rubber shoes that most runners consider critical to their performance, no single size will fit all when it comes to form. Striving for a more natural running style will require you to go through trial and error to discover the finer points of your own form. A handful of drills are discussed that will help you in the next chapter.

ON YOUR TOES

When first attempting to improve the way you run, take it one step at time. Try not to focus on too many details or overthink the process. Practice techniques with drills in this and the next chapter that will help you develop new skills. Improvements will surface with time as you continue to follow your training plan.

To run well, you need a grasp of the basic principles that will help the body and mind adjust for new habits. The progression involves learning new skills that will intrinsically change the way you run.

All of this is not to assume that certain runners do not develop good form on their own. Numerous runners who have developed good technique most likely found their way through trial and error, whether they realized it or not. People in some parts of the world simply grew up running as a way of life, perhaps even barefoot. Discovering your own natural running potential is what the quest for perfected form is about. After you've learned the basics, it is up to you to perfect your personal running style while monitoring and maintaining exceptional form.

The Foundations of Form

At its most basic level, running is honestly quite easy and can be done in many ways. For humans, running is fundamentally an act of motion in which both feet are off the ground during one cycle, usually in an attempt to move forward, perhaps faster than a normal walking speed.

Runners occasionally develop habits that can be detrimental to their hopes of improvement. Some runners might swing their arms from side to side, while others hold them stiff at their sides. Others might stride out as far as they can in an attempt to elongate their legs' reach—a perceived feeling of covering more ground with less effort. Even more runners rely totally on their legs to get them from point A to point B without considering that other parts of their bodies are involved in the procedure, namely the core.

Almost everyone can run, but not everyone runs correctly. Bad running habits can take the place of sound running form over time. Running with proper technique can be the decisive factor that makes or breaks a performance. Optimum form is pivotal at all levels of the sport.

Runners with good form have the potential to run faster. We will talk about the general aspects of form later in this chapter, but those who have a more relaxed stature, increased cadence, and the ability to use their overall core strength to allow gravity to naturally carry them forward are able to hold a faster pace than those who do not. If you want to achieve better running times, then you must break your running down to its essential parts, study your technique, and then pinpoint what you need to focus on to perform better.

Barefoot Running and Good Form

Barefoot running is important when talking about developing good form. When barefoot, the feedback of improper form can be rather immediate. If, for example, you discover a blister after your first 10-minute barefoot run, then you have to consider several theories. Were your feet skidding on the surface? Have your feet been conditioned slowly through barefoot walking and other exercises? Perhaps you were going too fast?

When combining form drills and barefoot running, you have little room to make a mistake. Shoes can seem comfortable when you are running in them, but they block the instant feedback that your feet provide, which means you might push yourself too hard, land forcefully, and overstride. Focusing on form while barefoot ensures that you will run slowly at first, land lightly, and increase the number of times your feet hit the ground, preventing the common mistakes that runners in shoes might initially make, or have a hard time altering.

The First Rule: Relax!

Runners, by nature, tend to have tight muscles, especially in the shoulders, back, and hamstrings. Before each run, and especially before jumping into formwork, try to tune in to your body's tight areas to relax them. It might seem odd that changing your form (or simply taking off your shoes) would cause any distress. Nevertheless, after you make the decision to run better, you will find yourself on a quest that is riddled with ecstatic ups, upsetting downs, new strengths, possible pain, enlightening discussions, and potential ridicule.

TIP TOES

Remember that running barefoot is a personal endeavor. It not only puts you closer to nature, but it will also keep you running for years on end. When you face doubts about running sans shoes, keep in mind that you are doing it, first and foremost, for yourself. Think about the time you have devoted thus far to barefoot running. Look over your training journal for a run that you really enjoyed. Recall that time, the good weather, the ambience, and the ground underfoot. Stick to your plan and it will pay off!

As with any major life change (and for passionate runners, barefoot running is up there), the result can be increased tension, anxiety, and uncertainty. This stress can wreak havoc on your body; tension in the neck, shoulders, back, and arms play an intricate part in the way your legs, ankles, and feet respond to the world below them. An inability to relax through the transitional period of barefoot running can ultimately hinder your ability to fine-tune your form.

Prior to heading out on a barefoot run, start by warming up, stretching gently, and doing some drills to help relax your body.

One hotspot for tension is in the neck and shoulder region, which can affect the rest of your body. Ease neck tension with the following stretches. Be sure to take it easy. Never use your hands or arms to push your neck in any direction. Additionally, do not go from one stretch to the other without returning the neck to a regular, relaxed, and upright position. When your posture is straight, move on to the next stretch. Keep the motions slow, careful, and easy.

Do this stretch gently. You should not overdo it, but gently bend and hold for a specified amount of time. Shutting the eyes can help with focus.
(Photo by Eric Lang)

This neck stretch helps the back part of the neck and upper shoulder blades relax. Imagine your chin resting on your chest, but do not push it to this position. Hold this stretch for 5 to 10 seconds, breathing in and out. Do this only two or three times per stretching session.

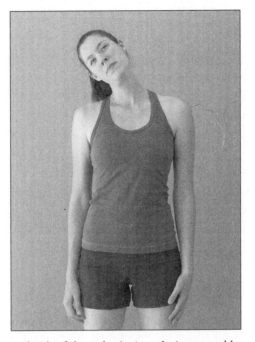

Do this stretch on each side of the neck. Again, take it easy and breathe in and out slowly.
(Photo by Eric Lang)

This stretch helps loosen the side of your neck while extending the benefits to your shoulders. Imagine your ear touching your shoulder, but don't push it that far. You can also bring your shoulder upward toward your ear. Hold this stretch for about five seconds on each side, breathing carefully in and out. Only do this stretch two or three times per stretching session.

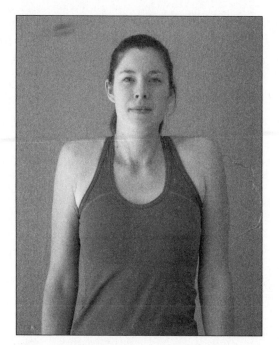

More than a stretch, scrunching the shoulders for a controlled amount of time helps to release tension in the shoulders and neck.
(Photo by Eric Lang)

While you hold your neck forward, your eyes should be looking straight ahead or be closed. Slowly bring your shoulders up toward your ears. Keep your back as straight as possible. Hold the pose for five seconds as you breathe in; exhale as you slowly bring your shoulders back to their resting position. This isometric stretch can help relieve tension in your neck, shoulders, and shoulder blades. Focus on doing this stretch once or twice with each session.

Beyond these basic stretches, runners tend to practice other forms of relaxation techniques that keep their upper limbs limber, legs loose, and body relaxed. If you do not practice any form of relaxation in your workout routine, consider adopting a method that allows you to be as relaxed as possible with each and every run.

Revolutions in Running Form

Over the last few years, various manuals on running have been published with the goal of helping runners overcome injury and enhance performance at a fundamental level. Some of these techniques have been studied and implemented by individuals, coaches, and even elite teams hoping to push their athletes to the top while avoiding injury. Most runners who pursue running excellence through barefoot techniques choose to adopt another program alongside their barefoot running program that can help them discover their own natural running form.

Talking about running form, especially barefoot running, without highlighting movements such as the Pose Method or ChiRunning, for example, would be to disregard techniques that have helped barefoot running gain so much momentum.

Pose Method

Based on the research by Doctor Nicholas Romanov, the endless search for learning about and perfecting the human runner led him to publish a book on his research called *The Pose Method of Running*. Focused on the biomechanics of running, Romanov demonstrates how altering your form will help eliminate injuries, increase endurance, and actually run faster while expending less energy. His research and revelations have caught the eyes of world-renowned athletes and coaches. With a focus on body posture, foot landing, increased cadence, and relaxed leg muscles, all while maintaining an astute center of gravity, Romanov's theories have worked well for both shod and barefoot runners alike.

When applied to barefoot running, the Pose Method promotes a forefoot landing where the heels do not necessarily touch the ground. As the cycle continues, the ankle lifting up off of the ground (the recovery foot) is raised by the hamstring, which creates what is referred to as a compact "pendulum." The resulting stride is quicker than a more elongated stride.

The Pose Method dictates that a runner should learn the skills that will allow gravity to do the real work, while the runner uses muscle elasticity, landing technique, and the body's core to allow the body to move forward efficiently. Visit www.posetech. com for more information about the Pose Method and how you can apply it to your training.

ChiRunning

Based on the Chinese concept of tai chi (or the art of "soft" human motion), ChiRunning was developed by Danny Dreyer, whose goal is to teach runners that efficient, natural form matters most. Fundamentally analogous to other schools that teach natural-motion techniques, ChiRunning uses the idea that the body should work with the forces of nature, namely gravity, to allow the runner to run more naturally.

ChiRunning uses the core of the body to maintain straight posture, a mid-foot landing (made possible while in a shoe with a contoured footbed) and a focus on placing the foot at the body's center of gravity. This is done with a slight forward lean (or a "fall forward"), bent knees, and a concentration on arm swing. The inherent idea behind ChiRunning is for runners to become mindful of their bodies by using body-scanning practices to relieve tension and discomfort. Visit www.ChiRunning.com to learn more about applying ChiRunning to your barefoot running program.

Both the Pose Method and ChiRunning promote natural running proficiency by teaching natural form while lowering potential injury rates. Numerous barefoot runners adopt facets of Pose Method, ChiRunning, or other techniques in their training programs. Adopting a certain technique does not mean you cannot alter it to fit your needs. Anything that helps you to think more deeply about form, body positioning, and energy efficiency is worthwhile, but as with any technique exploration, you should experiment carefully, implement slowly, and increase activity gradually.

Natural Barefoot Running Form

For the majority of people, running changes drastically once they throw their shoes to the wayside. Though the philosophies of the Pose Method and ChiRunning view running from different perspectives, both teach the rudiments of natural form. Focusing on some basic elements of form will help you find your own natural running style.

Besides relaxing, the most important factor in running proficiently is keeping your body well aligned. Having a straight posture ensures the whole body is engaged in carrying you forward. Poor posture results in poor running form (and slower performance times). Runners with poor posture place too much emphasis on the legs to "carry" the dead weight of the upper body through a run. Starting from the head downward, the keys to good posture while running are all about alignment.

Your Head

Beginning barefoot runners tend to look at the ground directly in front of their feet, but you should learn to look 10 or more feet ahead as you get better at navigating the terrain. Looking directly down at your feet brings your chin toward your chest, which results in neck stiffness and improper alignment for the rest of your body. The human head weighs an average of more than 10 pounds (4.5 kilos), which is quite a block of weight for the neck to support when not held in a straightened position.

You also need to relax your jaw muscles when you run. Refrain from holding any expressions (other than a smile, of course), and avoid clenching the teeth tightly together. When running, you can maintain a relaxed jaw more easily if you allow air to be exhaled naturally along the cheeks and through the mouth as if sighing.

Additionally, your head should not swing from side to side. In longer events, when your body is tired, your head might begin to feel heavy. Warming up, stretching, and keeping your upper body strong will help carry you through prolonged activity. Runners whose heads bobble back and forth when they are running are not using physics to their advantage. To run forward smoothly, make certain that your entire body is helping you with forward momentum. A bobbing, bouncing, or swinging head will throw off the entire balance of your body and can potentially lead to other problems with your shoulders, neck, and upper back.

Your Shoulders, Arms, and Hands

Keeping your shoulders relaxed while you run might feel a bit awkward at first, but after several sessions of holding a nice, relaxed, yet straight posture, you will begin to feel the benefits.

When running, your arms should swing in line with each respective shoulder. Imagine a line drawn directly in front of your body, dividing you right down the center. Your arms should never cross this central line. The unnatural twisting of the thorax led by your arms tightens your core and restricts forward motion, throwing off the forward momentum of your body.

Swimmers and triathletes in particular often have a problem with maintaining good posture when they run because extensive swimming exercises can actually pull the shoulders slightly forward.

Allow your arms to swing forward and backward without bent elbows. Avoid twisting your thorax.
(Photo by Yasmine Bennis)

To practice arm swinging, stand up with your hands at your sides. Gently swing your arms forward and backward with no bend in your elbows. Allow your arms to swing naturally back and forth.

Now bend your elbows to 90 degrees as you continue to move your arms back and forth. By bringing your arms upward, you are allowing your shoulders to remain relaxed. Your hands will come in slightly, pushing your elbows slightly outward. The placement of your hands is in line with the top of your stomach or bottom of your chest. As you run, your hands might approach the centerline of your body, but they should never cross it. Doing so encourages twisting, which will throw off your forward momentum.

When your elbows are bent, tuck them up into a relaxed position without scrunching your shoulders, which helps keep your entire upper body relaxed.
(Photo by Yasmine Bennis)

By relaxing the hands, you can actually prevent the upper body from becoming so tight.
(Photo by Yasmine Bennis)

All the tension that can build up in the upper body while running can ruin anyone's form. Relax your hands by bringing your thumb to rest on top of the index finger or by bringing the index finger and thumb lightly together (as in yoga).

You can encourage your upper body to relax by integrating a fun drill known as Sloppy Waiter into your workouts. As you continue moving your arms forward and backward with your elbows bent at 90 degrees, rotate the palms of your hands so they are facing upward. With each step, bring the opposite, open palm up to your chest, as if you are a sloppy waiter spilling soup on yourself. This drill is especially effective as you run, to help eliminate that dreaded heavy feeling of the forearms or tightness of the shoulders.

The Sloppy Waiter helps you relax your hands, elbows, and shoulders. It gives you a moment to ensure no part of your upper body is tense.
(Photo by Yasmine Bennis)

Your Back

When talking about posture, most often it refers to the alignment of the spine. Good posture is best maintained by keeping your spine aligned with your neck, shoulders, and hips. Slumping over when you run most often occurs as you begin to fatigue, which feels better than holding your upper body straight but is detrimental to fluid movement. To ensure proper posture even when you are tired, work on strengthening your core stomach muscles, which is discussed in the next chapter.

Slumping disengages the core of your body and it becomes dead weight for your legs. This is poor running posture.
(Photo by Yasmine Bennis)

An example of proper, erect running posture. Keeping your body aligned allows you to engage your core while using gravity to help maintain momentum.
(Photo by Yasmine Bennis)

Your Torso, Hips, Glutes, and Pelvis

Your torso or upper body includes the back and needs to remain as straight as possible. This straight posture is often called running "proud" or "tall," but the upper body also needs to remain as relaxed as possible. Your diaphragm should be elongated to allow for optimal breathing and forward motion.

The center of gravity for runners is the hips, glutei (buttocks), and pelvis. Whatever direction this mid-section of your body is pointed will be the direction you will go. You can aid forward momentum greatly if the core region of your body is properly engaged, so keeping this area conditioned will help you perform more efficiently.

When running, it is essential that the hips do not move from side to side, but instead remain relaxed and pointed straight forward. Also, your buttocks need to remain in line with the rest of your body. Avoid pulling your butt inward or pushing it outward as you run.

Finally, your pelvis should be held in a neutral position. Avoid leaning forward or pushing outward. Pivoting the pelvis in any direction is an undesirable running trait that even professional runners develop if they do not monitor their form closely. The result of a forward lean of the upper body that keeps the lower carriage, or legs, straight is a potential injury for the entire lower body, including the hamstrings, knees, ankles, and feet. To keep the pelvis neutral, your front waistline should be in line with your back. Imagine a leveling rod held at your waist. When you run, the movable marker inside the liquid should not move from its center position.

Swinging your body from side to side results in a twisting motion, which goes against your natural forward momentum.
(Photo by Yasmine Bennis)

Your Knees

One of the most important components of running more naturally is keeping your knees slightly bent throughout the entire running cycle. If done properly, your knees will not suffer from (or absorb) any shock, regardless of the surface. For barefoot runners and even those in minimal footwear, shock is decreased dramatically (almost entirely) thanks to proper landing, feedback, and intuitive musculature adjustments.

Maintaining bent knees throughout the entire running cycle will ensure that you are not overstriding. It also helps prevent your knees from absorbing shock with each step.
(Photo by Yasmine Bennis)

ON YOUR TOES

As you focus on keeping your knees bent, keep in mind that you should not force the movement. Pushing your butt outward causes unnecessary extra pressure on your lower legs. Maintain good posture, ensure that your feet land below your center of gravity, and focus on proper stride with a high turnover rate.

Your Ankles and Feet

It may seem difficult to relax your ankles, but it's important to keep them loose when running without shoes. Loose ankles will help ensure proper foot landing with each and every step. Before starting off on a run, perform the ankle stretches described in Chapter 6. If you experience pain or swelling in your ankles, back off from running, allow them to heal, and then assess what could be causing the issue. Leaning forward too much can cause ankle strain and even shin splints.

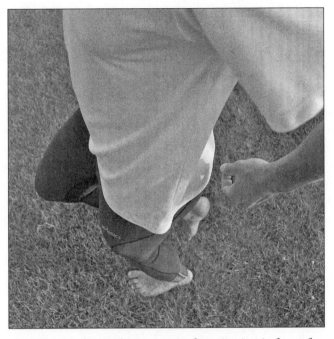

Your feet should land in line with your center of gravity, just in front of your hip line.
(Photo by Yasmine Bennis)

Your feet, too, should be relaxed, yet ready to quickly adjust to changes in the terrain. Focus on landing as quietly and lightly as possible without pushing off. The drills described later will help you develop "quick feet."

Because most mainstream running shoes promote a heel-first landing, runners actually roll the foot forward, as if in a rocker. The resulting movement causes runners to push off into the next step because of the braking action that a heel produces. This is a movement that takes extra time, energy, and force.

When no shoes are worn, the foot takes on a completely different role. Running more naturally involves tossing aside your previous inclinations about the purpose of the foot. Your foot should not push you through the next step, but simply provide your body with a well-adjusted, light landing. When barefoot, no propulsive force is applied by the feet, which results in no energy being wasted.

Knowing Newton: Gravity's Role

Both the Pose Method and ChiRunning discuss how you can use gravity in your favor to help carry you forward. In our experience, a slight forward lean of the whole body helps move you forward without any extra expenditure of energy. This forward lean, however, should not adversely affect your posture.

You can start to use gravity in your favor by simply standing in place in front of a wall. Maintain a straight posture as you begin leaning forward. From your ankles, move your whole body, which should be held tightly aligned with the core. This will create an angle from your feet on the ground with the tilt of your entire body forward. If you do this without a wall directly in front of you, at some point you will have to put a foot out to catch yourself. To create forward motion, you must lean forward until the point where gravity insists you catch yourself with the next step, but this movement cannot be counterproductive to an erect body position, otherwise you put extra strain on your lower legs.

An example of running with a slight forward lean. This enables gravity to assist with your forward momentum. Notice the slight forward angle that is created from the ankles upward.
(Photo by Yasmine Bennis)

Falling with Style

Gravity isn't always on your side, especially as you take your barefoot running to new heights by attempting different types of terrain. Tripping, stumbling, or falling over roots, stumps, knobs of downed trees, curbs, or simple changes in the ground are all possibilities with or without shoes. Such objects on and off the road can make barefoot running slightly more dangerous no matter the time of year.

It goes without saying that, to avoid tripping, one should pay careful attention to the ground ahead—another point where mindfulness in barefoot running is highlighted. For barefoot runners, practice using the information your feet and eyes gather to accurately guide you over the ground. Trust your feet to relay the subtlest differences in the terrain to your brain while using your eyes to help navigate safely. You will be surprised at how quickly you can adjust your landing as needed to avoid any tumbles.

There are two types of falling: slipping and tripping. Knowing how to fall safely is a way to keep yourself out of harm's way. Practicing (or even visualizing) what to do when you begin to trip will help decrease the likelihood of injury.

The impact of falling or slipping backward can be decreased if you avoid using your hands and allow the body to roll and absorb the blow.
(Photo by Fazia Farrook)

When slipping, you tend to fall backward as your legs come out from under you. It can occur anywhere but usually occurs while running down steeper grades or when you lose traction on loose or wet leaves or pavement. People falling backward will often try to catch themselves with their hands on the ground in an attempt to brace the fall. Hence, most injuries from slipping involve sprains (or breaks) occurring to a part of the arm, usually the wrist.

To avoid injury when falling or slipping backward, practice falling without using your hands to catch yourself. Landing on the buttocks is one painful option. Rolling backward from your lower hip (and onto your shoulder if needed) while keeping your chin tucked (which prevents your head from hitting the ground) is another. If you are not able to, you can use your arms to absorb impact by bringing them out to your sides and forcefully catching the ground as you land.

The impact of falling forward can be decreased if you practice rolling from the upper arm to the shoulder.
(Photo by Fazia Farrook)

When tripping, you tend to fall forward as your foot is snagged or caught on something. Tripping is more common when running because of the increased momentum of forward motion. When falling forward, you often tense up, attempt to grab something (or someone) to keep you from falling, and sprawl out when hitting the ground.

There are several ways to fall forward. Many of these, based on martial arts, suggest that you *practice falling*, so you are not scared of it. The more skilled you are, the more relaxed you will be, and the more your reflexes will take over to ensure a safe landing.

Like falling backward, you need to avoid landing on your hands, which can injure your wrists. With any sort of forward or backward fall, the best way to avoid injury is for the body to roll over (similar to a backward or forward somersault). At the basic level, rolling from the upper arm to the shoulder best absorbs the impact of falling forward.

If you fall and are not injured badly, check yourself over, walk for a few minutes, and continue jogging. Sitting down and thinking about the fall may unnerve you, while continuing to run will help calm you down.

Leg It: Three Keys to Barefoot Form

Maintaining good posture while allowing gravity to assist your forward motion is one of the key factors in running naturally, but there are other things you should do to ensure proper form. Developing your natural form requires an intense focus on your entire body. Because running involves extensive use of your legs, it is important to become proficient in using your legs to help you move gracefully forward. As you begin perfecting your barefoot running form, keep three important things in mind.

Natural Springs

Natural springs do not imply that you should bounce up and down when you run, which is a major culprit of energy loss. Working to eliminate bounce is an important key to running more naturally.

When referring to natural springs, we're talking about elastic energy stored with each step. The springs come into action after the foot has touched the ground. The springs of the legs help you to continue your stride and give the legs time to recoil (and relax) before the next step. When combined with a slight forward lean, which allows you to work with gravity, you are using natural elements in your favor to help the body store energy throughout your entire run.

Cadence

The number of times your foot touches the ground during a period of time is known as your cadence. Cadence is important in energy conservation, injury prevention, and speed. If you watch the elite runners participating in big city marathons, you will notice that they all hold a high cadence throughout the entire race. Their feet are touching the ground many more times per minute than those farther back in the pack.

Admittedly, those runners are running as fast as (or faster than) a sprinter, so of course their legs are moving faster. The point is that, no matter their speed or distance, elite runners maintain a high cadence with each and every run, from 1,500 meters to ultra-marathons. What you can learn by watching the crème de la crème of runners is that they are very efficient, natural, and relaxed athletes.

TIP TOES

Calculating your cadence is an easy math problem. While running on a flat sur-face, count how many times one foot touches the ground per minute. Multiply this by two. Do this exercise three times, then find the average of those three results by adding them together and dividing by three. How close do you come to matching an elite runner's cadence?

Elite athletes maintain an average cadence of 180 to 210 on a flat course; that is, these runners are taking approximately 200 steps per minute. Going uphill, this average number of steps decreases by about 20; going downhill it increases by 20 to 30 steps. It is important to emphasize that, regardless of whether these athletes are warming up or racing, or what distance they are running, their cadence always remains constant.

If you have a low cadence, consider working on increasing it to run barefoot more naturally. Drills designed to increase your cadence are discussed in the next chapter. A higher cadence ensures that you are not overstriding, and that you are limiting your foot's (and ultimately your body's) contact with the ground, which results in less impact force with each step.

Ultimately, this reduced contact with the ground results in an increase of power (and energy) for you, a proven method of running faster without expending extra energy. Energy will only be lost if the bottom foot lingers too long underneath or behind the body as it continues forward (caused by pushing off or overstriding). Therefore, cadence alone will not necessarily determine speed, but an ideal cadence of 180 or more, combined with reduced contact time with the ground, will aid you immensely in the long run.

Stride

Another major component of running more naturally is stride. Stride and cadence are closely related in what they do for you, and are most often talked about together. For the purposes here, cadence is how often you touch the ground in a given amount of time; stride is the distance covered with each step.

An athlete wanting to increase cadence while fine-tuning stride should proceed with caution. Overstriding can wreak havoc on your leg joints; it occurs when the leg is too far extended in front of the runner's center of gravity, which means the knee is no longer in its optimal bent position.

When you have undergone a good portion of your barefoot training program while working to develop proficient form, you will feel more energized, balanced, light, and in tune with your body and the elements. The numerous advantages of better form are realized over time with increased energy, potential resistance to injury, and heightened bodily awareness, coordination, and strength. Running without shoes over a carefully planned transition period while focusing on form allows you to discover, adapt, and inherently acquire the skills necessary to run the way Mother Nature intended humans to move.

The Least You Need to Know

- Understanding the mechanics of form can help you greatly as you adapt to a more natural way of running.
- One size will not necessarily fit all when talking about developing barefoot running form.
- Staying relaxed is an important component of running more naturally.
- Other components of good form include excellent posture, an engaged core, relaxed arms, bent knees, a straight torso, proper foot landing, and the ability to use gravity in your favor.

Improving Your Running Form

In This Chapter

- Why mental focus is as important as proper technique
- Why a strong body core is important in barefoot running
- What drills are important to enhance running efficiency
- How to tackle hills with correct form

A huge misconception is floating around out there that running causes injuries. The human machine is well designed to run long distances over a long period of time; the cause of most injuries is actually improper running and training techniques.

This chapter does not claim that running barefoot will solve all your running woes, nor that wearing mainstream shoes will either. But it does contend that barefoot running reteaches the body how to run, in turn transforming runners into stronger athletes. Running without shoes is not a miracle cure for injuries or flawed running techniques, but it is a way to view your own running life through a different lens, one that will allow you to build yourself anew from within.

She's Got Legs

You can often tell elite, professional runners by certain striking characteristics. The first is physical appearance. Professional runners have perfectly slender bodies. Like a beautifully sleek greyhound, these elite runners have lean muscle mass. Their legs and arms are often thin, yet amazingly durable and strong. These same barrel-chested runners have a robust core, or midsection, that allows them to run longer distances with lightning speed, endurance, and efficiency.

In the United States, a focus on strength training (or power training) has gained attention for the quick results it produces. Strength training's main focus is on short, intense workout sessions that build strength and bulk.

The belief that athletes need to be bigger to be better is counterproductive to injury prevention and (especially with running) performing at your peak. A runner with thick legs competing against a well-trained, slender runner will never win a race. The larger runner's muscles are actually working against him by creating more *lactate* (or lactic acid), requiring more oxygen, and using up more energy with each heavy step.

DEFINITION

Produced and used during exercise, **lactate** (measured as lactic acid concentration) was once thought to cause soreness and muscle fatigue when produced. Lactate is actually fuel for muscle. Changes in lactate production occur as a runner becomes more fit. These changes are measurable by observing a runners' lactate curve. Runners who reach their max performance are said to have reached their lactate (or anaerobic) threshold.

Serious runners should limit power training. At some point, with a focus on pure power, your body will succumb to injury. For many people, running is a way of life with long-lasting benefits. True runners think carefully about their athletic futures to sustain themselves in the sport. They don't push themselves in and out of sickness and injury. Continue to plan your running future, gradually meet goals, perfect your technique, and you'll begin to see the results and rewards of calculated planning and mindful running.

Mindfulness in Barefoot Running

Seasoned runners tend to become (extremely) devoted to their scheduled runs for a variety of reasons. Many claim they are addicted to endorphins. Others use their runs as an opportunity to reflect, away from a busy work or home life. Barefoot running in particular adds another dimension to the sport because it has the potential to put you closer to nature.

Being immersed in your natural surroundings has a way of calming any day-to-day internal strife that you might be experiencing. Runners who are committed to bettering their form by going barefoot will discover the meditative aspects of running are multiplied by the simple act of running without shoes. Allowing the foot to feel, react, and become stronger while tuning in with the Earth brings great awareness, focus, stimulation, and satisfaction. No longer can you blame your running addiction wholly on endorphins, but you will also develop a passion for being connected with the elements.

And, because barefoot running promotes natural form, a multitude of mistakes are corrected inherently when the tactile sensing of the terrain takes over through proprioception. Barefoot running also promotes better form, so you may notice an increase in energy rather than exhaustion after a run or workout. By treating your body better (through proper form and a well-developed running plan), you will begin to eliminate the aches, pains, and soreness that characterize many runners' life span.

As you continue with your barefoot running program, be mindful of the mental (and possibly even spiritual) transitions that you undergo, and keep track of these changes in your barefoot running journal. Running without shoes has a way of focusing the act of running from the external to the internal, from measuring your own heartbeat with the heart of everything around you. As you make barefoot running a part of your overall running toolkit, it becomes a part of who you are more than a part of what you do.

From novices to world-record contenders, barefoot running takes nothing away from training. In fact, the initial dedication needed to transition properly and the skills you've developed while doing so will add a whole new dimension to how you run. It improves your form, cadence, stride, energy exertion, shock absorption, and even breathing patterns. Fine-tuning these aspects is beneficial, regardless of a runner's expertise.

Just like Earth's terrain, you will experience peaks and valleys on your barefoot pursuit. Expect to experience good and bad moments when you run, and have a game plan for each. When you're down in a valley, keep in mind that the next peak is right around the bend. On a day that stands out, ask yourself: *Why do I feel good? What was the terrain like? The weather? Did my form feel natural? What was on my mind? Was I focused?*

Sticking with barefoot running and taking advantage of the mental, emotional, and physical benefits makes those days atop the mountains even better.

Mind Over Manner

The previous chapter focused on the idea that running more naturally will improve the way you run. Your mind cannot control everything around you, but it can control how you react to it. Barefoot running requires a diligent focus on the fundamental skills that will enhance not only the way you run, but how you feel when you run.

Controlling your body's positioning, being more self-aware, and staying focused not only allows the meditative aspects of barefoot running to surface, but also helps to keep you safe and injury-free. If you look away for even just a moment, a stubbed toe or gnarly scrape could be in your future! Running barefoot allows you to control your body in a way that running in shoes does not. You literally control the *manner* in which you run without giving much thought to the *matter* of the situation, the end goal, or other diversions that will lead your concentration astray.

To ensure that you are maintaining good form, get in the habit of performing a self-scan to check aspects of your form as you run. One way to do this is to set your watch as if you were doing interval training. Program the watch to beep every five minutes, and when the watch beeps, check your form from the feet up. This becomes especially crucial toward the end of a longer outing when you begin to feel fatigued. And don't forget to keep an eye on the terrain in front of you!

Here are some key points to keep in mind as you scan your form. Start by focusing on one or two main areas. Then, with each run, add in an extra checkpoint.

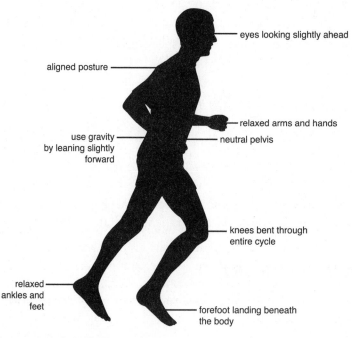

Barefoot running form checkpoints.

❑ Forefoot landing in line with the body

❑ Relaxed ankles, allowing a slight lean forward

❑ Lifting the feet rather than pushing off

❑ Bent knees throughout the entire cycle

❑ Pelvis tucked under the hips

❑ Back, neck, and face aligned with good posture

❑ Arms swinging loosely with a 90-degree or more bend

❑ Hands loosely cupped, as if holding an egg

❑ Breathing in rhythm to bodily movement

❑ Calmly inhaling and exhaling fully

If you identify any areas of pain, tightness, or soreness, feel free to stop, relax, breathe, and lightly stretch the area. If you are tight in the arms, shoulders, stomach, or chest, drop your hands and shake your arms slightly as you take your run down to a slow jog or brisk walk for one to two minutes. If breathing is a problem, slow down and relax your body. Give your body time to adjust, balance, and get back on track.

Doing a self-scan at regular intervals as you run helps you avoid bad running habits. As you increase your distance and training and begin to meet your goals, do daily running scans to ensure that you maintain proficient technique with each and every run.

Building Core Strength

Strengthening your core will help you run with better technique, greater efficiency, and more energy. The core is where true running power stems. A strong carriage is pivotal to proficient forward movement because it holds the body in alignment, uses gravity in your favor, and carries you through even the toughest of events. A sturdy mid-section is literally the "core" of perfect form.

Most people do not enjoy working out in a weight room where you have to pay for a membership, adhere to specific hours, and work out with others. The great aspect of developing a strong core is that you can do many of the workouts in your own home with a simple weight set, at your convenience. You can do several of the stretches, drills, and exercises in 15-minute sessions once or twice per week. As with any new exercise, take it slow at first.

TIP TOES

With most of the workouts discussed, starting off doing five repetitions is recommended. As you become more used to the movements (especially with weights), you can increase this gradually to 8, 10, 12, and even 15 or more repetitions up to 3 sets. Give yourself a few months to build yourself slowly. It's best to build muscle endurance with lighter weight and increased repetitions. Avoid strength training with heavy weights that will only add bulk with no real increase in endurance.

While outlining and implementing your running plan over the next several months, begin incorporating core workouts into your running workouts. If you need more time to do them, deducting a few minutes from a run to work your mid-section is a worthwhile trade-off. A strong posture supported by a lean core will do more to carry you through an event than a few extra minutes on the road. Strength training, especially in this part of the body, will truly benefit you in the long run.

Working on Posture

Regardless of your daily schedule, you can make time to work on your posture throughout the day. Make the effort to sit, stand, drive, and even sleep with a well-aligned carriage. Try to continually remind yourself to keep a straight back, neck, and shoulders. Place a reminder note on the screen of your computer at home and in the office. While driving, put the seat in an upright position where the knees are higher than the lower back. When lifting heavy items, lift with your legs and keep your back straight. Doing these things will help you improve and maintain a straight and strong body.

TIP TOES

Invest in an inflatable exercise ball to sit on at your home desk and at work. Start with half an hour per day and work gradually over the next three to four months toward sitting on it for most of the day. An exercise ball makes the perfect chair by helping keep your back straight, improving your core strength, and even burning up to 350 extra calories throughout the day!

One of the best ways to improve your posture (besides focusing on it throughout your day) is to strengthen the muscles that surround the spine, namely the deep abdominal muscles, as well as the middle and upper back. Weak muscles in the region make you slump forward. Strong muscles, however, will allow you to engage them over a longer period of time, and you will find that it is actually more comfortable to walk or sit straight instead of slumping.

If you have ever experienced any back pain, give yourself some extra time to become stronger, and proceed with extra caution. Before beginning a weight-lifting program, talk with your doctor or sports practitioner about your strength-training goals. When you have the green light, consider hiring an experienced trainer to teach you the skills that will work best for your long-term objectives.

ON YOUR TOES

Look for a professional trainer who has coached or currently coaches runners. A trainer needs to relate to and deeply understand your vision. Avoid fitness experts whose goal is to bulk you up by increasing weight and pouring protein shakes down your gullet!

Do the following drills with light weights. At first, do no more than 8 to 10 repetitions of 2 to 3 sets each. After a few weeks, begin increasing repetitions to 10 to 12 before increasing the weight. Make your muscles stronger for stamina and endurance, not to build bulk.

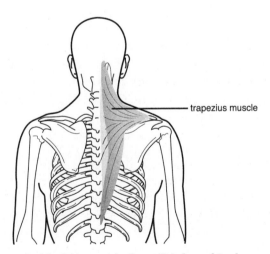

The trapezius muscle (also known as the "traps") is located in the upper-middle back.

Here, you can see the location of the trapezius region of the back. Being strong here helps to counterpoise the front, often tighter muscles of the body. Balancing the back muscles with the core will help promote good posture and upper-body balance, especially when you run.

The Upright Bar Lift will help you work the trapezius muscles. Start out practicing the movement without weights.
(Photo by Yasmine Bennis)

To do the Upright Bar Lift, stand with your feet shoulder-width apart, holding the bar in front of your body at your waist. Your hands should also be shoulder-width apart. Begin by raising the bar to a point just below your chin as you inhale. Your elbows should bend outward as you raise the bar. Hold for one second and then gradually exhale as you return the bar back down to your waist. Start out doing two sets of five repetitions. Increase the weight and repetitions gradually over the next several weeks to 8, 10, and 12. Muscle endurance requires several repetitions of medium weight.

To Fly Like an Eagle, start by bending over slightly so that your stomach is perpendicular to the ground while keeping your back straight. Keep your neck in line with your back. Your knees can be bent slightly. With your arms hung below your chest, bring them out to your sides as if you are getting ready to take off for flight. Do not extend your arms past the point of comfort; this puts stress on your shoulders. At the apex, hold slightly, and then exhale slowly as you bring your arms back down to their resting position. Start out doing two or three sets of five repetitions with little or no weights. Gradually increase the number of repetitions over time, never bringing the weights too high.

This lift works both the middle traps and shoulders. It should be done with very little to no weights at first.
(Photo by Yasmine Bennis)

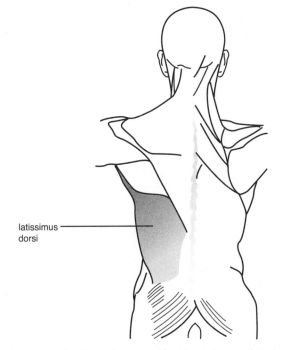

latissimus
dorsi

The latissimus dorsi muscle group (the "lats") is one of the largest bundles of muscle tissues in the entire back.

The lats are located on both sides of the spine. Having strong lats helps the upper and middle back maintain a poised posture throughout your daily activities.

This classic lat exercise requires special equipment that you can find at most gyms.
(Photo by Yasmine Bennis)

While sitting, this Back Lat Pull Down is best done by placing your arms on the bar above your head. Your hands should be slightly more than shoulder-width apart. Pull the bar down slowly behind your head while inhaling, hold for a count of one, and allow the bar to return upward as you exhale slowly.

For the first couple of weeks, do not use much weight (if any) for this routine. It is important to get a feel for the machine and the motion involved, as well as using the correct technique. Avoid doing more than two variations of this routine for the first few weeks. This will allow the lats to become acclimated to the new movement. Start with two sets of five repetitions using light weights. When you can easily do 3 sets of 10 repetitions, start adding weight over the next few weeks.

In addition to lat pulls, regular push-ups can also work this area of the back while toning the pectoral (or chest) muscles. Balance any push-up workouts with a light shoulder workout.

You can also do a variation of this pull called the Front Lat Pull Down by bringing the bar in front of the body to a point above your chest.
(Photo by Yasmine Bennis)

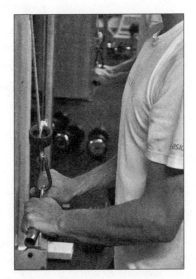

A third alternative is the Hand-to-Hand Lat Pull Down. Place your hands close together while pulling the bar down in front of the body. This also works the tricep muscles on the back of the upper arms.
(Photo by Yasmine Bennis)

Hard-Core Workouts

Interestingly, people with six-pack abs may not necessarily have a strong trunk—the rectus abdominus muscle that makes up the front stomach muscles are superficial in regard to their effect on overall torso strength. According to Michael Fredericson, Ph.D., a running biomechanics expert at Stanford University, nearly 90 percent of runners who exhibit inefficient form do not have strong, deep abdominal muscles. Having overall proficient, natural form requires that your legs not do all the work when you run.

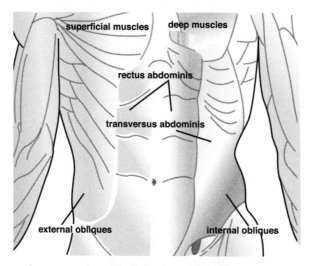

In addition to the upper and middle back, the muscles of the trunk surrounding the front and back regions of the stomach play an intricate role in the way you run. For the purposes here, core strengthening includes the upper, middle, and lower stomach (including the diaphragm) as well as the obliques and lower back.

FROM THE SOLE

Famed magician and escape artist Harry Houdini (Ehrich Weiss) boasted of his strong abs. One of his claims was that he could take a punch above the belt by anyone without being harmed. When a university student repeatedly punched Houdini, who did not have a chance to tighten his abs and was not ready for the blows, Houdini was taken aback, and historical rumor has it that this was the cause of Houdini's death. Although the jabs were not helpful, Houdini had been suffering from appendicitis for several days prior, but had refused medical treatment. It was this that actually caused his eventual demise.

The torso is the nucleus of your entire body, so if it is weak, then your whole body is not as strong as it should be, especially for running. Having a strong midsection promoted by exercises such as *Pilates* allows the legs to work in sync with the rest of the body's movements. The forward lean combined with excellent posture is best maintained with a strong, balanced torso.

DEFINITION

Pilates is a workout system that focuses on strengthening the core, or torso, of the body and spine. Similar to yoga, Pilates works on the connection of mind and body to promote the exertion of the muscles through graceful movement and breathing. Starting Pilates with a certified instructor is one of the best ways to learn various routines that will increase your core strength while helping raise awareness between your mind and body.

As mentioned in the last chapter, an important part of running more naturally involves keeping the pelvic region as neutral as possible. This is one of the jobs of the transversus abdominis muscle, or deep abs, which wraps around the entire torso extending from the ribs to the pelvis. Of all the six major muscle groups that make up the abdominals, it is located closest to the spine and assists in the stabilization of the entire core. The deep abdominal muscles also aid in keeping your pelvis aligned with the rest of your body, allowing you to utilize more of your energy for forward motion rather than losing it in pelvic rotation.

Properly conditioning the core takes both time and energy. As the trunk of the body becomes stronger, you might notice the role your deep abs play when you run. Focus on this area during your body scans while running. Try holding your pelvis neutral as you use your legs, gravity, and core strength to keep you moving gracefully forward.

The Ab Crunch exercise is a good warm-up before working the deep abs. Start by lying on your back. Bring your knees upward and cross the ankles. Place your hands on your chest and tuck your neck slightly upward toward your chest. Avoid straining your neck by locking it to your chest, or by placing your hands behind it for support. Next, steadily lift your upper body toward your knees. Your knees will also move slightly toward your chest. At the "crunch" point, hold for an instant before returning to a relaxed position while exhaling slowly. Do these methodically and carefully. As with any anaerobic strength exercise, taking your time and focusing on breathing are more beneficial than rapid, uncontrolled movements. Doing this exercise on a yoga mat may be more comfortable.

The classic Ab Crunch works the abdominal muscles in beneficial ways. It is also a good warm-up before working the deep abs.
(Photo by Eric Lang)

An exercise that is good for the lower back, chest, and abs, the Pelvic Tilt will help you feel the placement of your pelvis.
(Photo by Eric Lang)

To start the Pelvic Tilt, lie on your back with your knees bent upward and your feet comfortably flat on the floor. You can place a small pillow underneath your head for added comfort. The movement begins by tightening your abdominal muscles while focusing on bringing your pelvis and ribs together as you press your lower back toward the floor. You can hold for one or two seconds before relaxing.

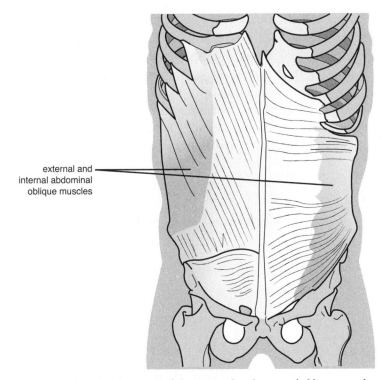

A diagram showing the placement of the internal and external oblique muscles.

The internal and external obliques are on each side of the trunk. Having strong obliques aids greatly in maintaining an aligned posture. The external obliques are less involved in spine positioning, but still play a role. The internal obliques affect the pelvis, spine, and ribs.

Plank Exercises help to strengthen the deep abs and oblique muscles of the core.
(Photo by Eric Lang)

The first Plank Exercise is an isometric hold that promotes core balance. Start by lying flat on a yoga mat. Place your forearms on the ground under your chest and lift yourself as if you are doing push-ups. Your elbows should be bent. Then, bring your toes underneath your ankles so they are supporting your legs. Your midsection (the "plank") should be held as straight as possible in the air. You can also do this in a sideways position, which works your internal obliques even more. Hold for a count of five before relaxing. Do two sets, holding each pose for 5 to 10 seconds when first starting out, eventually leading up to 30 or more seconds.

Side Bends work the external obliques.
(Photo by Eric Lang)

Start the Side Bend by positioning your feet shoulder-width apart. Place one hand gently behind your head with the other extending down to your side. Lower your extended arm toward the ground. Next, return to an upright position by recoiling your opposite side. Keep your body straight and do not bend forward or backward as you continue. Start by doing two sets of five repetitions. You can eventually add hand weights to this exercise for an added challenge, but keep it very light.

Barefoot Running Drills

Triathletes often train their swimming form so that they move through the water as smoothly as possible. In the same way, efficient running form will help you move easier through the elements. Landing properly, having a streamlined stride, maintaining posture, maintaining a strong core, and working with gravity will help you immensely as you continue to grow as a sound runner. Unfortunately, none of these components means anything until they are combined to work fluidly together. The best way to ensure that is to perform routine drills that combine the elements you have been working so hard to master. Form drills serve to make athletes more aware of their bodies through physical, mental, and even emotional repetition.

As you continue to improve your form, run longer distances, and increase your speed, allocate time each week to practice running drills that focus on proficient running techniques. Additionally, drills are best completed after you have warmed up but before you are too fatigued to concentrate.

Form drills can also allow you to better scan the body in finding early warning signs of tension, stress, tight muscles, or fatigue before these small issues develop into more serious problems.

Your Own Barefoot Drills

Completing drills without shoes will promote better sensory feedback in regard to form and landing. Some of the drills described here ask an athlete to undergo movements that you would not normally do while running, such as pushing off the ground with explosive force. The benefit of such drills is an increase in overall flexibility and strength in the foot.

Many coaches often have their athletes do various drills in the grass without shoes. This works the leg and foot muscles in different ways than running in shoes does. If you have running warm-ups or drills that you enjoy doing, try them barefoot. You will be surprised at how different it feels. Any running drills you can do without shoes allows the foot to become stronger, the legs more robust, and the body more aware of its movement.

Improving Form and Economy

Coaches, self-taught runners, and even triathletes use drills to improve their ability to run more efficiently and perfect their running form. Such workouts help runners focus on flexibility, relaxation, and the feeling of how to run naturally. Feel free to do the following drills on grass, but start on a dirt road or track to learn them. You will be able to monitor your landing and body positioning much easier. As always, you should execute them with caution.

High Knees is used to emphasize the role of and strengthen the quadriceps, hamstring muscle, and hip flexor in running. For barefoot running, the focus is on alignment rather than how high you can bring the leg.
(Photo by Yasmine Bennis)

To start High Knees, begin jogging normally. As you continue at a nice easy pace, bring the knee of each leg up to the front of the body, higher than you would normally while running, which will thoroughly work the *hip flexor*. For this particular drill, you do not need to bring the knees to the chest, but rather keep the upper leg parallel to the ground. Attempt to maintain a relaxed stature as you increase your pace. At first, do this drill for two sets of 10 to 15 seconds followed by walking briskly for 15 seconds between each set.

DEFINITION

Anytime you pull the knee upward toward the body, such as in the high knees drill, you utilize the **hip flexor.** These skeletal muscles help you fully move the femur bone up toward your pelvis. This is a common place for pain or injury in runners, and lightly stretching the hip flexor after you have warmed up (and before a workout) is one way to avoid stiffness later.

Skipping barefoot feels great on the feet, helps strengthen the lower extremities, and promotes proper foot landing.
(Photo by Yasmine Bennis)

For those not familiar with the movement, this skipping drill involves moving forward and hopping on one foot while the other foot is brought up into the air. Doing the same motion with high knees is another variation beneficial to runners.

Power Skipping exaggerates lift, while focusing on your center of gravity. As you begin, pay attention to how high you go rather than how far. The goal is not to overstride, but to drive each leg upward before bringing it down softly under the body. Start out Power Skipping for 10 seconds, increasing time and distance gradually.

Power Skipping involves pushing off of the ground with explosive force.
(Photo by Yasmine Bennis)

Backward Running is one useful and fun way to work on the biomechanics of form and strengthen the lower body.
(Photo by Yasmine Bennis)

Your legs and feet continually serve to move you in a forward direction. You might never consider that running in the opposite direction makes you stronger. For runners working on form, it is vital to hone the antagonistic muscles, even if you do not use them the same way when running forward.

Running backward works the hamstrings, buttocks, and feet. It also helps stabilize the joints of the legs and feet, especially those in the knees. If you are prone to knee pain, check with your coach or trainer to see if it might aid in the strengthening of your upper leg muscles, and start the drill slowly.

FROM THE SOLE

Known also as retrorunning, retropedaling, or reverse running, backward running has been used as a training drill by running legends throughout the latter 1900s. In the 1980s, running backward really took off, and Doctor Robert K. Stevenson published the book *Backwards Running* in 1981. The movement accelerated even more in the 1990s as runners claimed to find even more benefits of the exercise in their training, such as helping to balance the muscle groups of the legs, speed enhancement, and better running posture. As a standalone sport, it is still thriving. The World Backward Running Championships are advertised on www.reverserunning.com; members hope to make backward running an Olympic event for the 2020 games.

You might not be able to keep yourself in a perfectly straight line while doing this drill for the first few times, so be sure to have ample space in which to run. Begin by kicking your heels up behind your body, toward your butt, and begin moving backward slowly. Stride back with your leg as far back as it is comfortable. Keep your knees bent throughout each stride so that the landing foot hits the ground below your hips. Start out doing this drill in 10-second intervals. When you have practiced for a couple of weeks, increase the time and distance you run backward.

Evolutionary Breathing

As reported in the journal *Science*, most four-legged mammals that run are constrained in the way they breathe. They cannot control their breathing frequency after they begin running. The strides per breath are a one-to-one ratio. Interestingly, birds have the ability to breathe independent of their bodily motion, and it actually takes two breaths for them to exhale. They do not breathe in and out as humans do, but rather air fills small sacs within their bones that connect to their lungs, so that oxygen continually flows through them.

Humans, on the other hand, can make use of several different ways of breathing as they run, which don't necessarily depend on speed or gait. A human runner does not need all the oxygen that is sucked in through the mouth. Moreover, carbon dioxide is not necessarily a waste product when it comes to performance, but it is a principal element of energy creation in the body.

Competitive runners have recently begun utilizing a system of evolutionary breathing, which focuses on the breath being inhaled and exhaled out of the nose. This helps to moisten, clean, and warm the air before it enters the body. In fact, coach-trained athletes and self-trained runners who employ nose-focused breathing techniques when training and in races have noted drastic improvement in their performances. Like barefoot running, the skill takes months to develop, especially as you begin increasing speed, which can often make runners feel like they need more oxygen. Focusing on breathing as part of your barefoot running program is another way to focus on the moment rather than the situation. You might be surprised by how well you do when running fast is not your only aim.

Running Efficiently Uphill and Downhill

The art of running uphill and downhill takes practice to master. When watching a race or a group of runners, you might notice that each runner has a different method for dealing with the obstacles before them. A high percentage of runners loathe hill workouts and hills in races. One reason hills have a bad reputation is that runners often do not know how to handle them in regard to body positioning, foot landing, and overall posture, making them difficult to conquer.

Running uphill can actually help you in your pursuit of natural running form. When compared to running downhill, going uphill will inhibit you from overstriding, as the foot naturally lands under your center of gravity. Additionally, when going uphill, the cadence of runners will increase slightly if they are maintaining the same speed as when they are running on a flat surface.

When training with hill repeats or encountering a hill on a regular run, approach the incline with a mental note that you are going to maintain the same proficient form as when you run on a flat road or trail. You only have to make a few changes, which you can practice. When going uphill, focus your foot landing on the front of the foot rather than with a flat-foot landing. Getting up on the balls of your feet even just a fraction more will help you counteract the grade, putting gravity back on your side. While checking that your knees are bent with each step, increase the cadence of your stride. Escalating the number of times your feet hit the ground will help you conserve energy and cover the distance efficiently. Going uphill should not make you feel like you must expend an exponential amount of energy.

When running uphill, your arms should come closer to your chest, and the 90-degree elbow bend that was discussed earlier will increase slightly. Avoid tightening your upper body when you bring your arms up.

In addition, be sure that you keep a straight posture and avoid slouching over from the abdomen. Slumping over will cause you to slog up the incline and you'll waste a vast amount of energy on each burdensome step. Focus your line of sight on the ground a few body lengths in front of you instead of the horizon. This means that your jaw line will not be held at the 90-degree mark as discussed before, but slightly lower.

Many coaches tell their runners to allow the downhill to take them forward, giving them a boost in speed. At the fundamental level, this is true. However, runners should be careful when running downhill so as to not increase the impact on the body. As stated, elite runners actually increase their cadence by up to 40 steps more per minute when running downhill. Barefoot runners will naturally do the same. Overstriding while landing on the heel as you run downward gives the body a shock that literally vibrates the musculature of the entire body. Focus on increasing your steps without launching the leg and foot in front of the body.

Using gravity to help you gain some speed downhill can help your race times, but don't allow your body to spiral downward uncontrollably—you'll put yourself (and others) in danger. When you increase your steps, keep your hips pointed forward. Avoid leaning back as if you are trying to put on the brakes. Leaning forward just a bit will give you all the gravitational propulsion you will need. Likewise, keep your line of vision on the ground in front of you. This will help promote the slight forward lean and keep you from leaning backward.

Running up or down hills shouldn't make you alter your form in major ways. Your aim should be to maintain nearly the same technique you use on a flat surface. Slouching over or leaning back while going up or down a hill will cause your gait to become inefficient and arduous. Overstriding either way can cause injury, as the body does not properly absorb the impact of each weighty step. Maintaining a good posture with the chin angled slightly downward while both going up and coming down can help immensely with keeping the body aligned. Practice running on hills and learn to handle them well, and you will increase the odds that hills of any grade will be your friend as you smoothly roll up and down them.

The Least You Need to Know

- Being mindful of your body while running is an important skill that enables you to better your form.
- Running naturally implies running more relaxed.
- A strong core will make you a stronger runner.
- Implement form drills that will translate to better technique.
- Running up and down hills is much easier when you know the most efficient and safe way to handle them.

Surviving the Elements

The great outdoors is a wild place indeed, especially for exposed feet! In this part, you see how to handle Mother Nature like a pro. At this point, you might opt to wear minimal running footwear, known commonly as "barefoot running shoes." Then you go off-road to learn about handling all types of terrain. Running on trails, natural paths, and even sand are all excellent ways to give your feet (and body) the variety, stimulation, and workout they need to keep you strong, light, aware, and injury-free.

Here, you also see how to run barefoot in all seasons. From hot pavement to running in the snow, you can continue your barefoot running pursuits no matter the weather. And if soreness or mishap strikes, all the essentials are covered to get you healthy so that you may continue your shoeless adventures.

Minimal Footwear Running

In This Chapter

- What "barefoot shoes" and minimal footwear are all about
- How running barefoot and running in minimalist shoes are different
- When you should use minimal footwear
- How to choose the best minimalist shoes for your needs
- A listing of recommended barefoot shoe manufacturers

For those times when connecting to the elements might be more difficult, using minimal footwear is one way to keep your feet protected and warm. Running in minimalist shoes allows you to sustain certain strengths gained through barefoot running and helps you accomplish your overall running goals.

Barefoot Shoes

The apparent oxymoron "barefoot shoes" is becoming an accepted term for minimalist footwear, or shoes that offer some protection for the foot, have little to no cushioning, and allow your feet to feel and flex to the ground. Barefoot shoes are hot consumer items these days, and big shoe manufacturers are jumping into the race to help you feel like you are running barefoot without actually running in bare feet.

As barefoot shoes become more readily available, more of the running public will hopefully make the switch. Chapter 5 discussed some of the reasons why you should consider not using minimal footwear as transitional footwear. As with other professionals in the barefoot running community, it is recommended that you first build yourself up purely barefoot, develop efficient technique, and try out various surfaces (both man-made and natural) before donning a spiffy new pair of barefoot shoes.

> **TIP TOES**
>
> A running friend from Spain recently bought a name-brand pair of barefoot shoes at a factory outlet. He took off running in them for his regular one-hour run. Upon his return, he could not believe how his feet felt. He told his wife that his feet felt alive yet sore at the same time. He tossed the shoes into his closet and had to take three days off to recover. A month later, he heard about barefoot running and discovered that his shoes were actually designed to promote that style of running. Because of how alive (yet sore) his feet felt from using the shoes, he decided to give them another go, but only after he had worked on his foot strength without shoes first. A few months later, he began using the shoes when he could as part of his regular (mostly barefoot) running program.
>
> If you are unsure whether a pair of shoes is supposed to promote a barefoot feel, ask the sales clerk or look at online reviews of the particular model. Some runners may not be aware that they purchased a pair of barefoot shoes.

One of the best ways to build yourself up to using barefoot shoes is to plan the stage in your barefoot training plan in which you might begin using them. Using minimal footwear could fall between barefoot periodization stages III and IV, increasing distance and increasing intensity respectively. At this point, beginning barefoot runners are potentially ready to begin extending their own barefoot abilities, preparing for events, or wanting to get off the beaten path and try tougher terrains.

If you decide to use minimal shoes, put them to the test by walking in them before using them for running. Just as you would break in regular running shoes, walking occasionally (start out with 10 minutes and work yourself up to an hour) on a hard, smooth surface will help stretch them out. It will also allow you to monitor your feet for soreness, blisters, or the formation of corns, which are hard areas of skin that appear on the sides or tops of the toes. It is very important to know when, where, and how to use these shoes before wearing them for a run.

Barefoot vs. Minimal Footwear

Both barefoot and minimal footwear running has pros and cons. The biggest argument against minimal footwear is the disruption of communication between your foot and the ground—a major concern for beginning barefoot runners who benefit from this immediate feedback. Even in the thinnest-soled running shoes currently available, sensory perception can be reduced by nearly 80 percent. This sensory information is of great importance as you toughen up your feet's padding and develop a more natural running stride.

Another important point is that running barefoot allows your feet to breathe. Although breathability is a main feature of minimalist shoes, nothing beats the breathability of the foot's own natural cooling mechanism. Composed of more than 250,000 sweat glands and releasing as much as several cups of perspiration each day, it's no wonder most shoes stink! Sweat cools the feet through evaporation, which can't happen when your feet are restricted by shoes. The cooling ability of the human body, even in the scorching sun, is one of the major features that allowed humans to evolve in all environments. Now, you have the ability to use it to your advantage on long runs or in endurance events.

Additionally, going barefoot is free (and freeing)! You don't need to buy an expensive product to experience the joy of running. Most minimalist shoes are well designed, distributed, and marketed—the cost, however, is passed on to you. Admittedly, high-quality minimalist shoes do have their place. One benefit is that they last longer than traditional running shoes, even for runners doing greater distances. Furthermore, running in minimal footwear is more socially acceptable; after all, only kids go completely barefoot, right?

> **FROM THE SOLE**
>
> Nike has promoted barefoot running since 2005 after experiments were conducted in Nike's Sport Research Lab. In the study, they discovered that barefoot training was an undeniable way to strengthen the lower leg and ankle muscles, "reawakening" the foot. The result was the Nike FREE shoe, designed for both running and cross training. Nike's catchphrase in their commercials: "Run Barefoot."

For many of us, the biggest incentive (besides protection) of minimal shoes is that they offer many of the same advantages as being barefoot, such as natural foot motion, landing, and strengthening. Moreover, people mostly feel better wearing *something* on their feet.

Surprisingly, some barefoot shoes stand out more than plain bare feet—you will learn about some of the top manufacturers and models later in this chapter. Even if you decide to buy the most outlandish minimalist foot attire, resist using or alternating them with your barefoot runs until you are fully confident in your pure barefoot running abilities.

When to Use Minimal Footwear

As contradictory as it may sound, the best time to use barefoot shoes is when you are already running without them a significant amount of time (45 minutes to an hour or more) over various terrains. Only when the foot, ankle, and leg are strong; your foot padding toughened and thickened; and your form perfected, should you bring minimal shoes into the picture. By doing so, you will make a worthwhile (and safe) barefoot transition where the sense of touch has fully guided your path.

Don't forget that you can carry your shoes with you. Carrying one in each hand will help balance you and give you an additional workout. You can also use an ultra-light backpack. If the shoes are thin enough, tuck them into your back waistband (or wear a cycling shirt with those handy back pockets). Here are 10 occasions when minimal (or regular) footwear would come in handy.

Exploring New Terrain

You are out exploring a new trail. You discover, well into the exhilarating adventure, that the craggy terrain is wreaking havoc on your foot padding. Throwing on a pair of minimal shoes will allow you to keep exploring, or at least help you make it back to where you started. Remember that it is better to start out in bare feet, especially because it will prevent perspiration from making your feet soft and susceptible to injury.

Be sure to walk new terrain a few times before you run it. This will help you familiarize yourself with it, and, when walked barefoot, your foot padding is given some time to partially adapt and prepare as well.

In an Urban Setting

In much the same way, having a pair of minimal shoes handy means you can throw them on whenever you need them, such as while running in unknown urban areas. Cities (and their parks) make wonderful barefoot playgrounds, but when faced with a precarious area (an alley or construction site, for example), you might rather have something on your feet. In the winter, city roads (and sidewalks) are often coated with rock salt to help melt the ice. Spend too long running on wet rock salt and you will quickly soften and break down any thickened padding. Avoid ever going out in the city in the winter without at least carrying something to put on your feet. Using minimalist shoes is better than nothing until you are clear from such dangers.

When Traveling

Minimalist shoes are good in airports (walking in them is healthy even when not running), and having a pair of minimal running shoes when you travel can ensure your feet stay protected, make you feel more confident than being barefoot, and allow you to explore new terrains. In some places, nasty organisms, standing water, or various waste materials could be an issue. Certainly wearing shoes may not help prevent sickness or contamination, but it will offer a slight barrier between you and any unpleasant surprises. As an added bonus, minimal shoes tend to be lightweight and backpack-friendly—another advantage with ever-changing baggage restrictions!

> **TIP TOES**
>
> If you travel for business or pleasure and find yourself spending a lot of time in various cities in the United States or abroad, consider locating some barefoot running groups online. Another option is to contact City Running Tours (www. cityrunningtours.com) in the United States or Global Running Tours (www. globalrunningtours.com) before you travel abroad and join a fun run in a new place. Ask them about running barefoot (or in minimalist shoes) before you land and set out on your course of interest.

In Wet or Cold Weather

Running in wet or cold weather can be exhilarating on bare feet. In the summer, dashing through a puddle can make you feel as free as a child. Plus, a nice muddy coating on the bottom of your feet makes for superb (and natural) minimalist shoes! In cooler temperatures, the feet will actually radiate heat to keep you warm. And, for the especially adventurous among us, running a limited amount of time in the snow (yup, it is possible!) without shoes invigorates every part of your body. (Chapter 11 delves more fully into running in various types of weather.)

Many runners enjoy their jaunts, no matter the weather. Being the first one to leave your prints on a snowbound trail provides quiet satisfaction. On the other hand, every runner sometimes hates heading out on a drizzly day to complete a workout, whether in bare feet or not. Coming to the rescue are certain types of minimalist shoes that can keep your feet dry and warm, yet still awakened. Finding a pair that works in any type of weather is difficult, and it can take some creativity to find the perfect pair.

To Work the Foot Differently

Wearing a pair of minimalist shoes is not going to wreck your barefoot running goals. In fact, rotating a couple pairs of barefoot shoes (during intense training, bad weather, or recovery days) might be good for your feet. Many novice (and professional) runners have two or three pairs of regular shoes (such as trail shoes, racing flats, and road shoes) that they use for different terrains, weather, and workouts. If you have the means, think about investing in two or three pairs of minimal footwear that will meet your various running needs.

Additionally, when it comes to regular shoes, athletes often rotate pairs to extend the life of the shoe's cushioning. This is not an issue in some types of minimal footwear because most have little to no cushioning. The downside to purchasing more than one pair of minimalist shoes is the cost and the risk that they may not work well for you. The upside is that they may last longer than regular shoes, are healthier for your feet, and will allow you (when you are ready) to slowly extend your barefoot running adventures.

For Daily Runs

After you begin extending your barefoot running to prepare for races or fun events, you might hope to run more than every other day. Some runners enjoy active recovery, which translates to daily runs with one day off per week (or less). Because the beginning stages of barefoot running include taking a day off in between runs to ensure recovery, you should increase to running every single day *gradually*. Using minimalist footwear for those extra running days is one way to save your foot's padding from being overworked. Wearing minimalist shoes for two of the five or six weekly sessions would be well balanced.

A Foot Injury or Foot Condition

If you cut, bruise, or injure your foot in any way, take time off to allow the injury to heal completely before setting off barefoot again. Minimalist shoes can help protect an area during recovery. The sweat and bacteria in any type of shoe are not beneficial to a wound, but wearing minimalist shoes might be better than coming into contact with certain elements you will encounter outdoors (or especially in public places).

For others with a foot condition, such as those who wear orthotics, certain types of minimal footwear might help to strengthen the muscles of the foot and arch without exposing it to the elements. Pay close attention to how your foot feels and do not overdo it. Talk with your doctor about your plans. For some runners, such as those with diabetes, running completely barefoot may not be possible due to sensory impairment.

During Intense Workouts or Racing

Increasing your barefoot workouts and racing barefoot is discussed later, but using minimalist footwear is one way to save your feet's skin and padding from harm during speed workouts or while racing. Both of these activities increase friction dramatically because you will be moving faster than usual, especially on a road. If you have not trained fast in bare feet, it is better not to chance it in a race. Running a race barefoot is both exhilarating and fun, but make certain that you are prepared to do so (and bring your shoes along just in case).

For Everyday Life

Choosing to wear minimal shoes is a healthy choice for your daily life. The role your feet play in the overall health of your body is undeniable. For those who work long hours standing up, you will be surprised how much less your legs, feet, and joints ache—a real benefit for both you and your employer!

To Make a Statement

Avoiding high heels that damage joints or cushioned sneakers that atrophy the foot is another way you can be an advocate for a healthier lifestyle. Wearing unique minimal shoes can be fun, spark conversations, and will give you the opportunity to share what you know.

Remember to work minimalist shoes slowly into your barefoot running routine. After a few weeks with one shoe, you may want to try another model. This way you can make certain that the brand/style you are using works best for you, causes no pain or discomfort, and allows your foot to feel and flex with the ground.

If the (Minimal) Shoe Fits

Minimal footwear for walking, running, playing on the beach, or simply bumming around is already a hot market item. Reviewing all the different brands and models could be a book in itself. The process is made easier for you by outlining the barefoot shoes of which we are aware, have tested ourselves, or have talked about with other professionals. Ultimately, we focus on those manufacturers both large and small that are producing high-quality, minimalist running shoes.

Before delving into various brands of minimalist shoes, remember that you are looking for a product that might work well with your current running program. You might already have a pair of shoes buried in your closet just waiting to be dusted off. Older running shoes with hundreds (or even thousands) of miles on them can actually make good minimalist shoes because the hefty cushioning is worn out.

Arthur Newton, one of the early twentieth century's most revered endurance athletes, is just one example of someone who wore thin-soled canvas shoes more than 3,500 miles in training before he would consider another pair. It often took him another 500 to 1,000 miles to finally make the switch. Perhaps he was on to something, considering that, at the age of 51, he broke the record for the 100-mile race from Bath to London in just over 14 hours!

At the very least, old shoes might work well for those times as talked about earlier, such as when exploring, in bad weather, or on recovery runs. Shoes that would otherwise be considered broken down by most running-store clerks might work perfectly for you. Even retired racing flats can do the trick. If you have not kept any of your old shoes, visit a local used-clothes shop. You will be surprised by what you might find. These shoes might need a sanitary dip, but there is no use in investing in new shoes when well-worn ones can work just as well (if not better)!

During the last 30 years, certain features of the running shoe's design have changed substantially. With a rise in barefoot and minimalist-shoe running, a partial reverting of the industry is occurring where consumer choices are guiding manufacturer's designs. Knowing what important features to look for when choosing a barefoot shoe empowers you to make a well-informed decision before spending your hard-earned money on a fancy new product.

How to Select Minimalist Shoes

Choosing a pair of barefoot shoes can be fun because of all the great models available. Although these shoes are becoming more and more popular, it is still hard to find an athletic store that carries a wide selection of brands. Generally, they will carry a couple of models from the larger companies. Certain outdoor-adventure stores stock bestselling designs that can be used for various pursuits, not only running. Most minimalist-shoe hunting is best done online, which can be easier because you can also read user reviews.

When beginning your search for a new pair of minimalist footwear, you first have to consider your price range. The minimum price of some of the most popular models is going to set you back nearly $100. Expensive minimalist footwear from world-renowned companies can set you back more than that. Even more costly are companies that will customize a shoe specific to your foot's dimensions. Don't let this discourage you, though, as there are cheaper alternatives.

When looking at all the types of minimal shoes, keep in mind the following parameters so that you will be able to choose wisely. In some cases, certain features will have to be weighed against others, depending on what you will use them for (trail running or road running) and also the time of year you will use them (cold, wet, or hot weather).

Feel and Flex

The first and foremost characteristic of a quality barefoot running shoe is that it allows you to feel the ground and flexes with the natural movement of the foot. Feeling the curvature of the ground is extremely important in barefoot running so that your feet remain strong, the ankles flexible, and the legs robust. All those tiny variations on the ground will work to make you a stronger, less injury-prone runner.

Try to verify the thickness of the sole, which will usually be measured in millimeters (mm). Anything between 2 mm and 4 mm should work very well. Look carefully at anything larger than 10 mm. See if you can easily bend the upper toe area of the shoe to the back part with ease. Then twist the shoe in different ways. See if there is any arch support. Avoid shoes with foam, plastic, or a tight midsection that might keep the arch from flexing. Certain racing flats will not be as flexible as other types of shoes, but can work well as minimalist shoes. If you are going to be doing competitive running on roads, weigh the options of such flats against other minimal brands.

No Built-Up Heel

For some reason, major shoe companies are having trouble designing, constructing, and releasing a running shoe without some sort of raised heel. It is as if they are waiting on someone else to do it first to test the market. European models of shoes (whether for running, walking, or everyday activity) produced by major international corporations do not have the same built-up heels as their sister shoes in the United States.

The feature that prevents us from raving about certain models in this chapter is that they alter the way the foot naturally meets and feels the ground. Find a shoe that keeps you as close to the ground as possible, which will help prevent ankle sprains, loss of balance, and even tripping. Welcome with open arms shoes that allow you to control how your foot lands.

No Extra Cushioning

Akin to producing a shoe with a raised heel, shoe companies are having a difficult time producing a shoe without engorged cushioning. Avoid shoes that claim to offer you freedom from impact. More cushioning means more weight, and more weight means more pounding, which adds tons of extra exertion and pressure to your joints after thousands of steps.

Motion Control

The high-tech claims of most modern shoes say they will keep you on track by controlling how your foot lands and your body reacts with each touchdown. Steer clear of shoes with pronounced indentations or fancy gimmicks that control the way your foot moves.

One of the best-known companies offers a shoe with a microchip control module that adjusts the shoes' variables with each and every step. After years of design and millions of dollars in research, they have literally taken the role of your brain out of the running equation. The shoe actually does the thinking for you. Avoid motion-control shoes and any high-tech, mind-numbing claims that promise you they can do better than you can naturally.

Weight

With added sole thickness, cushioning, and even microchips, the weight of shoes is compromised. After a month or two of barefoot running, put on an old pair of the heaviest running shoes you can find (trail shoes are often the most gargantuan). Try running in them for a few minutes. The added weight you feel is a startling wake-up to how modern shoes are being made and marketed to you. Added weight is prohibitive, so choose the lightest barefoot shoes you can find. We suggest choosing a shoe that weighs less than 10 ounces. As with any purchase, a certain balance of features that fit your needs must also be taken into consideration.

Breathability

Remember those 250,000 sweat glands in the feet? Pure barefoot running allows the feet to naturally perspire, breathe, and adjust to variant temperatures, and you should search for shoes that help promote the breathability of your feet. Certain leathers breathe better than others. Breathable, moisture-resistant fabrics might make a good choice. Some shoes have handy mesh vents that promote air transfer with each step. Some shoes even aerate through the sole, allowing air to enter freely, but keeping water out (good for the foot pads). For the summer, consider *barefoot running sandals* or anything that offers as little shoe as possible.

> **DEFINITION**
>
> **Barefoot running sandals** are designed for running with a minimalist approach. The most popular brand is currently Huaraches Barefoot Running Sandals for both running and walking. First used by the Tarahumara of Mexico, the simple sandal was first composed of old tire rubber and tied around the foot and ankle with a thin cord. Modern versions are on sale at www.barefootted.com and www.invisibleshoe.com. These and other websites also show you how you can make your own indigenous types of footwear designed specifically for your foot.

Toe Movement

Minimalist shoes should allow the toes to move freely. Avoid tight or snug shoes that inhibit the movement of the toes. Some shoes will have a raised front, curve inward, or have a snug toe box (the area where the toes and upper foot rests, sometimes called uppers). A natural stride is dependent upon the movement, grasping, and splaying of the toes while running. Avoid shoes that attempt to control or deaden the natural reaction of the feet when you run. Shoes should be straight, have wide uppers, and rest flat on the ground.

Craftsmanship

Verify the quality of the shoe you are purchasing. If you cannot test the shoe yourself, search online forums to see if anyone has had any trouble with a specific brand you are considering buying. If you can actually test the shoe, do so while in the store. If fabric and a rubber sole are sewn or glued together, double-check the edges to ensure they are held together well. Don't pull too hard, but double-check the quality of the seams.

Return Policy

No shoe will last forever, but verify the warranty of the shoe and the return procedure. Will the store handle returns or only the manufacturer? If so, can you submit a
ticket online directly to the vendor? Who pays for shipping?

If worn indoors and kept clean, then returning a recently purchased pair for another
type or a full or partial refund should not be difficult. Read the manufacturer's
return policy before purchase. Sending a note with your feedback with the return will
also be helpful in receiving a prompt response; it might also help the company with
future designs.

Types of Minimal Footwear

When you begin looking at all the options of minimalist running footwear available,
you will understand how hard it will be to select the pair that will work best for you.
We have tried to make it a little easier by searching out some of the most outstanding
shoes and shoe manufacturers, both at home and abroad, and offering some insight
about why they may or may not work well for your running needs.

For our purposes, we will focus on those shoes that are best for barefoot running.
We will also point out some shoes that serve well for other purposes, including minimalist sandals and slippers. Some of the smaller enterprises will have models that will
work well for your toddler. The health of your kids' feet might depend on it!

FROM THE SOLE

Some of the greatest runners in the world come from Kenya. Training differently from their Western counterparts, elite Kenyan runners grow up running
(for the most part) completely barefoot, and they continue to run without
shoes for many of their workouts even as adults. Many runners do not begin
wearing shoes until their late teens, giving their feet enough time to fully
develop and mature. Having shoes is considered a luxury in some areas, and
many do not have shoes to train until they can afford them, but they do credit
barefoot running as one of the numerous variables that has helped to make
them world-class professionals.

Minimalist running shoes will continually evolve based on consumer demands. It is
our hope that the companies designing, producing, and marketing such shoes will
strive to stick to the barefoot basics outlined in the previous section. Make a shoe
that truly takes us to our barefoot roots and it will get noticed, raved about, and worn

time and time again. Some of these (and other companies) are discussed next, where they are rated on a 0- to 10-foot scale (0 representing heavy clods and 10 representing barefoot heaven).

Vibram Five Fingers

Rating: 10 feet
www.VibramFiveFingers.com

Vibram is a well-established company in the business of making high-quality rubber soles for shoes in the fields of recreation and industry. They took a leap of faith when deciding to enter the shoe-manufacturing world, but their creation of Vibram Five Fingers has become the most popular minimalist shoe today for a variety of activities, including water sports, trekking, yoga, and barefoot running. Designed as "foot gloves," they have a barefoot mission to keep their customers' feet happy, healthy, and free. Remember we mentioned that certain pairs of minimalist footwear might stick out more than bare feet? These are shoes sure to get you noticed.

ON YOUR TOES

Before buying any pair of minimalist shoes online, be sure to flee the fakes! Make certain the company you have researched manufactures the product you are purchasing. Because of their popularity, low-quality copycats of Vibram Five Fingers have emerged, ready to take advantage of unknowing customers. Check that the site you are using is the company's actual page, verify online reviews, and pay attention to the domain address. You can always access real distributors through www.VibramFiveFingers.com.

Most models available from Vibram meet (and even surpass) the criteria for selecting minimalist shoes from our list. They're not for everyone, but they are revolutionary in their design and scope. *TIME* magazine even awarded Five Fingers as one of the Best Inventions of 2007 in the category of health. Customers report improved foot strength, agility, aligned posture, and a lessening of past running pains.

One of the most raved-about models is the KSO (Keep Stuff Out) Trek. Different than the regular KSO, the Trek is composed of a breathable and light kangaroo leather upper (available in different materials). It is great on rocky and craggy terrain, as well as backwoods trails. The EVA sole is protective and a bit thicker than their other models at 4 mm. The materials are robust, the craftsmanship superb, the leather smooth and soft, and the shoe is light (less than 6 ounces). The only downside is the slightly supported arch that is partially held taut with the top Velcro strapping mechanism. If you need an extra sweat-wicking layer or secondary insulation in colder temps, consider purchasing a pair of Injinji (www.injinji.com), toe socks that fit Five Fingers well.

Newton Running

Rating: 7 feet
www.newtonrunning.com

Although we speak out against shoe companies making lofty scientific claims about their shoe designs, the folks at Newton have given us pause. Their shoes are designed to help make you a more natural runner by not only allowing you to feel the ground better, but also to land with a more natural foot strike. Their patented rubber lugs (called "actuators") on the bottom of the front of the shoe are supposed to rebound energy to the foot to help move it through the running cycle. Any shoe that allows the foot to land properly is appealing!

The look and flexible soles of the various Newton shoes available are top-notch. However, the shoes have unnecessary motion-control features. Current models weigh around 10 ounces, but the hefty price tag (U.S. $100+) will give recreational joggers a real run for their money.

Terra Plana

Rating: 9 feet
www.terraplana.com

A company founded in the UK, Terra Plana (which means "flat land") has a wide variety of high-quality footwear for both casual and outdoor pursuits. Their Vivo Barefoot models are the most appealing for barefoot runners. In particular, the Evo is great due to its minimalist features. They offer a 4 mm sole that allows the foot to breathe, lets the toes move freely via a wide toe box, and flexes well. The shoes stay cozy in temperatures just above freezing, but go below that and you might need socks.

The Evo is a decent shoe for trail running, handling both muddy and snowy terrains with plenty of grip. The downside is the price at around U.S. $160. In regard to these shoes, you truly get what you pay for: quality craftsmanship, a shoe with a true barefoot feel, and no gimmicks. Plus, the company is at the forefront of sustainability by being eco-friendly and made of recycled materials. Terra Plana's shoes truly make a difference both on and off your feet.

inov-8

Rating: 5 feet
www.inov-8.com

The inov-8 design philosophy is based on barefoot movement, allowing wearers of their shoes to freely move and function with nature. With a plethora of models from which to choose, the inov-8 brand's true market is extreme trail runners and racers.

On the trail, whether rocky, muddy, snowy, or plagued by sharp rock, these shoes receive rave reviews from racing pros and recreational runners alike.

When held to our criteria for what makes minimalist shoes shine, most of inov-8's shoes would be considered too rigid, too high off the ground, and created with too much support. Their racing flats weigh around 10 ounces, so it's worth taking a look at what they have to offer. These shoes are designed to help you run naturally in the world's most extreme environments, harsh terrains that can wreak havoc on under-prepared feet.

Nike

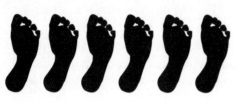

Rating: 6 feet
www.nike.com

A shoe that laid the groundwork for the barefoot shoe revolution is the Nike Free. Used worldwide by the running greats for training, these shoes come with a small user's manual because of the radical difference in the way they function and feel. Over the years, the shoe has gotten better thanks to feedback from thousands of runners.

Unfortunately, Nike uses a confusing numbering system to decipher various models. Originally, the shoes would have a number rating of 0 to 10 (where 0 is essentially barefoot and 10 is a mainstream, supportive shoe). Basically, shoes that are marked 3.0 are more barefoot in feel and flex than 5.0 or 7.0 models. The Nike Free 5.0 offers the best of both worlds. Nike Free models still have built-up heels, partial motion control, are a bit too high off the ground, and are too snug for full toe splay for those with wide feet (various widths are currently not available).

Other Barefoot Shoe Options

Several other companies are answering the call to create a better barefoot world. Here are a few companies offering minimalist shoes, whether for running, walking, or just healthy living.

Skora Running

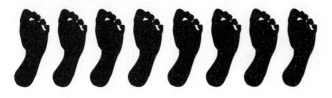

Rating: 8 feet
www.skorarunning.com

A brand-new running shoe company set to debut their models in 2011, Skora will offer shoes that mimic running barefoot. We will see if they hold true to their mission. We have given them an 8-feet rating for good intentions.

FROM THE SOLE

Before simply tossing out your shoes to make the minimalist switch, why not share your sneakers by donating them (and by making a financial contribution) to Give Running (http://giverunning.org)? Started by Mr. Greg Woodburn of California, shoes are collected, cleaned, and distributed to underprivileged children and others at home and abroad. If you have other sports items to donate, contact (and donate to) Sports Gift (www.sportsgift.org), which ships equipment around the world.

Feelmax

Rating: 7 feet
www.feelmax.com

Offering shoes for women, men, and children, Feelmax has a mission to make the most flexible, light shoes on the planet. They offer some great deals for kids, too. Their European designs and quality are sure to catch on in the United States.

Ecco

Rating: 7 feet
www.eccousa.com

Known for their high-quality, comfortable footwear, Ecco has entered the natural-running world with the release of their cutting-edge BIOM. Without "excessive cushioning or motion control," the shoe may very well help runners reach new heights if they can part with the necessary funds to purchase a pair. With models designed for competitive runners to fitness joggers, you can download a BIOM Training Guide from their website to help you carefully make the transition.

Soft Star

Rating: 10 feet
www.softstarshoes.com

Shining in the world of alternative foot health, Soft Star makes family-friendly, minimal shoes for kids and adults alike. Based in Oregon, they have been creating shoes for nearly 30 years. This eco-friendly company even has vegan shoes and accessories available. Try out their designs or personalize and design your own. Their minimal running shoes receive our top rating of 10 feet for surpassing several of our barefoot standards.

Zem

Rating: 7 feet

www.zemgear.com

Zem has a unique take on footwear—a versatile bootie! Designed as beachwear and for other activities, Zem gear has put a lot of technology and durability behind their products. Walking, running, and playing beach volleyball are some of the handy uses of this snazzy minimalist attire.

A few other shoe manufacturers producing minimal footwear also include …

- Merrell (www.merrell.com)—Merrell is releasing its Barefoot Collection in partnership with Vibram in early 2011 and will definitely be worth checking out.

- Puma (www.puma.com)—In Europe, Puma has a nice hold on the minimalist market, especially with the Puma K-Street series, which are also available in the United States.

- Water shoes and slippers—The Teva Proton (www.teva.com) and Sockwa (www.sockwa.com) are water shoes that work well as a slip-on minimalist running shoe. Zinetic Pocket Slippers (www.pocketslippers.com) or Sanuk (www.sanuk.com) are similar and comfortable for extreme lounging. Such models are super flexible, affordable, come in a wide range of sizes, are breathable, and dry fast. Also popular is Earth Footwear (www.earthfootwear.com), which promotes a variety of shoes for work and play.

- Kigo (www.kigofootwear.com)—Last but not least, an eco-friendly company that deserves at least a 9-feet rating is Kigo, which makes light, thin, comfy, and stylish minimalist shoes for active and leisure activities.

Other well-known companies who have entered the minimalist market include Brooks, Adidas, New Balance, Mizuno, and Asics.

Making Your Own Barefoot Running Shoes

For the jacks-of-all-trades out there, designing and constructing your own barefoot footwear is a worthwhile venture that might lead you to some interesting discoveries. Taking a pair of old sneakers, cutting off the bottom sole, and gluing or strapping on your own might open up a whole new world. That is where Dr. Craig Richards (co-author of this guide) began. He developed a model called Barefoot On Grass (http://barefootrunningshoe.blogspot.com) that has helped many people think differently about the connection between our feet, minds, and bodies.

It would not be surprising if some of these better-known shoe companies started out as one-man shows, designed their own footwear, and then turned it into an enterprise worthy of our feet. If you are a do-it-yourselfer, making your own pair of barefoot running sandals is a great place to begin—imagine having the perfect, customized pair! If you decide to do this, think about your running needs (snow or trail, or both?). Start with some string, cardboard for initial sole designs, a hot-glue gun, and some duct tape, and see what happens. Keep minimalist criteria in mind and be creative.

The Least You Need to Know

- Barefoot running shoes are a type of minimal footwear that helps protect the feet while still allowing you to feel the ground.
- Barefoot and minimal footwear running can work together in a balanced way if planned, implemented, and done carefully.
- Certain times are better than others to use minimal footwear for running, including in inclement weather, on rough terrain, and when your feet need a break.
- Educate yourself on sales gimmicks for running shoes before shopping so that you buy the highest-quality minimal footwear available.
- Various types of minimal footwear are now available on the market; these include models from well-established companies and others from small, eco-friendly, and visionary manufacturers hoping to make their mark.

Barefoot Trail Running

Chapter 10

In This Chapter

- How to properly transition to barefoot trail running
- How to best handle terrain, regardless of difficulty
- Why you should rotate trail running surfaces
- How to avoid and deal with dangers on the trail

After you overcome the initial phase of transitioning to barefoot running, you are set to discover a whole new unpaved world. Whether you walk, hike, or jog, going barefoot on a trail toughens your foot padding, strengthens your legs, balances your body, and connects you to nature in ways that running on man-made surfaces cannot. Trails offer a new, interesting, and challenging place to learn, practice, and elevate your newfound barefoot skills. So what are you waiting on? Let's hit the great outdoors!

Getting Off the Beaten Path

For many runners, escaping busy lives on a zigzagging forest trail is heaven on Earth. For barefoot runners, feeling the terrain underfoot is the zenith of shodless experiences. The cool dirt, a smooth rock, or a muddy patch take on a whole new meaning when you allow your feet to steadily guide you over what were once viewed as pesky obstacles.

Barefoot runners who really want to connect with the environment should spend as much time as possible on natural surfaces. Steven Robbins, M.D., makes a valid point that the safest ground on which to go barefoot is naturally deposited ground, such as what one would find on the African savanna, where humans first began subsistence hunting for survival. Such grassland pathways have firm ground, offer little resistance, and are not inundated with rocks, sticks, or other unforeseen hazards.

Finding a perfectly smooth and naturally packed trail might be hard for runners who live in certain areas. Because of this, it is essential that you become used to the ground before you actually attempt running on it. It is even better to know the nuances (or any potential dangers) of the trail before you leave your shoes completely behind.

To safely begin barefoot trail running, start by trail walking (see Chapter 5). Not only will this get your feet used to the terrain, it will also allow you to spend time in the woods without necessarily having to run. In just a short amount of time, you can begin jogging carefully on your favorite trails for small periods of time, slowly building yourself up to longer and longer sessions.

If you're hesitant about going into the forest without foot protection—good. Runners who want to try barefoot trail running should be extra cautious, observant, and more alert. Heed this advice: take your time. Do not allow the elation of the experience to prevent you from listening carefully to your feet. When your feet say they are done, do yourself a favor and listen!

Trail Shoes Versus Trail Feet

The beauty of trail running is the slow development of trail-running feet. When exposed to the elements, the thousands of nerve endings on the bottom of each foot will become even more stimulated than when you run barefoot on a road or track. With all the subtle differences from one step to the next, your feet will naturally strengthen and become more alert.

There's a big difference between barefoot trail walking and running. When walking, your eyes and feet have plenty of time to react to changes in the surface. A pointed rock or a gnarled stick is easier to handle because you are moving slower and landing with less impact. One foot is always in contact with the ground, which helps to decrease the weight coming down on the landing foot. When running, both feet come up off the ground in one cycle, which means you will be landing with increased weight with each step.

When you first begin trail running, your feet will be hyper sensitive to the terrain. Each and every rock, stick, or pebble will offer its own challenges, but your feet will eventually adjust. When wearing shoes, your feet may be more protected, but the foot will feel and react less. Although certain shoes stick to slippery surfaces such as a moss-covered rock better than the human foot, only the uncovered foot can offer you enhanced balance control through landing adjustments and unsurpassed toe grip.

> **TIP TOES**
>
> Continuing to run on different kinds of trails will allow you to acclimate to a variety of surfaces; it's all about safeguarding your body and listening to your feet. Calibrating your landing, controlling impact, and determining where to plant your foot before it hits the ground are important reflexive skills that will boost your trail-running confidence and ability immensely.

It is best to start barefoot trail running without any sort of shoe. Your feet won't take long to become used to the nooks, crannies, and natural objects underfoot. You will also become readily skilled at moving your feet out of harm's way by quickly recoiling the leg, jumping sideways, or adjusting your landing or stride. After your feet have gotten used to the more rugged terrain, your new trail-ready feet will read, respond, and guide you innately in a way that no shoe can.

Wearing Minimalist Shoes on the Trail

When you are exploring new areas or trying new techniques, or when you want to keep going without turning your foot pads into hamburger, a pair of minimal shoes is worth their weight. Stubbing a toe, scuffing your padding, even breaking skin are all possibilities in the wild outdoors, so toting a pair of shoes is a smart back-up plan. Minimal footwear is probably the best choice, because it provides protection and flexibility without controlling the way you land. Plus, they weigh much less than regular shoes.

When you bring shoes along with you, do not feel you have to use them right away. Start out completely barefoot so that the shoes do not soften your foot pads from sweat. When your feet have had enough, you can throw on the shoes to help get you back to the trailhead. Or, as an alternative, slow down and walk for a while (three to five minutes usually does the trick) to allow the foot muscles to cool down, skin to rest, and sweat to evaporate. While walking, pay close attention to how your feet feel. Putting on shoes while your feet are hot could cause the skin to moisten up, which works against your goal of toughening the foot's bottom skin.

If you bring a pair of shoes along with you, ensure that they are clean and free from debris, especially if you are running in a few different parks. Dirt on your shoes can contaminate an area that has not been exposed to certain plants or bacteria. Certain pairs of shoes (even of the minimalist variety) will hold more dirt than others. When you are done with an outing, clean the bottom of your shoes with soap and water, using a knife to scrape off debris if necessary. It does not mean that you have to wash them completely; wash just enough to keep what grows naturally in one area from infesting another. Limiting contamination is good for the environment and the future of your favorite running trails.

Trails Are Good for the Sole

Not only do trails help runners connect even more with nature, they are also good for the overall health of your feet, legs, and body. Just as you should work different muscle groups on different days when you lift weights, you should also work different parts of your feet and legs by varying the terrain when you run. Trails are wonders at working nearly every part of your body evenly; with small inclines, dips, turns, twists, and bumpy sections, they're the epitome of a full-foot workout. A trail's small changes offer a greater flexing of the tarsal and metatarsals that make up the arch of the foot much more than a flat road. When the tendons and ligaments supporting the region are engaged, the overall sole of the foot is strengthened.

That said, spending too much time on rugged terrain (especially in the beginning) could result in aches and pains that you have never felt before. The best way to counterbalance a rigorous foot workout and prevent injury is to rotate surfaces. Because running off-road can give the foot a thorough beating, getting back on a flat surface allows the foot to relax, recover, and recuperate. Spending all your time on trails can cause an overuse injury. For the first several weeks, allow two running days off the trail for each day spent on it. If you're running three days per week, you could opt for a trail run every Monday, followed by two days on easier terrain.

Conversely, spending too much time away from natural surfaces can also cause problems. If you run on the same road day in and out (even in shoes), you will not be offering your legs or feet any new challenges. Working the same parts of the body the same way each and every day can spark fatigue that can lead to overuse trauma, not to mention burnout and boredom. Varying your barefoot runs will ensure that your legs and feet are kept refreshed, alert, and well balanced. This recovery time is essential to ensure the strengthening (and not a breaking down) of the lower extremities. Alternating surfaces will also allow you to concentrate on aspects of your form.

Trail Running Techniques

Everything you learn about natural running form will hold true when you are trail running. As on any surface, proficient technique involves an aligned posture, high cadence, short stride length, bent knees, upright head, and alert eyes, all while maintaining a relaxed upper body.

When trail running, a few other helpful hints will ensure that you handle the varying terrain with grace and efficiency. Keep the following pointers in mind to handle trails like a pro.

Keep Yourself Aligned

When trail running, avoid bringing your neck to your chest to stare at the ground directly in front of your feet. It is more beneficial and healthier to keep your neck and spine comfortably aligned while looking ahead 5 to 6 feet or more in front of your body. Lifting your head to look farther down the trail every so often will give your eyes and neck a break from the wearisome task of only focusing on one point.

ON YOUR TOES

When running on or off-road, practice looking ahead of your shadow. Because your shadow is moving with your body, you might be led to pay attention to it rather than what is on the ground ahead. Also, test trail running with and without sunglasses. In certain cases, darker lenses coupled with shadows might impede you from seeing rocks, roots, or other objects. Polarized, yellow amber, or other lighter shades may brighten up the trail for you.

Adjust Foot Landing

When running on a trail, try different types of foot landings to see what is most comfortable in different situations. For example, when running up a boulder-laden mountain pass, you might find it easier to get up on your forefoot to spring from one step to the next. When running downhill, you might find it necessary to zigzag with quick steps to handle the terrain. Prepare yourself for the types of terrains you will encounter.

Springing up a trail is one way to handle the terrain. As the forefoot lands, use your upper leg muscles to spring upward.
(Photo by Fazia Farrook)

Use the Full Foot

When you encounter an especially rough patch on a trail, such as an area of sharp gravel, rather than getting up on your front pads, try to land more flatly, using the entire surface area of the foot to spread the impact more evenly. Do so by slowing way down, relaxing the feet, and practicing a full foot landing. Be sure that the heel does not land first.

It will feel safer and perhaps more natural at first to run through difficult areas on your front pads, as if you are tiptoeing around rocks, sticks, or roots. However, running all the time on the forefoot (or front pads) through difficult areas can cause problems for you down the road. Putting too much sharp, upward force on the toe bones (metatarsals) can cause deep tissue or bone damage (whether barefoot or in minimal shoes) if done repeatedly or forcefully enough. When you begin barefoot trail running and as you continue to pursue it, take time to feel the different landings you can do on a variety of surfaces.

Lower Your Center of Gravity

Lowering your center of gravity will give you more stability over particularly knobby or agonizing terrain. Lower your center of gravity by slightly squatting as you run, putting more of your weight on the upper leg muscles. Lowering your arms down to the hips will also help increase balance. Maintain good posture, keep your torso engaged, and remember to use as much of the foot as you can on landing.

Run-Walk

Moving slowly and safely over a rugged area is better than speeding through it and praying you do not damage your feet. The combination of using more of the foot and lowering your center of gravity will make you feel like you are moving slower. In actuality, you are moving smarter.

If you do not want to walk while on a treacherous bit of terrain, slow down to a run-walk. The difference comes when you propel yourself from behind with the hamstring leg muscle rather than simply lifting the foot up using the quadricep muscle for the next step. This increases your stride and decreases impact, which still gives the foot a good workout.

Shuffling along a rough part of a trail will help you get over the terrain without your feet taking a beating.
(Photo by Fazia Farrook)

When you feel the need to walk, do so. This is particularly true for those new to trail running. You might find this particularly appropriate when running downhill on rocky terrain. Walking over a taxing stretch still gives your feet and foot pads a great workout. If the entire trail proves to be formidable, walk part of it, throw on your shoes, and have fun enjoying nature. Rather than becoming discouraged, plan on building yourself up slowly so that you can handle intimidating terrains. Within a short time, what once seemed impossible to traverse will be child's play.

Develop Trail Skills

Developing the ability to walk, jog, or run in bare feet on the trails in your area will heighten the connection you feel with the environment. Even the smallest bit of litter on the ground might affect this connection. One barefoot runner in Connecticut became so bothered by litter on the trails that he began taking a small trash bag on each run. He would stop and pick up any trash and toss it into the bag—with his feet! Over time, he developed the dexterity to pick up old plastic cups, cigarette remains, or even straws with one quick swipe of his foot. The ritual became something of a game and did wonders for his toe agility. By the end of the summer, all of his (and other people's) favorite trails in the neighborhood were pristine.

- **Sticks and Stones:** Trail games are fun to play while you are out and about. One of these is called Sticks and Stones, which enhances rest periods on barefoot hikes. Similar to using building blocks, attempt constructing something with your feet while you sit enjoying the scenery. Make teepees, log cabins, and small fire pits, or simply toss rocks into the water with your toes to strengthen your feet as you relax.

- **Tree Balance:** This game helps develop foot and ankle strength and the skills you need to traverse difficult areas. Find a downed tree and practice your balance while walking across it. Gripping the tree with your bare feet helps progress foot pad toughening, and working on balance is an important skill for forest running.

  Skillful balancing is easier with good core strength. Doing such balancing acts, whether on trees, a slackline, or on boulders and rocks, will not only help you hone your barefoot balance but will also help reinforce your core strength. And better balance will ultimately make you a stronger athlete and runner, on or off the road.

- **Side Gliding:** A final game you can do in or out of the woods involves jumping from one side of a sloped area of ground to the other while maintaining forward momentum. As the slope increases, so does the workout for your ankles, feet, and core.

You can make up your own fun games as you explore new trails. Mixing up your runs with games, fun challenges, or random diversions can be a way to keep your entire body engaged, enlivened, and attentive to the elements.

TIP TOES

Another way to really develop barefoot balance is to try out the new sport of slacklining (www.slackline.com). Made of nylon webbing that is 1 to 2 inches in width, the line is stretched between two anchor points (such as two trees) and most often walked barefoot. The slackline can be made as loose or tight as the user would like. Slacklining involving stunts, jumps, and other tricks is often referred to as *tricklining,* while walking at low heights is called *lowlining.* If you purchase a slackline, also invest in a tree-padding pack, which protects your gear and the bark of the tree from wear and tear.

Types of Trails

When talking about trails, in general it is about a natural path in a forest, in a meadow, on a mountainside, or even in the desert. This path might be man-made and maintained (such as in a park), an animal footpath, or even one made by bikes, 4×4s, or motorcycles—the examples are limitless. Two factors seem to affect a trail more than any other, namely, the type of traffic on it and the time of year it is used.

Similar to rotating general running surfaces, if possible, you should also rotate trail types to ensure maximum benefits. For those who do not have a wide variety of trail choices out their back door, do not fret. Spending even one day a week on any type of naturally packed surface will give your feet the workout, variety, and stimulation they need to stay robust.

Rocky Trails

Rocky trails are among the most difficult to run, and they make up a good percentage of trails located in mountainous regions. They are often made up of large, smooth boulders buried deep under the surface (like an iceberg, where all you see is a small portion of the top), volcanic rocks, or loose, scattered stones.

Training on trails crowded with rocks can offer you the challenge, variety, and workout to keep you and your feet in tip-top shape. Plus, running such a stony path helps you build truly quick foot-to-brain reflexes. When you find a rhythm, you will be able to bounce, adjust, and find the best place for the feet to confidently land with each step.

Even if you are now able to run an hour or more on a variety of surfaces without hindrance, when taking on an unusually rocky trail, go half or less the distance you are used to covering. Do this for the first three weeks on new terrain so you do not fatigue or injure your feet. Bring along your shoes and put them on as soon as you have covered a predetermined distance or time.

Muddy Trails

Muddy trails are another order of trails altogether. Mud, caked on a shod runner's shoes, can be frustrating due to the additional weight. For barefoot runners, muddy trails are fun to run. Not only do the toes add substantial grip, but also as the mud dries, it offers a natural and protective barrier between you and the elements.

On trails that have the occasional mud puddle, enjoy it as long as you are not damaging the local habitat. Certain parks try to keep people, bikes, and dogs from strolling off-trail or through the mud, which creates erosion. If you must make a choice whether to go through a muddy section or get off the trail, choose the muddy path first.

ON YOUR TOES

Many trails are designated for either mountain bikers or hikers and runners, but not usually both. Get caught running on a mountain bike trail (or vice versa) and you might get berated. Runners like their trails smooth; bikers like their trails challenging. If you are exploring a new trail and discover that it is for mountain bikers, consider returning to the start to find another path. If you are scolded by a mountain biker, but see no signs that indicate the path is reserved for two-wheeled enthusiasts, talk to a park official. Avoid any confrontations and admit mistakes when you're in the wrong. Nearly all trails are regulated for safety, fun, and the local environment.

Swampy Trails

Swampy trails are different than muddy ones. If you want to run in a swampy area with or without shoes, be sure that no dangerous organisms reside within the muck, and especially be certain that no parasites are transmittable through your bare skin.

Running paths around ponds or lakes engage the senses more intensely than other environments. Bodies of water have sounds, smells, and often soft, grassy, or sandy terrain for your bare feet to enjoy. If fishermen frequent an area where you run, watch out for bobbers and hooks. Also, pay attention that no hooks hung in trees are in your way. If the trail is short, walk it first or wear a pair of minimal shoes the first few times you run.

In Coniferous Forests

If you live in or visit certain regions, especially at higher altitudes, you might spend time in coniferous forests. Whether running in pines or firs, at certain times of the year, the resin produced from the tree will splatter to the ground on the trail. This sticky material always finds its way to the bottom of your feet. For the first few minutes, it can cause you to pick up small stones, pieces of cone, or pine needles, which can penetrate the skin easily. After the sticky stuff has become saturated with dirt, then the gummed gunk does your foot pads a favor by coating them for the rest of your run.

When returning home, you might find the dried resin hard to scrape off the bottom of your feet. Warm water and soap tends to do the trick. Scrape lightly with your fingernails, a sponge, or a soft brush. Using a pumice stone is not recommended as this will scour away the toughened skin you have worked so hard to build and maintain.

In the Desert

Running in more arid areas offers its own challenges as well. Although the dry earth provides a good workout for your foot pads, the dryness prevents moisture from softening your foot's bottom skin. If you live in a desertlike region, running barefoot on back-road desert trails can be a mesmerizing experience, especially as the sun is going down. Walk an area before you run it, if possible. Watch out for cacti spines and other similar inconveniences.

At Night, a Trail Runner's Delight

Many famous names in barefoot running love to get on the trails at night. Barefoot Ted often takes his dog Hercules (the fat dog) with him on such nightly scoots. The draw of running in the darkness is the heightening of your senses. When you enter the forest for a barefoot walk or jog at night, your primordial skills take over. Your feet become true guidance systems; the small sticks and stones that you try to avoid during the day become beacons by night.

Barefoot trail running at night is not as dangerous as it sounds. In the dark, you will surrender and let your feet be your guide. You will run more lightly than usual. Your ability to respond quickly means that when the foot lands, the body immediately reacts. After you are no longer dependent upon sight to guide you over a trail, the automatic adjustments to your landing style, stride, and awareness will help you gently land and move gracefully forward.

TIP TOES

Running in full darkness can be an eerie, yet mesmerizing, experience. If you're nervous, bring a running partner along. Other options for nighttime running include wearing a headlamp, running in the moonlight, or completing a run at dusk before it is totally dark.

Prepare yourself for nighttime trail running by walking in the dark first. Because your eyes are made up of two types of photoreceptors in the retina, called rods and cones, you need to give them time to adjust. You might notice that you can see the trail better by not looking directly at it. From the sides or at the bottom of your field of vision, the trail will be easier to read. This is due to the adjustment of the rods, which aid sight in low-light situations. The time it takes your rods to adjust to low-level lighting is roughly the same amount of time from sundown until total darkness.

At first, it is a good idea to stick to a trail that you know very well, though at night it will seem brand-new. Avoid running more than a few hundred yards on the first attempt, although you will likely want to go farther. After several sessions of walking in total darkness, begin running. If you are running with a partner or group, give each person plenty of space. Try to let silence prevail so that you (and especially your feet) can pay attention to the world under toe.

A Trail Runner's Survival Kit

When going out to explore a trail, consider taking a small survival or first-aid kit with you. Pack it in your ultra-light runner's backpack, stuff it in your waistband, or wear a cycling jersey and stuff it into the back pockets. Ultra-trail runners who wear a waist pack that holds water and other goodies can rig the kit onto their belt.

The kit should contain some basic items, including minimalist shoes or sandals. Consider leaving a bigger first-aid kit in your vehicle as a backup measure. You might also bring along any items to treat yourself if you are prone to allergic reactions (such as from a bee sting). In your car, leave a note with your running route, estimated time of return, and your phone number. Bring a cell phone along if you are alone. At a minimum, your survival kit should contain:

- Alcohol swab
- Saline wash
- Sports tape
- Gauze
- Adhesive pad (moleskin)
- Waterproof bandages
- Sewing needle or tweezers (for splinters)

If you're really going off the beaten path, consider adding:

- Headlamp
- Bungee cord
- Waterproof matches
- Compass
- Nutrition bars
- Knife
- Water-treatment tablets
- Light umbrella
- Long-sleeve shirt (not cotton)

- Insect repellent

- Snake bite kit (if a concern)

With this kit, you'll be able to tidy up cuts or scrapes, remove a thorn or splinter, prevent a blister, and even survive the night if you have to. Bringing an extra long-sleeve shirt is a good idea if unexpected weather is common in your area. You should avoid cotton not only because it is heavy, but also because it actually pulls heat away from your body when wet. Even a small layer between you and the elements can be a lifesaver.

Last but absolutely not least, remember: if you are badly injured on or off a trail, seek medical attention as soon as possible.

Potential Perils in Your Path

Whether in city parks, county reserves, or millions of acres of nationally protected land, trails offer a way to get closer to nature. Sometimes, though, nature can get a little too close for comfort. Because barefoot running exposes you in new ways to the ground, you must make sure that what is on the ground does not endanger you. New barefoot trail runners are often wary of exposing their feet to nature. This is normal and means you are thinking of safety first—the principal rule in dealing with potential perils.

This section discusses some of the risks that many barefoot runners should learn more about.

Cuts, Punctures, or Splinters

Whenever you get an opening in the skin, you should stop running to fully assess the situation. Continuing to run on any wounded area might cause a minor abrasion to worsen or increase the likelihood of infection, especially with exposure to unsanitary materials. Your main objective is to clean, cover, and protect the wound. If you are carrying a first-aid kit, use sports tape, moleskin, or gauze to cover the region.

If you can or must continue running or walking back to your starting point, do so carefully. If you have nothing available to clean and cover the region, remove or tear a layer of clothing to wrap the foot. In certain scenarios, using saliva or water from a nearby creek to clean the area might be better than nothing. If you are within

20 minutes of safety, you can skip such measures as long as you clean the region promptly upon your return. After you've cleaned the area, apply antibiotic ointment and avoid running until it has healed completely.

Hypodermic Needles

A real risk in certain areas, stepping on a hypodermic needle can potentially puncture the skin of shod or shodless runners alike. Stepping on a needle with or without shoes is a scary thought due to the potential exposure to various diseases.

If you live in an area with an increased risk of hypodermic syringe waste, it would be better to run somewhere else, or choose minimal footwear that might offer some protection. If anything, footwear might relieve some anxiety.

Scorpions, Spiders, and Snakes

If you live in an area where other types of nasty critters might live, such as snakes, scorpions, or spiders, practice scanning the ground carefully as you run. Scorpions tend to hide under rocks off trails, so they may not pose a risk, but watch out for them (or venomous spiders) if you decide to sit on a rock to rest, drink, or put on a pair of shoes. If you leave your shoes on a trail to pick up later, shake them out before wearing them.

If you are stung by a scorpion or bitten by a spider, remain calm. As soon as you can get back to civilization, wash the area with soap and water and apply ice covered with a cloth. Common symptoms include stinging pain and inflammation. Worse symptoms include nausea, rash, muscle aches, or spasms. Whatever the case, death is highly unlikely, but you should seek medical attention right away. Bites from certain spiders, such as the brown recluse spider in the United States, can cause tissue damage.

Snakes will come out in the direct sunlight during cooler days to warm up, but they tend to avoid trails where larger animals and humans move about. Increased risk of being bitten comes while hiking through the backcountry through tall brush rather than running on trails. When basking, snakes tend to be unaware of oncoming intruders and can be caught off guard, although they will usually try to move out of the way if they sense you coming.

In or out of shoes, being bitten by a snake may be a risk in certain regions of the United States, namely the Southwest. You may be able to avoid a run-in with a snake with a quick sidestep or jump. If you are able to stop before encountering the snake, back up slowly to stay out of its reach. If venomous snakes pose a significant risk where you run, carry a snakebite kit as a part of your first-aid kit. One of the lightest (and cheapest) kits is the Coghlan's Snake Bite Kit (www.coghlanscampinggear.com).

Woodland Creatures

Wildlife won't purposely get in your way. Generally, if you encounter a wild animal, that animal is going to flee to avoid you. For smaller animals, your risk of being bitten or attacked is minimal. If you live in an area with wild dogs, bring along dog repellent. Stepping on a bee or being stung by a wasp is frightening, and you should take necessary precautions if you are allergic to such insects. Various types of flies, gnats, or mosquitoes are annoying, and some people have more severe reactions to being bitten than others. Take precautions, such as using bug spray, before your outing.

For medium- to larger-sized animals, you may be in danger if you scare them, happen upon their young, or get too close during mating season. If wild animals live where you run, wear a small bell that will warn them of your presence on the trail. If you run with a pet dog, ensure she has a bell, too. If you do not have a bell or other warning system, chant your favorite song lyrics or clap your hands every so often. Carry bear spray if you live in an area where bears might be a risk.

The most dangerous type of creature that trail runners should be made aware of is a hunter. If you run in a park or reserve that is also used for hunting, be sure to avoid the trails on days when the area might be closed or during hunting season; officials do not always post signs at every trailhead. If trails are open to the public, but nearby areas are also being hunted, be diligent about being seen and heard. Avoid wearing gray or white-colored clothing as this can often be mistaken for the hind ends of larger game. Instead, wear colors that stick out, such as bright orange.

Visit the information center (or bulletin board) of a wildlife area you are visiting to verify hunting seasons. Avoid listening to headphones on trails, especially during hunting seasons, and remain aware of your surroundings. If you encounter an injured animal, stop and back away slowly. After you are out of its field of vision, turn around and take another path. Running with a partner can also decrease your risk. Respect hunters and their grounds and they should respect you.

Using Topographical Maps or GPS Units

When you are exploring a new area, using a *topographical map* to help you navigate the terrain is one way to keep yourself from getting too far off track. Topo maps come in varying scales or ratios, depending upon how accurate you want them. Generally, you can get a map of 1:100,000; 1:50,000; or 1:25,000 (or less); the latter is the most detailed version.

DEFINITION

A **topographical map** is a representation of an area drawn to a certain scale that shows contour lines that relate to surface and altitude of a location. They also often relate information about the location of rivers, woods, and areas where people reside.

Combining a topographical map and compass is one way to navigate, although GPS (global positioning system) units are becoming even more practical, user-friendly, affordable, and available. In fact, most mobile phones now have color GPS maps to help you navigate the world in a car or on foot.

Using either of these handy navigating tools while barefoot hiking is one way to explore a place and pinpoint certain parts of the trail that you might like to run again (or avoid). Getting off-trail with either instrument is also possible, but without shoes, you are better off sticking to the trail.

When you use navigational apparatuses, you should stop frequently to calculate your position correctly. If you look at the screen of your GPS unit while running, with or without shoes, you may end up injuring yourself.

Trail Running Resources

Do not feel that you have to venture into the wild country alone to find the best hidden trails in your area. The following list of resources should help you locate and map routes and trails in your region:

- Trails (www.Trails.com)—One of our favorite trail websites, this site is easy to navigate, has an excellent resource for trail books, lists available topographical maps, and allows users to share trail information. If trails are your passion, this is a good place to start.

- Run (www.Run.com)—Part of the LiveStrong family of websites, Run.com is just coming out of its beta testing. This site offers a library of roads and trails, with a preference for loops over out-and-back routes, as well as a listing of trails around the world if you plan on traveling while training.

- Map My Run (www.MapMyRun.com)—A website that not only allows you to find running routes, Map My Run allows you to log your training, find races and other events, talk with others, and read inspirational running articles.

- USA Track & Field (www.usatf.org/routes)—This website has a lot to offer its members, and one of the most valuable features is the route search, which has nearly 400,000 routes for you to explore. Users can rate routes on a gold, silver, and bronze scale.

- Serious Running (www.SeriousRunning.com)—This website does promote heavy trail-running shoes, but it has an ever-expanding list of trails across the United States and a growing list of those abroad. Other features include a listing of top-rated trails, as well as up-and-coming races.

Additional resources include the American Trail Running Association (ATRA) (www. trailrunner.com), Trail Space (www.trailspace.com), as well as TrailRunner (www. trailrunnermag.com), a glossy magazine dedicated to the sport.

The Least You Need to Know

- Running on natural surfaces barefoot works the entire body in beneficial ways, potentially prevents overuse injuries, and enhances a runner's connection with the elements.

- Carrying a pair of minimal shoes when you barefoot trail run is a good idea, especially if you are exploring new areas.

- Running on trails can be made easier by adapting one's technique, namely by maintaining an aligned posture, lowering the center of gravity, and allowing the foot to spread fully by shuffling.

- Barefoot trail running at night is made possible through the enhanced sense of feel of the feet.

- In certain areas, runners should take precautions for wildlife.

Four Seasons and Two Feet

In This Chapter

- Running barefoot through all the seasons
- Handling barefoot running in extreme weather situations
- Avoiding the perils of each season
- Acclimating yourself to different temperatures and terrains

No matter what you choose to wear or not wear on your feet, weather will play a crucial role in planning your runs. Barefoot runners are especially affected in extreme conditions, such as when it is too hot or too cold. Roasting your feet on the asphalt or freezing your toes off in slush by pushing your abilities beyond your limit is no way to keep your feet or body happy and healthy. Slowly adjusting your feet to a wide variety of temperatures on assorted surfaces is the best way to build up resistance to the elements. It is the only way to enjoy barefoot running no matter what the season brings.

Running in the Spring

Running through a verdant meadow filled with blooming flowers is not only the stuff of daydreams, it's what spring is all about. At no other time of the year is nature so fresh and so alive. The awakening of the trees, rebirth of the plants, and creatures discovering their new world are all reasons to get outside and explore, and there's no better way to enjoy nature in her prime than in bare feet.

Running barefoot in the springtime is one of the first opportunities to put what you have done in the winter to maintain your barefoot running to the test. It will take some time for your feet to get used to the various elements (road, trail, and even gravel) again, but not as long as when you first began your barefoot activity. Remember to carefully increase distance while slowly varying terrain.

If you have not been doing much in the way of barefoot running (or any running at all) before, then be sure to take your time getting used to running again. Because you have not run (in or out of shoes) for a while, you may actually be at an advantage. At this point you can make a decision about your running future. If running barefoot (which implies perfecting your overall technique, efficiency, and ability) is important to you, then it is a perfect time for you to consider how barefoot running might play a part in your running goals.

Come Rain, Fog, Hail, or High Water

Running in the rain or mist can be exhilarating. If it is warm enough, the rain can cool you down, awaken your senses, and give you a new view of places you run often. Plus, when done barefoot, running free of wet sneakers is a definite bonus!

Running in the rain with or without shoes, however, does have its downside. Running in a downpour can decrease visibility and is slippery, and running in a thunderstorm can be downright dangerous.

TIP TOES

Lightning is a danger any time of year, but it is possible for you to calculate how far lightning is away from you. This way you can determine how long you have to get home. To do so, when you see a lightning bolt strike, immediately count in seconds (use a watch if possible) until you hear its accompanying thunder. Divide that number by five to calculate miles, or by three to calculate kilometers. If, for example, 20 seconds pass between the moment you see lightning until you hear its thunder, the lightning would be 4 miles (or about 6.5 kilometers) away.

One of the most hazardous times to run is when it is foggy. Fog is basically a cloud that hovers near the Earth's surface and limits visibility. On trails, you might lose your sense of direction. While running on roads, the dangers escalate because cars may have trouble seeing you. If there is a chance of fog when you set out on a run, wear a bright-colored or reflective poncho, vest, or shirt. If you wear a headlamp for low-light or nighttime running, consider wearing that as well. You might also want to wear a blinker.

If you find that cars are getting too close for comfort, then get off the road as far as you can. Some roads have grass or concrete ditches for water or snow flow. Running barefoot on the sides of these is possible; however, you should stop if you experience any aches or pains due to the gradient of the slant. Walking will keep your body steady and give you slightly more time to react should you encounter any obstacles.

Running in the rain, mist, or fog can also cause hypothermia, even on warm days. If you begin feeling chilled, cover your head, neck, and hands. Put on shoes if you have them. If you are walking, begin jogging to warm up the body as you make your way home.

TIP TOES

Running barefoot on wet pavement or asphalt should not keep you from covering your regular distance as long as you maintain good technique. Though your feet will soften to some extent, do not push off or slide over the road or sidewalk. This will cause friction, resulting in abrasions and potentially blisters. Lift your feet, land gently, and keep your cadence high. If you will be running more than one to two hours on a wet surface and your feet become irritated, throw on a pair of minimal shoes and avoid running on a wet surface the next day.

Running in hail is another threat. The size of hail can vary greatly, from pea-sized granules to chunks as big as baseballs. Hailstones can plummet to the Earth at speeds of more than 100 miles per hour. Due to atmospheric friction, collisions with other particles, and wind, hail never tends to pick up much momentum, which the National Severe Storms Laboratory refers to as "terminal velocity."

Regardless of its speed or size, hail wreaks havoc on cars, houses, structures, and people every year. The potential for injury or death from being caught in a hailstorm is real. If you are out when hailstones start falling, seek cover immediately. Choose trees or shrubs for protection as a last resort. If you are out in the open, squat down and cover your head with your clothing while putting your arms over your head. In certain regions, hail can serve as a warning sign for an oncoming tornado. If you continue running (even with your arms covering your head), you risk the chance of being injured primarily due to the lack of coverage for the rest of your body, including your feet. Hailstorms often move through quickly, so if you cannot get to a safe place within a minute or two, find cover and wait it out.

Finally, flash floods are another potential danger that can happen anywhere at any time of year. In fact, they are the main cause of deaths associated with water every year in the United States. Local weather channels often mention if there are flash flood warnings that day, but not always. Flash floods can happen in every region, including mountains, forests, plains, and even in the desert. If you live in an arid climate, even a short rainstorm can cause a flash flood. Whereas most cities are built to handle some flooding, many desert towns flood even with a minimal amount of rain. If you are running in a low-lying area, near a dammed body of water, or near a drainage ditch, take extra precautions if there is a chance of flooding.

If you are caught in a flash flood, do not wait! The swift movement of water carrying all sorts of debris can sweep you along its path. If the water is rising around you, find higher ground or climb high into a sturdy tree. Don't climb on top of your car or attempt to drive away; floodwaters can easily carry you and your vehicle away in a matter of seconds.

Overall, the chance that you will be injured during a storm is slim. You must, however, run smart and be aware and prepared to stay safe. Then, whether you are barefoot or not, inclement weather will not keep you from your daily run!

What's Your Poison?

Though pernicious plants begin sprouting in the spring, they do not seem to pose a greater risk to barefoot runners than those wearing shoes. Most often, runners come into contact with poisonous plants with their lower legs near the knee, calf, or shin. A few of the most common types of poisonous plants in the United States are poison ivy, oak, and sumac, which contain an oil called urushiol that can cause a rash on those who come into contact with it. An old saying holds true for these plants: "Leaves of three, let them be." The chance for contamination from urushiol increases as you move from the West Coast (least chance for infection) to the East Coast (increased chance of infection) in the United States.

If you are severely allergic to such plants, consider purchasing bentoquatam over the counter, which acts as a barrier against urushiol. To treat exposure, wash the area well with soap and water. Also be sure to wash any clothing that could have come into contact with any such plants separately from your other clothes. For prevention, protection, and treatment, obtaining products such as those offered from Ivy-Dry (www.ivydry.com) complements a first-aid kit well. If you develop a severe rash, it spreads internally, or you have difficulty breathing, call 911 and go to the emergency room right away for medical treatment.

Running in the Summer

Running barefoot in the summer will take some planning and preparation. During this season more than any other, you might contemplate running earlier in the morning or later in the evening to avoid the hotter parts of the day—especially for your feet. Although humans possess the ability to run in extremely hot temperatures, doing so without shoes day in and out is not recommended. Slowly acclimating your feet to hotter surfaces is an essential step to enjoying barefoot summer fun!

Like trail running, getting your feet used to various terrains at different temperatures will help toughen your foot pads immensely. It may not seem hot to you outside, but if it's sunny the ground temperature can be much hotter than the air. Consequently, it is possible to burn the bottoms of your feet on scalding surfaces. Avoid going too far for too long on hot surfaces without steadily habituating yourself to the practice.

ON YOUR TOES

When you first begin running on a hot road or trail, be sure to bring a pair of shoes along. When your feet feel hot, put them on right away. Do not push yourself too far while transitioning. Running on extremely hot surfaces can result in first, second, or even third-degree burns.

Get used to running barefoot on hotter surfaces by walking on them for two to five minutes, two times per week. If you cannot handle the surface for even one or two minutes, then the surface is too hot and you should stay off it until later—or altogether. Slowly build your time by adding a few minutes to each session with each week's outing. Do this for a few weeks before trying to run. While walking (and as you begin running), bring your shoes along in case the surface gets too hot to handle.

Because surface temperatures can vary greatly depending upon the type of terrain, test those areas where you will run. Get your feet used to different terrains at various temperatures gradually. A patch of sand is generally hotter than mud-cracked earth, and pavement heats and cools faster than a cement sidewalk, for example. Mix your running routes to include sun-soaked surfaces with shady areas of respite. A dash of planning ahead will get you through any sizzling run in the sun.

Gradually introducing your feet to hotter and tougher terrains while giving your body a rest a day or two in between is the only way to guarantee that your feet will have time to build, recover, and prepare for future runs. Running on hot sand, dirt, rock, and even pavement will do wonders for your foot padding, but only if you allow time for recovery.

If your feet feel like they are smoldering following a run, or at night after a day spent on piping hot terrain, it is a positive sign that they are receiving an increased amount of bloodflow, forming new blood vessels, and becoming stronger than before. If your feet feel scorched, however, you may have pushed yourself too much. Soak them in cool water for 10 minutes, and then lather on ointment or pure aloe vera gel. Use a salve rather than a lotion or cream; you do not want to moisturize the feet, but simply provide relief. One of our favorites is Badger Balm (www.badgerbalm.com), an organic foot ointment.

After your feet feel soothed, wash them again in cool water with a gentle soap while allowing them to air-dry completely. Avoid wearing socks, allow your feet to breathe at night, and wear sandals if you have to walk around outside. Your feet need to stay dry and moisture-free to ensure the skin heals and the pads thicken.

TIP TOES

If you find yourself running on a burning road without footwear and it becomes too hot to handle, rather than moving to the gravel side completely, try running on the painted lines marking the sides of the road. These lines are usually made of thick, white (sometimes golden-yellow), reflective paint that is much cooler than the pavement. If no such lines are present, then getting off to the side, hitching a ride, or tearing up a t-shirt to wrap around your feet are all options.

All this hard work you have done in the summer heat will pay off as cooler temperatures approach. The foot's padding does not only protect you from heat, but also insulates you from the cold. The increased circulation of blood to the foot will serve you well all year long, keeping your feet cool in the summer and warm in the winter.

If you are able to increase your barefoot time gradually on various surfaces throughout the summer, you will gain more barefoot ability than in any other season. However, you must still take it slow. Pay extra attention to your feet. If they become hot or tender while you are out and about, put on shoes. Summer is a time to worry about your tan, not your scalding feet.

Run and Squeal, It's Chip Seal!

Chip seal is a surface treatment that helps roads last longer, a combination of asphalt and small (often sharp granite) rocks that are layered like a cake. Chip seal is later covered with a coat of thin asphalt called fogseal, which helps hold everything together. The real job belongs to traffic, which over time helps to compress the rocks into the asphalt even more.

Running on newly asphalted or chip seal roads is not recommended for barefoot runners. The fumes can cause nausea and the chemicals, an oily tar combo, tend to stick to the feet. Small, pointy rocks tend to stick to feet as well. Plus, these surfaces are black, which means they absorb heat like nothing else.

Too much time running barefoot on new or old chip seal roads can wear down your hard-earned foot padding. You can eventually get used to running on just about any type of surface, but chip seal roads take longer. Regular paved roads, trails, and even sand will feel like heaven in comparison.

Even though all of this can make your feet more resistant, you really have to land lightly without scraping. This is good for practicing form, but vary your runs away from chip seal roads if you spend a lot of time on such a surface. Your feet need to respond to the slight changes on other surfaces more than they need to be punished on surfaces that can really make you squeal in pain!

Running on the Beach

When most people think of summer, they think of the beach. When barefoot runners think of the beach, they think of running in the sand. As discussed, running in the sand is one surefire way of building strong feet and thick foot pads. Not only does the texture of the sand toughen the skin, but it also works to strengthen your foot, ankle, and calf muscles like no other surface because each step is different than the last.

ON YOUR TOES

Do not forget about your feet when you put on sunscreen. Because of their direct exposure to the sun, the tops of your feet can burn just like any other part of your body. Applying sunscreen with an SPF rating of 15 to 30 will keep your feet protected adequately. Try to purchase a sunscreen that contains no perfumes, is hypoallergenic, and will still allow your feet to perspire. Use it on the ankles and even on the tops of the toes, and allow it to dry before running. Don't treat the bottoms of your feet with sunscreen, as this may soften the skin too much before a barefoot run.

When you begin running on the sand for the first time, do not overdo it. Even if you are able to run barefoot on a variety of surfaces (at differing temperatures), test your ability on the sand with just 5 to 10 minutes at a time. Allow a day in between each run to see how your feet and body feel. Running on the sand will alter your form to some extent, so you want to be careful to prevent injuries by not pushing yourself too far too soon.

At first, try to run close to the water's edge where the sand is compact, slightly wet, cooler, and at its flattest. Running back the same way you came will ensure that each leg is worked equally if the slope is uneven. As you get used to the sand, move farther away from the water line and try your skills on the drier, hotter, slipperier stuff. Digging your feet in under the surface of the sand will help you find a cooler layer if the surface is too hot to manage.

As you run, watch out for small pieces of glass, wood, or other objects. Even if the sand looks clean enough, debris can wash up at high tide and get buried. Some runners enjoy wearing aqua shoes while running on the beach. If you run in an area where added protection is necessary, consider a minimalist shoe that will not become heavy if wet, is breathable, and allows the feet to flex.

Hydration and Heat-Related Illnesses

Running in the summer brings its own set of challenges compared to other seasons, and staying hydrated is one of them. Working through your hydration needs is something you should do at the individual level during different trainings at various temperatures. Carefully get used to running in the heat through gradual exposure. For longer walks (and eventual runs), bring along a hands-free water belt or running pack so that your hands remain free to carry your shoes (one in each hand to maintain balance). Drink a few sips of water when you feel thirsty, but avoid overdoing it.

Over-hydrating is actually a problem in many events in the United States. Runners completing a short race often ingest too much water, which actually slows them down, sloshes around in the stomach, or can cause *exertional hyponatremia.*

DEFINITION

Exertional hyponatremia is a disorder that can occur to athletes who drink too much during exercise. Too much water causes the body's salts and electrolytes to become imbalanced. When it is hot outside, the body loses even more salt through sweat. This salt loss combined with too much water intake can cause serious reactions, including nausea, vomiting, and even coma and death. The body simply cannot absorb or expel as much water as is being taken in.

In his book, *Why We Run: A Natural History,* Bernd Heinrich explains that camels can survive even if they lose up to 40 percent of their body weight in water. When a water source is found, they can quickly drink that loss back up. Humans, however, can lose just more than 10 percent of their mass in water before they begin to desiccate. If you try drinking that loss up too quickly, then you can suffer water toxicity, or hyponatremia. If salt, sugar, or other elements are present in the water, then the body can absorb it more slowly, but you still need to be careful about ingesting too much of any liquid too quickly, even when dehydrated.

Several groups of people, such as desert nomads, can survive a long time in extremely hot conditions on only a glass of steaming tea, for example. The tea, which can also contain a copious amount of sugar along with herbs, is digested slowly, lasting hours on end. With their loose clothing, adjusted metabolism, and water economy, they are living proof of our capability to survive, and thrive, in extremely hot conditions.

Following the nomads' and their camels' lead does not mean that you should strive to push yourself on less water (these nomads are probably quite dehydrated by a runner's standards), but it does give you a measure of two extremes. It shows that your body is adaptable to extreme environmental conditions—much more than we give ourselves credit. Finding your level of comfortable hydration while preventing dehydration in various climates is something you can practice and measure in training.

TIP TOES

Running in the evening or at night is one way to avoid overheating. One fun way of telling the temperature during this time is to count how often a nearby cricket stridulates, or chirps. Dolbear's Law states that one should count how many chirps a cricket makes in 15 seconds. Add 37 to that number. You now have the outside temperature in degrees Fahrenheit. To figure out what this is in Celsius, subtract 30 and divide the result in half.

However, because of the chance of heat stroke (or sunstroke), heat exhaustion, stress, cramps, or fainting, it is better to err on the side of caution in regard to water consumption and activity. It is important to hydrate 30 or more minutes before running or racing in hot weather so you will be ready to sweat when needed. When the event begins, simply drink when you feel thirsty. Sip water often rather than gulping it infrequently, especially if your activity will last longer than 30 minutes in exceedingly hot conditions.

If you feel hot, dizzy, or disoriented, or your skin begins to feel clammy or you have stopped sweating, seek an area out of the sun immediately. Sit down while taking in liquids slowly. A sports drink mix containing sugars, salts, and other electrolytes such as potassium might help restore your internal fluid balance. Douse your hands and feet in water. Wet an article of clothing and place it around your neck. Avoid pouring ice-cold water over your body as this can throw you into shock. Focus on relaxing, but if symptoms worsen, seek medical attention promptly.

Another facet of hot-weather running is choosing your apparel wisely. When it comes to the heat, we often think less is best. However, after the sun begins cooking your skin and evaporating your sweat rapidly, that is not the case. Wearing a bright-colored, long-sleeve, moisture-wicking shirt can help. Consider wearing a sun visor and sunglasses to help protect your face and eyes.

Running in the Fall

In certain parts of the United States, running, hiking, and other outdoor pursuits become very popular in the fall. The cooler weather, crisp air, and palette of colors beckon before the cold winter approaches.

With each season, a barefoot runner has a whole new array of sensations in which the feet can bask. In the fall, the crunching of the leaves and time away from scorching temperatures gives us a break to truly enjoy trails, backcountry roads, and city parks.

Running in the fall does present the same dangers as other seasons. A period of warm to hot weather in the fall is not uncommon (often called an Indian Summer), so be cautious if you have not run in the heat for a while. Additionally, rain and hail can still come tumbling down.

Late in the fall, be careful of colder mornings and evenings. Running through cold mud or puddles can make the feet numb if you are not yet attuned to colder temperatures.

Another consideration in the fall is the apparel you will wear. Because it is not as hot as the summer or as cold as the winter, certain gear will help keep your body adjusted to the variety of temperatures and possible fluctuating weather.

Layering your clothing is one way to ensure that you are prepared for any run. For any season, one material that has become widely popular is CoolMax fabric, which helps wick moisture away from the body. Using this in the fall as a base layer helps to keep sweat from saturating your clothing, which can cool the body below a comfortable zone. Add outside layers to this, such as a long-sleeved running shirt (avoid cotton) followed by an outer wind- or rain-resistant layer that can be taken off and tied to your waist if needed. This will help regulate your body temperature during your runs.

ON YOUR TOES

As the days get shorter in the fall, try to stay off busy roads as much as possible after dark. Trails or school running tracks can make suitable alternatives. If you cannot avoid running in trafficked areas, try to run in the daylight hours so that local commuters will see you. Solo women runners should also vary their schedules to avoid harassment or potential attacks.

Because of busy work schedules (and the turning back of clocks), your runs may begin before the sun sets but not end until after dark. Plan appropriately during the shorter days so you do not have to rush your training. Wear bright, reflective clothing, carry a stocking cap in case it gets cold, and wear a light or reflective vest if you are running on roads.

Running in Winter

In the United States, winters vary drastically from one state to the next—Floridians and upstate New Yorkers have very different winters indeed! More than in any other season, barefoot runners need to cautiously and gradually acclimate themselves to running in the cold (and on cold surfaces) to prevent harm or injury. With that said, just as your body gets used to the increased heat of summer, so can it get used to the decreasing temperatures of winter.

Unlike your hands, which can become quite chilled and lose heat in colder weather, your feet maintain a more constant temperature, due to increased circulation and the expanded fat deposits that have contributed to the thickened pads you've formed after several months of barefoot running. If you transitioned to barefoot running before the winter months, you will be even more ready for cold weather. It is still advisable, however, that you take every precaution to ensure that your feet are accustomed to the cold before you schedule a longer jaunt without shoes.

To run barefoot in colder temperatures, you will have to adjust even more carefully and slowly than you did in the summer. Like the dangers of hot surfaces in summer, freezing surfaces can also cause problems, such as frostbite, which can lead to a whole slew of *other* problems, such as gangrene.

Start out running only a few minutes per session in colder weather. Five minutes outside (you can finish the rest of your run in shoes or indoors) with a day off in between for the first few weeks should be enough. If the temperatures are near freezing, run only two to five minutes. Initially, take two days completely off from running after spending increased time in near-freezing conditions. This will allow your feet to build resistance, while giving you time to make sure no damage to the skin has occurred.

Before enjoying winter's wonders without shoes, it is imperative that you spend time getting your feet (and body) warmed up. Doing jumping jacks or running on a treadmill should do the trick. After your feet feel warmed up, head outside. For your first few runs, aim for dry, man-made surfaces with some sun exposure. And don't forget to bring along your shoes to throw on when needed.

Record both the temperature and time spent outside in your barefoot running journal. Making a graph comparing these variables will allow you to see your improvement over a prolonged period of time. It will also help you plan future runs.

As the weeks progress, temperatures will likely go up and down, which is why keeping track of it on paper will help. If the temperature goes well below what you're used to from prior running sessions, then cut back on your time appropriately. You might discover a formula that works for you. For example, with every 1-degree drop in temperature, you might find that you need to decrease the time spent barefoot by 10 percent or more.

Say you can spend 20 minutes running on a sidewalk at 38 degrees Fahrenheit. If the temperature drops to 33, then you should decrease the barefoot portion of your run by 50 percent. In this example, you would run only 10 minutes at 33 degrees. Following such a formula will help keep your feet out of danger.

This manner of calculating how long you should spend without shoes does not take into consideration the type of terrain, its conditions, or the actual ground temperature. You will have to determine what your feet can and cannot handle. What you might notice in due course is the inverse relationship of cold-weather running. That is, with less time spent in colder temperatures, you may be able to increase the time you can spend at higher ones. Your ability to run 20 minutes at 38 degrees may go up to 25 minutes if you have slowly acclimated at colder temperature zones hovering near freezing.

Running Barefoot on Snow and Ice

Running barefoot in the snow is also feasible after you acclimate your feet to it. Because of the inherent dangers of snow, ice, and extremely cold temperatures on the feet, you must take time and adjust carefully. Pushing even a minute or two past your ability (or comfort zone when the foot first begins feeling numb) can damage the tissue, nerves, or ligaments of the foot forever. So even though running in freezing temperatures, in snow, and on ice is possible, it should be reserved for individuals who truly have the patience to habituate themselves over several seasons of cold-weather running.

If you have snow during much of the winter where you live, then you can prepare in all kinds of conditions. If, however, you live in an area that only gets some powder a few times during the season, then plan your runs even more carefully. When you're first getting used to it, consider running close to home so you can get back quickly if you need to. Or rotate a few minutes outdoors followed by time inside to complete your run. If you are away from anyplace where you can warm up, carry your shoes (and perhaps socks) with you. Ensure that your footgear is loose-fitting so that your toes can still receive an ample supply of blood to help keep them warm.

Running on ice and slush or through near-freezing water is possible with toughened and adjusted feet; it might actually be warmer than trotting through the snow. Depending on the ground temperature, the surface underneath, and other conditions, you might have to switch running surfaces a few times during one run to find the warmest areas. Areas exposed to the sun will be warmer than those in the shade.

When exploring, remember to steer clear of melting snow mixed with halite, or rock salt. This is one way to tear up your feet fast. If your feet start burning or going numb after running through rock salt (or in snowmelt containing it), wipe them off and put on your minimalist shoes to finish your run.

Running in deep snow is also possible, but it is better to stick to snow no more than a few inches deep (or about up to the ankles) when you first begin. Exposing too much of the lower extremities to the cold might mean less blood reaches the toes. When acclimated, feel free to experiment with gradually deeper snow runs.

Just as you slowly adjust to different surfaces and snow depths, you will also have to test different temperatures your feet can withstand. The more winter seasons you run without shoes, the farther you will be able to go at colder temperatures. Running at 40 degrees Fahrenheit will not be all that difficult after you have done it for a few weeks. But when temperatures approach freezing (32 degrees), the barefoot game changes drastically. Over the course of several weeks, you will find that you can handle colder and colder temperatures. Running in the snow with temperatures around 25 degrees Fahrenheit (without a wind chill) will be manageable. Runs below this range are also possible, but should be reserved for individuals who have spent several months (or seasons) running in freezing temperatures.

Running on snow-covered trails is also within the realm of possibility for barefoot winter runners; however, the activity should be considered of the "black diamond" variety—an activity reserved for experts only. Because it is difficult to see the ground, you must pay close attention to how your feet feel. Like running on a trail covered in leaves, you will have to navigate carefully.

Running cautiously on a path while barefoot tends to slow runners down. In warmer times of the year, this is not a problem, but when you slow down in the winter, you cool down quickly. This means less bloodflow throughout your body, including your feet. Although the skin of your feet is toughened and thick, and the tissue is robust, less bloodflow combined with the cold means less elasticity overall. Your feet will still handle a certain amount of natural bending, flexing, and force, but they will be more sensitive to the terrain. Proceed carefully while running on frozen or snow-covered trails, and only do this when you are 110 percent ready.

Avoiding Frostbite

Frostbite is the freezing of body tissue due to cold. Generally, frostbite affects the fingers, nose, ears, and even toes of people who expose these areas to continued freezing conditions. Frostbite has different levels of severity depending upon how deep the tissue is frozen. If you believe you have acute frostbite, seek medical attention right away.

For both barefoot and shod runners, frostbite is a real danger in the wintertime. Running barefoot does not mean that you will get frostbite on your feet or toes, nor does wearing shoes prevent it. A runner in tight shoes (and even socks) has the potential to get frostbite due to restrictive footwear cutting off the flow of blood to the feet, which prevents them from warming up. Barefoot runners have nothing preventing bloodflow when acclimated to the cold, so their feet can potentially stay warm with continued, steady physical exertion.

When it comes to frostbite, prevention is, of course, the best medicine. On extremely cold days, try to run at the warmest time of the day. Also, run out of the wind or at a time when the wind speed has died down. Pay attention to the forecasted wind chill, which is a measure of how cold it will feel with the wind added to the temperature. This greatly affects heat loss for your whole body. For example, if it is 20 degrees Fahrenheit, a wind speed of 15 miles an hour will result in a wind chill of below zero, or –5 Fahrenheit. Don't rely solely on temperature to give you the whole picture.

Also, when running in exceptionally cold weather, avoid running yourself into exhaustion. Doing so will cause you to perspire, and your clothes will become saturated with sweat, which will cool your body even further. And if you run yourself into fatigue, the body decreases bloodflow to the appendages—increasing the risk of frostbite—so that the body core remains warm.

If any part of your body loses sensation or becomes numb, find a place to warm up the area right away. For hands, place them inside your clothing, next to your skin. For feet, put on socks and shoes and continue moving so that blood keeps flowing to the area.

In the case of deep-tissue frostbite (where it has changed color, and where you cannot move or feel the affected area), seek medical attention right away. If that is not possible, thaw the area only when you are 100 percent sure that it will not be exposed to cold temperatures again. Refreezing frostbitten flesh can result in permanent damage. Avoid rubbing or massaging the area. Immerse the affected area in warm water as soon as possible. Avoid scalding water as it may burn your skin though you won't be able to feel it. Fully thawing out the area will bring about severe pain, but it is essential to slowly warm up the area, no matter how painful. This is the only way to prevent lasting damage. When the area is warmed up, wrap it loosely in bandages, keep it clean, and seek medical attention.

Minimalist Winter Running Shoes

A high percentage of barefoot runners who continue training in the winter use minimal footwear to help them through the coldest part of the season. There aren't currently many options for those seeking a minimalist shoe for running in the snow or ice, or made specifically for keeping you warm in below-freezing temperatures.

Finding out what will work for you is an individual undertaking. As you try out different types of shoes, proceed with caution. Different shoes will change the way your foot responds to the ground, which can ultimately alter your landing style. Start out slowly and cautiously when trying out new winter gear for your feet, and spend no more than 15 to 20 minutes in a new pair for the first few outings. As always, take at least one day off in between runs to give your feet adequate time to adjust.

The important factors when searching for or making your own minimal winter running shoes are added insulation for warmth, looseness for optimal circulation, and a thin, flexible sole that will allow your foot to at least partially feel the ground.

Moccasins are one of the best solutions for many barefoot runners in the winter. Like mittens that help keep the entire hand warm, moccasins can help the entire foot enjoy the warmth being generated as you run. Contact Soft Star Shoes (www.softstarshoes.com) about their winter running moccasin options. Additionally, Arrow Moccasin Company (www.arrowmoc.com) has several models of regular moccasins from which to choose that might be suitable for winter running.

Many runners tout Vibram FiveFingers (www.vibramfivefingers.com) as one of the best minimal shoes, even for winter. Both KSO Treks and the company's neoprene models tend to work in colder types of weather. For added insulation, Injinji (www.injinji.com) socks tend to partner well because they have separate slots for each of the toes. Other runners have used aqua socks combined with wool socks in an attempt to stay as minimal as possible. Bear in mind that adding socks to already snug-fitting shoes might inhibit circulation, which can cut off bloodflow and go against your goal of keeping your feet warm. If you plan on using socks with a pair of minimal shoes for winter use, get a pair of shoes one to two sizes bigger than normal to allow plenty of room for your feet and toes to move about.

Depending on the temperature, some runners simply wear their racing flats with or without socks for winter running. Carrying warm booties along in case it proves too cold is always an option. If you are running on ice, choose a pair of flats with track spikes, which will help you maintain your grip. You might also consider thin-soled, flexible trail shoes with the insoles removed. With or without socks, you will at least have a grip on winter terrain while sticking to the minimalist agenda as best you can.

Do not feel that you have to buy new shoes to be able to run barefoot in the winter. Making your own minimal winter footwear is also an option for those willing to test their own design theories. From gluing thin soles onto wool socks to fashioning their own moccasins, barefoot winter runners are coming up with all sorts of solutions to help bear the cold. In the world of winter barefoot running, the room for innovation is large, warm, and welcoming.

The Least You Need to Know

- Spring is a great time to begin barefoot running because it is a time of awakening both nature and your feet, but beware of certain weather conditions, such as rain, hail, or fog, that can make running dangerous.
- Slowly increasing the time you spend running on hotter surfaces is one surefire way to build up your foot padding, but be extremely careful to prevent burning the bottoms of your feet.
- Carrying your shoes and using them when your feet have had enough in any season is one of the best ways to prevent skin damage and deep-tissue injuries.
- Due to foliage and other natural debris blocking your vision, you should be careful when barefoot trail running in the fall.
- Because of increased bloodflow and thick padding, your feet can handle barefoot running in cold conditions, including on snow and ice, after they have been acclimated through carefully planned sessions.

Dealing with Soreness and Injury

Chapter 12

In This Chapter

- Recognizing soreness that might lead to injury
- Handling common injuries to the foot
- Managing injuries to the legs

Being able to recognize the difference between aches, pains, and injury is crucial to being a successful runner. During your barefoot transition, you will be acutely aware of what your body is telling you. Managing the pain that is a part of the transition to barefoot running will determine your overall success and enjoyment as a barefoot runner.

On the Scale: Measuring Soreness

As a rule, pain is a protective response. It tells you when a part of your body is under too much stress or if any tissue or structure has been damaged. Some soreness is normal, particularly when increasing your training or trying out challenging terrain without shoes. When you feel sore, it means that you have broken down tissue. The damage must be repaired before the body can come back stronger. Only with time to recover will the body build itself to handle other challenges you might present it with, namely running farther or faster.

As a barefoot runner, you must be able to differentiate between various levels of soreness and be willing to adapt your training as needed. A low level of soreness could mean that you trained just right. You can probably enjoy your scheduled recovery run. A medium level of soreness might mean you should substitute your next intense or long training session with an easy recovery run (or an extra day off). Soreness that borders on pain requires rest and observation, and if it doesn't ease, should be assessed by a sports doctor to determine what injury has occurred.

Soreness not only tells you when you might have had enough, it also tells you how to run. For the barefoot runner, this can be helpful by giving you the feedback required to modify your stride, cadence, or if you need to make other changes to compensate for rough terrain, hills, or other variables.

You must respond to soreness appropriately so that it does not cause detrimental alterations to your gait, which could cause even greater problems for you down the road.

- If you develop any significant pain while running, slow down or stop until you can establish the source. If the pain subsides quickly, continue walking to see how you feel and then try resuming your run. If in doubt, the best option is to stop running for a day or two and see if it goes away or continues to get worse.

- If you develop milder pains that feel like they are coming from one of your muscles, continue running, slowing your pace if necessary and wait to see if it subsides. Stop if the pain progressively worsens, begins affecting other parts of your body, or causes you to alter your form or breathing.

- If you develop milder aches or pains that do not feel like they are coming from a muscle, but originating from joints, tendons, or bones, then continue with caution. If the ache does not dwindle after five minutes, or is getting worse, then end the session.

- In the days following a more intense or longer-distance run, the soreness you feel should not be severe. It should peak after two days and then ease steadily. Begin running again when you are able to walk without pain and you feel recuperated.

- If by the end of a warm-up muscular soreness is preventing you from running fluidly and easily, do not attempt a hard workout. It is much better to continue with an easy run to help your body recover. If this is not possible, walk or simply give yourself an extra day of rest.

Running After an Injury

The most common cause of injury in the world of running is athletes pushing themselves too hard without building up to it, or not giving themselves enough time to recover after intense workouts. Most often, injuries start out as a small ache or pain. If ignored, then an injury will require rest, rehabilitation, and up to several weeks or months away from the sport.

When practicing barefoot running, form is important. But don't focus on consciously altering the way you run with every session. How you think you should run is usually different from how your body thinks you should run, especially as the terrain changes. Deliberately overriding this subconscious control for too long can trigger an overuse injury.

Occasionally people have genuine structural problems with their legs or feet, but this is rare. If this is the case, it may limit how hard you train but is usually not in itself an unavoidable source of injury. Cross training, which promotes the use of other muscles, can also help prevent injuries. Both swimming and cycling can help to balance weaker parts of your body that are not as active when you are running.

A final and very important point is that running is not the source of all ills in your feet and legs. If you have an injury that will not go away, talk with your doctor about the potential causes. You might also see a specialist who can help you come at your problem from another angle.

Injuries to Your Feet

The skin on your feet adapts rapidly to running barefoot, but is initially delicate after a lifetime of wearing shoes. As a result, most barefoot runners have some sensitivity problems in the first few months until their skin toughens up. You can overcome all these problems with time and patience!

One of the most common types of injuries for barefoot runners is blisters, which result from friction and skin that is not yet toughened. Additionally, because your form is slowly developing, you may not actually land as lightly as you could. Moreover, the small accelerations and decelerations will cause you to drag your foot forward and backward, placing stress on the skin. Unfortunately, when you start barefoot running, weakness in both your skin and form may mean that you get occasional blisters.

Blisters will heal without interference. If you find a blister extremely painful or collecting a large amount of fluid, avoid opening it if possible; the chance of infection increases. If you do open a blister, do it with a sterile needle and then cover it with a sterile dressing. Avoid running until the skin has healed. Doing so when it is sensitive could alter your form, causing a more serious injury. If you are used to running in minimalist shoes, give that a try, as long as the area is protected and you feel no pain.

ON YOUR TOES

If you have recurring blisters, make sure you are not weakening your skin by allowing your feet to remain moist for prolonged periods. Avoid soaking them in a hot bath or wearing shoes and socks that do not allow the feet to breathe.

Bruised to the Bone

When you land on a rock or anything else that puts substantial pressure or force on an area of the foot, you'll get a bruise. More serious bruising underfoot can be surprisingly painful or show up as a fluid-filled cavity deep in the skin.

Similar to blisters, it is best to allow such injuries to heal on their own. Avoid running and stay off the foot as much as you can. A doctor should be able to help you more if you begin noticing a significant collection of fluid. Common treatment includes washing the area with disinfectant, using a sterile scalpel or a needle to open the cavity, and draining the fluid. This will help to relieve the pressure, making it more comfortable to walk. However, a break in the skin increases the chance of infection, so do not run completely barefoot until all the signs of an injury have subsided.

Clearly, prevention is the key. Stone bruises teach you very quickly to scan the trail or road ahead to watch where to place your feet. Novice barefoot runners should avoid running on rocky trails until their feet have adapted well to running on less-demanding surfaces. Alternatively, you can wear minimalist shoes, but bruising or other mishaps can still occur. Experienced barefoot runners can run on the harshest rocky trails without difficulty, but this level of barefoot adaptation can take years to achieve.

Jams and Fractures

Bones are incredibly malleable structures that are continually shaping themselves in response to stress. Unless you have a medical condition that weakens your bones, they are more than capable of adapting to the needs of barefoot running.

The injury that strikes fear into all distance runners is stress fractures. These are simply micro-fractures of the bone that have developed due to excessive stress placed on the region. Usually, this is the result of repeated cycles of bony breakdown without inadequate recovery. However, on occasion, stress fractures of the foot can occur to the small bones of the foot when too much force is put on the region during a single session.

The common sites for stress fractures in runners are the metatarsals, the talus, tibia, and occasionally the femur. You'll feel an ache at the affected site that worsens with activity and improves with rest. Diagnosis usually requires a radionucleotide bone scan because stress fractures are often unapparent on an x-ray. The treatment is to rest for 6 to 10 weeks.

Acute fractures are not commonly seen in runners, although anyone can have a nasty fall, and broken toes are not unheard of when barefoot runners jam a toe on a rock or a stump. Although bruising and scraping are more likely than a break, if you do suffer a significant toe injury, then a fracture or a dislocation is a possibility. Get the toe checked out by your doctor. An x-ray is one of the surest ways of locating the problem and differentiating between a fracture and a dislocation. If you dislocated a toe, you can try to put it back in place, but that probably isn't advisable without having an x-ray to rule out a fracture.

TIP TOES

If you are thinking of waiting to see how the toe settles before seeking medical attention, make sure you still have adequate bloodflow to the tip of the toe. You can do this by pressing on the skin and then removing the pressure—the skin will go pale as you push on it and then the color will return within two seconds if the bloodflow is adequate. If you don't have enough bloodflow or if the toe feels numb, you should immediately seek a medical assessment.

Fractures to the little toe are usually treated by buddy strapping, or taping the fractured toe to an adjacent one. In some extreme cases, surgery may be necessary. Fractures of the big toe are particularly important to have properly assessed. If you don't take care of them in time, they can lead to ongoing complications.

Penetrating Injuries

Puncture wounds from hypodermic needles might be at the top of your most-feared list while barefoot running, but the more mundane stuff—glass fragments, thorns, and sticks—are probably what will really cause you pain. In Australia, "bindi eyes" are particularly common and annoying. These are very sharp, particularly in summer when they have hardened and dried. Pulling them out leaves a multitude of tiny thorns that remain embedded in the skin.

With any such penetrating injury, you need to remove the foreign body and clean the wound. The tiniest thorn or glass fragment embedded in your skin can be extremely irritating and difficult to find. Examine your sole under a bright light and run your finger over the affected area to try to locate the fragment. If you cannot find it, then you might need to recruit someone else to look for you. If still unsuccessful, visit a doctor or podiatrist to remove it.

After you identify the offending object, use a sterile needle or blade to remove it. Use alcohol or heat to sterilize your tools for objects that have pierced the first layer of skin, called the epidermis; in most cases you will only be removing superficial embedded objects for which a clean needle is often enough. Impaling the shaft of the splinter with a needle and then pushing it back out of the skin along its path of entry can remove long splinters. After it emerges, a good pair of tweezers is invaluable for grasping the end and pulling it out in one piece.

In terms of prevention, keep your eyes peeled, scanning the ground ahead of you for potential threats. If you are planning to run a new trail, do so in daylight rather than venturing out at dusk. If you are planning a relaxing run where your mind is more likely to wander, run a route you know is safe and you are familiar with.

Foot Infections

If you develop pain, redness, or ooze from a wound, there is probably a degree of infection. Superficial skin infections as a result of scrapes or puncture wounds are usually minor and resolve themselves as long as the wound is cleaned and allowed to heal. However, more serious infections do occur and require immediate medical attention.

ON YOUR TOES

All barefoot runners should ensure that their tetanus and hepatitis B immunizations are up-to-date. If it has been more than five years since your last tetanus shot, and you suffer a deep penetrating injury in the foot, request a tetanus booster shot as part of your wound care. Hepatitis B immunization requires a course of three injections and will provide both protection and peace of mind if you are unlucky enough to step on a used needle.

If you develop pain deeper in the foot, pain or redness is spreading either within the foot or tracking up the leg, or you become unwell with fever or nausea, antibiotics plus or minus surgical explorations and drainage of the wound are urgently required. These more serious infections may spread within the skin or move deeper into the foot. There have been at least two reports in recent years of bone infections resulting from thorns penetrating deep into the foot.

Heat and Cold

Take care to avoid thermal injuries due to very hot road surfaces or ice and snow. Unless you have successfully adapted to running in such conditions, avoid temperature extremes. Significant burns to the sole of the foot can occur if you ignore the orders from your feet to get off a hot road surface. Similarly, frostbite can have severe ramifications, including amputation of toes.

Treat burns initially by running your feet under cold water. The skin may blister and, if severe, will probably require dressings and medical attention. If the burn is minor, applying antiseptic and waiting for it to heal is usually sufficient. Keep a careful eye on the burn to make sure it doesn't become infected, in which case antibiotics may be required.

If you get frostbite, you should elevate your feet and warm them using water just above body temperature. Avoid rubbing the feet as this can cause tissue damage. Seek medical attention if there is persistent pain, numbness, or discoloration of the toes after rewarming. Most importantly, don't allow the skin to refreeze by going back out in the snow.

Injuries to Your Springs

Your spring muscles and tendons are under significant pressure when you run. When transitioning to running barefoot, the previously unused elastic tissues in your foot and ankle will be particularly susceptible to becoming overloaded and inflamed. When this happens, these injuries often require significant rest to heal properly. Therefore, preventing these injuries is crucial.

In most cases being conservative and listening to the feedback from your body is enough to prevent such injuries from occurring. Planning a gradual introduction to barefoot running is important, but equally important is your ability to change your running plans if you feel any pain. Allowing the area to heal completely is the best way to prevent injury.

Plantar Fasciitis

The plantar fascia is an elastic membrane that links the three points of the tripod (see Chapter 4) of your foot. Pain in the sole of the foot—particularly in front of the heel—is often attributed to inflammation of the plantar fascia.

Whether the plantar fascia is actually the source of the pain is controversial, as is whether the plantar fascia actually becomes inflamed or merely degenerates. Irrespective, soreness deep in the sole of the foot is very common when learning to run barefoot.

Weakness in the muscles and elastic tissue of the feet from wearing shoes makes the foot initially susceptible to injury when you go barefoot. Therefore, you should take pain in the sole of your foot seriously and monitor it closely. Stop running when your calves or feet *begin* to fatigue; don't push them to the point where you have to stop because you are tired. Similarly, if you develop an ache deep in the sole of one or both feet, make sure you're on the mend and can at least walk comfortably before attempting to run again.

TIP TOES

A traditional therapy for pain coming from the bottom of the foot is to walk barefoot in cold water, such as walking in a creek. This both ices the region and provides beneficial stimulation by contracting the muscles of the foot, which helps build up strength.

If you are learning to run in minimalist shoes rather than bare feet, you should take particular care. If you cannot progress because of recurring deep sole pain, consider learning to run in bare feet before gradually reintroducing minimalist shoes.

Standard therapy for plantar fasciitis includes anti-inflammatories, orthotics, and steroid injections, but it's not clear how effective these therapies are. Plantar fasciitis usually heals with time, although this can take 12 to 24 months. Prevention in this case is better than any cure.

Achilles Tendonitis

If an Achilles tendon becomes inflamed, you will feel pain and stiffness in the area. Diagnosis is usually clinical, but may require an ultrasound scan.

Treat an angry Achilles with rest, ice, anti-inflammatories, and physiotherapy. You might receive corticosteroid injections around the tendon in chronic cases. Wearing a shoe with a raised heel, like your old sneakers, may settle down severe cases of inflammation in the acute phase but should be accompanied by calf stretching so that shortening of the Achilles and calf muscles doesn't occur. This will make the tendonitis more likely to recur when you start running again.

Calf Muscle Soreness

Everyone experiences significant calf soreness when learning to run barefoot. This rarely causes any ongoing issues and will resolve with time. However, you must take care to ensure that you do not overload your calf muscles to the point where they can no longer perform their spring functions, predisposing yourself to other injuries.

Your calf muscles develop significantly over the first three months. You can see this low in the calf due to enlargement of the soleus and also high in the calf due to enlargement of both the deep calf muscles, which support the arch of the foot, and the overlying gastrocnemius.

With these structural changes, you will gradually develop a smoother, more efficient gait and will no longer feel as much strain and jarring when running on hard surfaces.

Shin Splints

Shin splints, also known as medial tibial stress syndrome, occurs when the point at which the soleus muscle attaches to the tibia becomes inflamed. Shin splints in shod runners is usually associated with runners who are just starting or are increasing their speed work or running on hard surfaces. Barefoot runners face similar challenges in learning to run with a forefoot strike, particularly on hard surfaces.

You should carefully monitor any shin soreness and adjust your workload accordingly. If in doubt, err on the side of rest and recovery rather than pushing on. Inadequate calf and Achilles elasticity and strength will increase the risks for barefoot runners, as will artificially trying to run with a pronounced forefoot strike. Make sure your feet and ankles are relaxed and that your footstrike is natural, more subconscious than conscious.

Treat shin splints with rest, ice massage, calf stretching with the knee bent, and a very gradual rehabilitation program that starts with walking, progresses to 50 m of easy jogging on a grass track, and then gradually increases in distance and surface hardness. You should not progress to the next phase until you're doing the current one without pain, either during the session or during your recovery.

Other Aches and Pains

Barefoot runners often transition from shod running to escape from common running injuries such as iliotibial band friction syndrome, runner's knee, or less common injuries such as compartment syndromes. Anecdotally, these injuries appear to be less common in barefoot runners. If this is true, it probably reflects the different mechanics of running in shoes compared to bare feet.

Runner's knee or patellofemoral syndrome is knee pain resulting from the kneecap tracking unevenly in the groove of the femur. It may in fact result from running with a heel strike and uneven activation of the quadriceps muscle as a result. Shod runners treat it with exercises to strengthen the medial quadriceps and taping to pull the patella medially.

The iliotibial band is an elastic spring that runs from the pelvis to the outside of the knee. It allows you to stand on one leg despite the fact that only one side of your pelvis is supported. The bouncing inherent in running significantly increases these forces. In shod runners the iliotibial band can become inflamed above the knee, causing clicking and discomfort, particularly when running downhill or walking down steps. Resting, stretching, and occasionally steroid injections or surgery treats it.

Compartment syndrome in runners usually results from increased pressure within the anterior compartment of the leg. This compartment includes the muscle that pulls your foot upward and thus acts as the ankle spring when you heel strike. In a small number of runners this results in the muscle becoming enlarged to the point where it actually starts to impede bloodflow into the anterior compartment and causes pain. Surgery to cut the fascia and allow the contents of the anterior compartment more room is the only proven therapy for this condition, but in a number of cases conversion to a forefoot strike has resolved this condition.

Champions Listen to Their Bodies

Becoming an accomplished distance runner requires enormous mental strength, but you must balance your desire to push your boundaries with an equal awareness of when you need rest and recovery. Recognizing that fine line between challenge and injury distinguishes talented runners who suffer recurring injury from the truly great runners who successively build their skills over many years.

How you handle overuse injuries such as shin splints is an excellent example. These injuries develop slowly and resolve slowly. The longer you ignore them and treat them as just another pain barrier to overcome, the longer they will take to resolve. Many talented runners are so driven that they lose sight of the fact that they are working against their body and causing permanent damage.

The Least You Need to Know

- Soreness is a crucial feedback tool that a barefoot runner needs to listen to carefully.
- If you suffer an injury, take plenty of time off to allow the area to heal.
- Acute injuries from running barefoot primarily involve the skin on the sole of the foot, with deep infections posing the greatest risk.
- Barefoot runners can best manage overuse injuries with rest and a gradual return to activity.

In the Long Run

Meeting your running goals takes careful training, no matter what you put on (or take off) your feet. If you wish to run longer or faster without shoes, this part delivers insight into how modern training theory with a barefoot twist can help you reach the finish line with a smile. And, because nutrition is so important to athletes, how barefoot runners should think about fueling their bodies is also discussed. A back-to-basics approach empowers you to become a healthier person and athlete.

Creating a Barefoot Training Plan

Chapter 13

In This Chapter

- Thinking about barefoot running for the long term
- Applying periodization training to barefoot running
- Designing and adjusting your own barefoot training plan
- Logging your training to help you reach your barefoot goals

Running is one of those amazing sports where the potential for improvement increases with age. The longer you run, the better, stronger, and smarter you become. A high percentage of runners excel in their 30s and 40s. The physiology of the human body is such that, when it comes to endurance sports, the muscles learn to adapt, transform, and perform better.

The human body undergoes changes over time as it runs, and that means it also acclimates to barefoot running. The skills you acquire will make you more aware of your body's potential and perhaps its limitations. Being smart about barefoot running means sticking to a meticulous transitional strategy—a barefoot training plan—that you can personalize to fit your goals.

The First Steps

The rewards of barefoot running depend on the dedication of the individual. Some runners may decide to only use barefoot running as a small part of their overall training program, such as when they warm up and cool down. Other athletes incorporate barefoot and minimal footwear sessions as a central component of their training, but may not give up conventional shoes entirely. For others, the goal is to eventually run completely barefoot or in minimal shoes for all their runs, workouts, and races.

No matter how you plan to implement shoeless activity into your running program, the first step is to consider how much time and energy you actually want to devote to transitioning. Those who only want to use barefoot running as a small component of a training program can reach their goal more quickly than those who aspire to run completely barefoot most of the time.

If your barefoot goals aren't clear at this point, don't worry. As you begin exploring the sport, your intentions will become clearer, especially when you begin to feel the benefits. No matter the scope of your barefoot goals, the preliminary stages are fundamentally the same for everyone. Only after you have prepared your feet and increased your barefoot abilities (as described in Chapter 8) will you choose your long-term barefoot running path.

Visualize Your Goals

Rob Johnson, a coach for the United States' track and field team in the 2000 Olympics, is a strong believer in visualization techniques for athletes. When he coached our track and field team in college, he had us visualize (without our shoes on) racing at our top pace at least once a week. During a deep visualization exercise, our hearts began pounding, sweat beaded up, and breathing increased rapidly, as if we were actually racing.

His mantra, "If you see it, you can achieve it," still resonates with us, and it is an important piece of advice for any runner interested in going barefoot. Seeing yourself achieve your goals through visualization is a powerful way to enhance your performance.

When you first start any sport, becoming immersed in it is one way to get more excited about it. By thinking or reading about it, and even watching or imagining yourself doing it, you learn how to participate in and excel at it. Picturing yourself running in your favorite spot or hidden trail without shoes is a great motivator to keep you on track. Use visualization to develop natural, barefoot running form and build the mind-to-body connection that will help you run fluidly, proficiently, and with greater ease.

Over the Long Haul

You will learn a considerable amount about your body and its abilities through barefoot running, but do not feel that you have to undergo a painful rite of passage to become an accomplished barefoot athlete. Beyond getting your feet used to the ground and building new strength in select muscle groups, suffering through the transition is not a prerequisite. If done slowly, the gradual changes you undergo can be a joyful occurrence—you will actually feel your feet, ankles, legs, and body becoming stronger and more efficient.

That is why formulating a clear plan that helps you meet your barefoot running goals is as essential as preparing for any long-distance race. In much the same way, planning to run barefoot for the long term is more important than simply running barefoot for the time being. If you do not map the way to your long-term goals, you may never reach them, and that is when you will discover the real advantages of barefoot running.

ON YOUR TOES

If you are taking up barefoot running after a recent injury, take it slow. If you don't pay attention to the finer elements of foot landing, form, stride, gait, and posture, or allow the foot to fully strengthen, you may cause even greater trauma to any previous injuries.

Barefoot running is a lifestyle choice as much as it is a tool for running more naturally. Learning how to properly run barefoot is a long-term investment for your running life. Careful planning now will result in more time to enjoy your runs later.

A Barefoot Plan of Action

A barefoot training plan written on paper is more than a schedule of when, where, and how you wish to run. It is also a place for you to outline your personal goals. If you have never planned your running future, now is a good time to start.

Runners have learned that long-term planning is essential to athletic success. If you do not plan ahead, you are exposing your body to mishaps and injury. Experienced runners plan for races well in advance so they are completely ready when race day arrives. If you are a well-trained runner, outlining a schedule for your barefoot running goals may require nothing more than adjusting some parts of your existing training schedule.

Most runners understand that time combined with well-implemented workouts allow you to increase distance, speed, and overall ability. Splitting running programs into blocks of time is one way that many runners map out their training routines.

Introducing Barefoot Periodization

Periodization (or periodic training) is a handy way to ensure that you schedule rest days between barefoot sessions. Having a day off between barefoot bouts when you first begin gives the body a chance to heal itself. It also allows your feet to get stronger and gives you time to assess how your training is going. An injury may take a day or more to manifest itself, so if you don't take time off from barefoot activity, you could exacerbate a problem before you even know you have it, which will end up worsening over time. A chronic injury is one way the body guarantees it receives the rest it needs.

> **DEFINITION**
>
> **Periodization** is the process of breaking up a training season into specific periods of time. Each period has its goals. With or without shoes, classic periodization is a plan to build up the body, increase intensity, taper down, and control when you will peak, or perform your best.

Counter to common belief, the human body does not get stronger while working out. Rather, it is only after the workout, when the body rests, that it heals, strengthens, and prepares itself for its next session. Only with rest can you become a better and stronger athlete.

Periodization involves separating your yearly training plan into periods of manageable time. Each phase of barefoot running has a main goal that builds upon the previous ones. In this way, a past accomplishment helps you work toward future ambitions. The idea of barefoot periodization is to stay focused on one goal per phase, even though other goals might be met along the way. When one objective has been reached, the next period begins.

The Finer Points of Barefoot Periodization

When we talk about periodization, we should also mention macro and micro training cycles. When a cycle is broken up into its smaller phases, each cycle has its own more specific goals that either maintain or build upon an athlete's ability. Using this method, you will always have an answer to the question: "What is the benefit of today's run or workout?"

A macro training cycle is usually made up of longer training increments (up to a full year). Micro cycles are smaller phases of training lasting usually one week. A macro cycle helps you accomplish a long-term goal, while a micro cycle tends to focus on the short-term goals of your overall plan.

For example, a one-month period where you want to work on speed is a macro training cycle. The four individual weeks that make up this month are its micro cycles. Each of these weeks has specific goals meant to make you faster. Utilize the workouts at the daily and weekly level (the micro level) to meet the overall objective.

The first week might contain two days at the track doing 200-meter repeats. The next week might contain three days, and so on. Each workout would be followed by a day of recovery running. If you are a distance runner, you might also maintain your long runs on the weekend. The last week of the month would be dedicated to less-intense workout sessions and slow runs, which allow your body to recover adequately. This is a simplified 3–1 macro cycle (three weeks of training with one week of recovery).

Stages of Barefoot Periodization

The periodization of barefoot running has a general purpose, which is achieved using short-term objectives that help you reach long-term goals. When it comes to preparing the body to run without shoes, the process is broken down into six distinct stages that have a specific goal, but without a specific time frame in mind. The following are the stages of barefoot periodization.

Stage I: Preparation

The aim of this phase is simply to get your feet used to not wearing shoes all the time. Walking around barefoot whenever possible will help to strengthen all the parts of your foot and lower leg. This period includes barefoot walking, building strong foot padding, adjusting to new terrains, and slowly increasing barefoot runs.

Stage II: Learning New Skills

Attaining the basic skills of running is not as hard as you might think; you start running soon after you walk. However, even elite runners have coaches to help them with components of their form. In barefoot running, form is critical. It is best to begin focusing on the finer aspects of barefoot running form after you have gotten somewhat used to actually being barefoot.

Perfecting your form comes from slowly adjusting the overall way you run, developing core body strength, and devoting time to drills. Focusing on form through barefoot running will result in greater efficiency and running economy, two key components of running light with more energy.

Stage III: Increasing Distance

Increasing mileage is a continuous part of many runners' goals, whether in or out of shoes. Many runners hope to attain the skills, muscle strength, and endurance needed to cover a predetermined distance in a race or special event. As you progress in this stage, form is still a focus, but not the central one.

Stage IV: Increasing Intensity

Everyone from recreational runners to world-renowned elites have goals they hope to meet within any given running season. If you enjoy racing, then this stage will be an important part of your overall barefoot periodization plan. In the same way that you have prepared for past races, you can also prepare to run them barefoot or in minimal footwear.

This stage requires you to prep yourself for running at a higher intensity if you wish to run faster than you have in the past. As you increase intensity, decrease distance. For barefoot running, you have to continue developing the padding of the feet to handle faster speeds while continuing to strengthen the legs, hips, ankles, and feet.

Stage V: Peak Performance

This stage is for those athletes who want all their training to culminate at a specific time or event where they are performing at their personal best. This might include one or two or more races in which you really want to do well, or it might be an endurance event you simply hope to finish.

No matter what your goal may be, this is the time to attempt to achieve it. During this phase, it is important to taper, which requires a careful balance of all the previous stages with no workouts that push you too much.

TIP TOES

As you develop your barefoot training plan, remember to keep things simple. The theories presented here are to help foster long-term planning. At the basic level, understand that training requires time, along with rest and recovery. If you wish to create a basic plan, follow a 3–1 training cycle: three weeks of slowly increasing distance followed by one week of easier running. If you want to perform at a higher level, learn to taper, or to gradually reduce mileage and intensity, during your peak performance period.

Stage VI: Rest and Recovery (R&R)

Athletes who do not give serious time to R&R will end up paying dearly later in their season. Giving your body and mind rest and recuperation allows it to process, build upon, and recover from the strenuous activity that you have undergone. Skipping this phase could result in repeat injuries during your next season. If your body is not given rest, it will find a way to make you take it.

This period might include a time where you do not run at all. For many runners, this is a difficult sacrifice. Some runners do not want to take extended breaks, so they undergo "active recovery." Although this type of training does have its place in the running world, taking at least a week or two off altogether will give your feet a much-deserved break.

Toward the end of your rest period, you might begin slowly incorporating barefoot stretches and drills (see Chapter 6) to awaken your feet to a new season. You might also continue walking barefoot to keep the pads of the feet as strong as possible.

Developing a Long-Term Barefoot Plan

You can plan an entire athletic year to meet your goals. Although recreational runners might compress a barefoot plan into a few months, knowing your yearly athletic goals is one way to take control of your training, ensure proper distance development, plan workout sessions, and reach your peak performance.

Consider your overall goals for the year ahead. Writing down and visualizing your goals are important, and now is the time to put it into practice. Write down three barefoot running goals that are honest, reachable, and somewhat challenging.

If you write down goals early in the spring, and you note that you want to run a 6-mile (10-km) race barefoot, that's great! But if that race is in two weeks and you have undergone no barefoot training, you simply do not have enough time. A better goal might be: "Run my favorite 5 km run barefoot on July 15." This gives you several months of preparation time.

Here are three realistic barefoot running goals you could make in early spring:

1. Run 3 miles (5 km) barefoot by July 15.

2. Run a 5-mile (8-km) forest loop barefoot by August 20.

3. Run 6 miles (10 km) barefoot on my birthday on September 25.

For the average runner, these goals are honest, reachable, measurable, and offer a specific challenge. If there are particular events you look forward to each year, you can compare your barefoot goals with your regular running ones to see if they might work well together.

Steps to Attaining Your Goals

Now that you have outlined your overall goals, create a list of smaller ones that will help you reach these. Using Goal 1 (to run 3 miles/5 km barefoot by July 15), you should write down the benchmarks that will help you measure if you are on track. These might be …

1. Walk barefoot for 20 minutes on gravel by May 10.

2. Enhance my cadence to 180 steps per minute by June 10.

3. Extend my barefoot time to 30 minutes on three surfaces—road, sand, and trail—by July 8.

By understanding the stages of barefoot running, outlining your goals, and breaking them up into achievable steps, you will have a better chance of accomplishing what you set out to do.

A Yearly Barefoot Outlook

As your barefoot endeavors progress, more advanced objectives (such as running longer, faster, or up a mountain) will seem more feasible. You will not think about being barefoot any more than you thought about wearing shoes; it will simply be the way you run.

When developing a yearly schedule, plan ahead for your favorite events. For races that occur too early, consider using those as training runs (or consider volunteering at the event). Make other, higher-priority events the focal point of your running year. You can even label these races low priority (C races), medium priority (B races), and high priority (A races). Following your periodization plan, you should complete a few low-priority events before medium ones, followed by the high-priority events.

ON YOUR TOES

When you are planning to take part in events to test your newfound running skills, be sure not to arrange too many high-priority events. Two or three events are enough for any season. In building up to these, you can sprinkle in three to six low- and medium-priority competitions exclusively for training. Avoid spreading yourself too thin with too many goals. Follow this mantra: if you want to keep running year in and year out, do not burn yourself out!

Depending on where you live, the weather may play a large role in setting your yearly goals. If you live somewhere with cold temperatures and snow during winter, you will likely schedule most of your higher-priority events in the summer and fall months. For a seasonal schedule, beginning barefoot runners can use the following model for their first season:

Months 1 and 2: These are good months to jot down your goals and research fun events you can participate in. In addition, you might want to find some barefoot running groups in your area. If you're in a cold-weather climate during these months, you might walk and run barefoot indoors on a treadmill. Consider taking some classes to build overall foot strength, such as yoga or Balletone. Participate in Pilates sessions if you want to build core body strength.

Months 3 and 4: During this period, you can prepare yourself for barefoot running by walking and testing new terrains without shoes. You might also be able to begin barefoot running while dedicating some time to the fundamentals of form. At this point, you can carefully begin increasing your barefoot running distance, but not intensity.

Months 5 and 6: In the heat, coordinate your barefoot runs to avoid hot roads or stick to trails. Mornings and evenings are good times to run. During this time, begin increasing your distance. You can slowly build on other areas where you might need improvement, such as altering terrains and increasing overall leg strength with drills. You might also schedule some events that you can use for training.

Months 7 and 8: If you want to run faster, gradually lower your overall distance so that you can increase your speed. This requires a carefully managed plan where you can begin running more hills, timed repeats, or fartleks, which are runs in which you vary your pace for better conditioning (see Chapter 14). Schedule this period as a macro cycle, filling individual weeks with micro cycle goals. This is also a good time to plan on doing some medium- to higher-priority events. It is also during this period where previous running ambitions (such as, "Run 3 miles [5 km] in 25 minutes") might merge with your barefoot abilities. No longer do you separate barefoot running and other running goals.

Months 9 and 10: You have now undergone all the stages of barefoot running that will allow you to run with confidence through any predetermined event. This is a time to complete some higher-priority events. This may be a half-marathon for charity or a quiet, two-hour trail run. The event is what you make it. Avoid overtraining right before an event; any extra training you do within two to three weeks of a high-priority event will not benefit you at performance time.

Months 11 and 12: This period is devoted to rest and recovery. This whole time frame need not be completely free of running, but you should take a couple of weeks off to give your feet, body, and mind a rest from a job well done. This is also a good time to think about what went well with your training and what you can improve over the next year. If cold weather sets in during this time period, you might have to continue barefoot activity inside, or outside using minimalist footwear.

Reaching Your Barefoot Goals

To reach any goal, you have to dedicate time, energy, and perhaps money to achieve it. You have to set benchmarks that will help you meet your overall barefoot goals. Objectives are like waypoints helping you to reach your destination on a map. To run that 3-mile (5-km) barefoot race on July 15, you have to allocate a certain amount of hours per week to barefoot activity.

When setting goals for any sport, consistency is key. If you don't stick to your training plan, your goals will be undefined, and your training will not be effective. If you go barefoot for three days, skip two weeks, and then attempt to start where you left off, your potential for injury increases dramatically and you will not be helping your feet, legs, body, or mind.

As you begin planning your barefoot sessions to match your goals, set honest, feasible goals on a schedule you can manage. As one week builds upon the next, knowing that you have mapped out the journey ahead of time makes the barefoot transition less stressful, more fun, and much more memorable.

Scheduling Weekly Barefoot Activity

When planning your training, the first thing to think about is the number of hours per week you can dedicate to barefoot running, or running in general. Figuring out how much time you have per week is best done at the beginning of the week when you are planning your week's other obligations.

Some of the best time managers in the field recommend setting aside time for family, sports, and hobbies before actually outlining your weekly work/life schedule. It is a sort of "pay yourself first" method of time management that ensures you spend time on those aspects of life that are important to you, but might not always get your attention. These methods of time management ultimately make you more productive and feel less stressed.

Similarly, scheduling time for barefoot activity lays the groundwork for a successful transition; even the smallest plans matter. Knowing that you have scheduled three 10-minute sessions for one week, for example, highlights those as truly important. Each 10-minute session will help you become stronger so that you can build yourself up from one week to the next. It's important to be honest about your time constraints, schedule barefoot activity in advance, and follow through with each week's plans.

Readjusting Your Goals

Keep in mind that your goals should build upon one another. If you do not stick to the previous week's plans, adjust the following week as needed. If you find yourself unable to follow your barefoot plan, rethink your strategy. Ask yourself what might be preventing you from meeting your objectives. Is it the weather? Work? Too much too soon?

If you miss just a few days of barefoot activity, simply move onward as planned. Do not attempt to make up the activity by squeezing in two sessions per day or two days in a row. If, however, you miss more than a week, revisit your plan to outline an updated strategy. For example, if you hoped to run 3 miles (5 km) by July 15, then you might have to push this goal out or eliminate it in favor of another. When two or more weeks of barefoot activity have been compromised, go back to walking outside barefoot, do strengthening drills, and run accordingly. At this point, reorganize your barefoot plan and reprioritize your events; some high-priority events might now become medium-priority ones, and so on.

Not reaching a goal by a certain time should not necessarily bring you down. It is an opportunity to reflect and learn about your own barefoot capabilities and how you can better organize, plan, and reach your goals. Stay positive and enjoy building your knowledge of how to train your own body.

Creating a Barefoot Journal

With unbelievable sensory capabilities, the feet are like organic GPS units fixed on the terrain. Not only do they offer immediate feedback during a run, they also relay information to you after a session is over. Wouldn't it be great if you had more control over the quality of your barefoot running experiences? Wouldn't it be even better if you could increase the chances that you would perform well at a special race or event while barefoot?

Shooting from the ... Feet

The best method of understanding what your feet are telling you is to keep a written record of your barefoot activity. This will help you to build upon the knowledge of what works well or not so well for you. It also helps you become your own barefoot coach. Recording both the physical and mental aspects of your training is a much more accurate and scientific way of analyzing your training—a handy guide that will help you determine whether your program is appropriate to your needs. It will also help you remain confident in yourself and your newfound abilities as you progress through the phases of your barefoot training plan.

Am I on the right track? How do I know if I am ready to move on to the next stage? Am I ready for my planned event? Keeping a journal and closely following a barefoot training plan will ensure that you are listening and reacting to your body's needs during each and every workout.

TIP TOES

Keeping a barefoot journal will serve as a compass as you work your way through your barefoot training plan. Similar to navigating new terrain, it is important that you work your way carefully from one point to the next. Whether you increase your cadence or start a new drill, test each new method one at a time. Record these changes in your barefoot journal. Testing too many variables at once could cause confusion if any problems arise that need to be explained.

A barefoot journal can be as simple as keeping track of your barefoot activity along with other workouts. By writing down those moments of success and those of tribulation, you will be able to develop good running habits. From time to time, you will find that you have to adapt, adjust, and even rework your training plan according to what you discover in your journal entries.

After you begin recording your barefoot sessions, you might find that you have reached your goals sooner than expected, or that you need to give yourself more time with a certain stage of transitioning. A written log ensures that you are taking the necessary time for the physical strengthening of your feet and legs, along with enhancing your overall form.

A barefoot journal is best kept by writing daily entries in a format that helps you to review one week at a time. When keeping track of your weekly barefoot activities, record the physical activities that you have completed, including drills, exercises, or stretches, alongside other notes that will help you remember what you have done.

Using a weekly barefoot journal like the one shown on the next page (you'll find a full-page copy for your personal use in Appendix C) will allow you to keep track of your own barefoot activity easily. You can see at a glance what each week's activities included. It is important to rate how you felt. On a scale from 1 to 5 (1 being excellent and 5 being stressed), score each day's barefoot activity. If you score a 3 or more for two barefoot sessions in a row, take one or more days off as necessary to avoid injury and mental fatigue.

In John's weekly barefoot journal sample, notice that neither too much nor too little information is recorded. Like John, it is important for you to find a balance for your entries (especially under the Notes section). Entering only necessary or pertinent information will help you learn from your past and easily plan (or alter) future workouts.

John's Weekly Barefoot Journal

	Monday	Tuesday	Wednesday	Thursday	Friday	Saturday	Sunday
Date	May 16, 2011	May 17, 2011	May 18, 2011	May 19, 2011	May 20, 2011	May 21, 2011	May 22, 2011
Weather	78°, Sunny	77°, Sunny	76°, Partly Cloudy	74°, Overcast	74°, Rainy	73°, Rainy	78°, Partly Cloudy
Activity	Off	Warm-up, Ran 35 min	Hurt - Off Day	Warm-up, Ran 38 min	Jump Rope	Off	Warm-up, Ran 43 min
Route		Forest Trail Loop		Neighborhood Loop			Mix Grass and Track
Distance		3.2 miles		3.8 miles			4.2 miles
Physical		2		1			2
Mental		2		2			3
Notes		Ran in place and did some light stretching as a warm-up. Took off too fast and stepped on a stick, but did not puncture through the skin. Trail was a bit muddy.	Foot a little sore from stepping on the stick. Wanted to do 5 sets of calf raises (both one- and two-legged) today. Instead, took it easy to monitor my foot.	Feet feel good today. I want to go on a trail, but need to stick to a hard surface to ensure my foot is OK. Focused on form, still noticing left foot scraping the ground every now and then.	Did 10 minutes of jump rope activity in bare feet before doing my weight workout.		Felt OK today. The grass sure felt good underfoot. Mentally tired from work, but feet feel fine. Looking forward to a trail run next week. Gave myself a nice foot massage. That felt great!

Physical and mental score 1-5; a score of 1 being excellent and a score of 5 being extremely sore/fatigued/stressed.

Week of: May 16-22, 2011

Planned Time/Distance: 120 min / 12 miles
Actual Time/Distance: 116 min / 11.4 miles
Planned Terrains: Trail, Sidewalk, Track

Barefoot Objectives:
1. Run more than 30 minutes on forest trail
2. Focus on form (left foot issue)
3. Keep working out sore calf muscles

Overview:

Weekly Barefoot Time: 116 min
YTD Barefoot Time: 682 min
Total Physical Score: 5
Total Mental Score: 7

Other Notes:

Overall, had a good week. Taking two days off this week helped a lot. I think I will be ready for the June Fair 5KM Fun Run. Can't wait till they see me in bare feet!

Weekly barefoot log.

Assessing the Data

With only a few weeks of training behind you, assessing the data will not be a gargantuan task. You can see in the preceding figure that John is blending drills, exercises, and barefoot runs into his schedule. After stepping on a stick on a trail on Tuesday, he felt some pain, so he was forced to take a day off. Instead of doing any barefoot drills, he simply monitored his sore foot.

This probably contributed to the decent run on Thursday. Running on the hard surface that day helped him notice that his left foot still scrapes the ground occasionally. This might be something he needs to work on in regard to his overall form, leg, or hip strength, or an issue caused from fatigue. Perhaps he should see a doctor about it. John will have to do some trial and error runs to work through it.

As far as John's goals are concerned, he is basically on track. He wanted to run on a trail, which he did. The muddy trail could have contributed to stepping on the stick, although he admits starting out too fast. Perhaps he needs to work on paying closer attention to the ground while running. In addition, John seems to have a slightly higher mental fatigue score, so he needs to figure out how to deal with this for his future outings. This might mean he simply needs to sleep more, associate with other barefoot runners, or take an extra day off the following week.

One good sign is this runner's optimism about the upcoming June Fair 5k Fun Run. He is excited that he'll be ready to do the event in bare feet. Moreover, it is also nice to see that he is taking time to pamper his feet on Sunday to feel both physically and mentally ready for the week ahead.

TIP TOES

If you start to notice physical setbacks, or are feeling down about your progress, take some time to connect with others about barefoot running. Visit some online barefoot running forums or websites to chat with others about your experience. The website www.barefoot-running.us has a wonderful archive of articles and weekly features that will keep you absorbed in interesting reading. Likewise, consider joining a barefoot group in your area at www.Meetup.com, or read a biography about a famous barefoot runner. Stay positive about your choice to run more naturally; hold your chin (and feet) up high!

Planning Future Workouts

Keeping an athletic diary of your past training will help you immensely when planning out each week's activities. Set aside time each week (for example, half an hour on a Sunday) to look over your previous notes and your barefoot training plan (discussed in the next chapter). You will then be able to adjust your schedule, verify that you are meeting certain benchmarks, and plan workouts accordingly.

After you have compared actual notes with planned goals, think about the upcoming week's objectives. Do you need to run a few more minutes on trails to help prepare you for the midsummer forest run? Do you need to take more time to focus on your form while running on a smooth track? Are there any future goals that might need readjusting due to setbacks? When writing down the next week's objectives, be sure to keep them in line with what you have already done. You wouldn't go out and run one hour on a trail after having only completed 35 minutes previously. Try not to increase any distance or activity more than 10 to 15 percent per week.

Planning the entire week is much easier than planning one day at a time. Admittedly, you will need to adjust certain days due to soreness, injury, or weather. If you find that other obligations (work or family, for example) are competing with your scheduled barefoot time, you might have to redesign your schedule to compensate. Design your workouts for the week in a way that allows you to meet your goals; rest and recuperate adequately; and keep your training moving forward, interesting, and fun!

Recording Events and Races

When you reach a goal, record it with a distinctive entry in your journal. Best written the same day you have taken part in an event, the entry should reflect back upon the training that allowed you to accomplish your goal. If the challenge did not go as well as you had hoped, write down your thoughts about why this occurred. How do your feet, ankles, calves, knees, hips, and so on feel? Is there anything you can focus on with future trainings? Was there a point where your form got sloppy because of fatigue?

Barefoot Event Log	
Event Name	June Fair 5KM Fun Run
Event Date	Apr 14, 2010
Event Location	Bend, Oregon
Distance of Event	3.1 Miles (5KM)
Weather	87°
Main Objectives	Goal 1: Run barefoot
	Goal 2: Watch terrain carefully, but relax
	Goal 3: Finish race with no blisters
Physical Notes	Felt good at start and allowed others to go ahead to avoid them stepping on my toes. Kept cadence at 180 steps/minute. Didn't over stride. Calves a bit sore.
Emotional Notes	The run felt enlivening! There were two runners wearing minimalist shoes and we exchanged phone numbers for barefoot runs. Race felt great. Had some annoying barefoot questions.
Positive Points	Accomplished my goals and had no blisters! The road was a little torn up in one section, but I ran over it well. People cheered as I crossed the line.
What to Improve	I need to relax, shake arms, and keep focused. I might need to do a few more runs on regular roads. Need to warm up my feet more before the start.
Other Notes	Overall, a good event. I look forward to the trail run coming up in another month. I will need to examine the course before race day. Time for a foot and calf massage.

Barefoot event log.

In this barefoot event log (a copy is available for your personal use in Appendix C), the runner had a good run at the June Fair 5km Fun Run. His goals were simple, realistic, and attainable. His notes reflect some things he might work on, such as calf strengthening, doing some relaxation drills, and ensuring that he warms up properly before the next event. His emotions were pretty balanced, except that he became annoyed with some people's questions about him being barefoot. Perhaps this runner needs to adopt a new perspective or have an arsenal of fun comebacks to common questions or comments he receives. He also notes that he should examine the next running course, which is a trail run, taking place the following month. This information will help him outline his central objectives for the next few weeks.

Regardless of whether you have planned to run in your town's annual fun run or compete in a half-marathon, planning ahead while logging your progress is one surefire way of increasing the odds that you will be completely ready when the special day arrives. Not only will you feel confident in your abilities, you will have proven to yourself that mapping out your way is one of the best and most fun ways of truly finding out what your *sole* is really made of!

The Least You Need to Know

- Planning for barefoot running is like preparing for any race—it takes dedication, patience, and time.
- Break down your barefoot transition from a yearly outlook to monthly cycles and scheduled activities.
- A weekly journal not only helps you record what you have done, it also helps you keep on track to reach your future goals.
- Keeping a separate journal entry for special events will help that event stand out and give you more time to reflect on how your training has helped you succeed.

Going for Distance and Speed

In This Chapter

- Taking your barefoot abilities to the next level
- Why recovery is the most influential factor in training
- How long, slow days can help you run farther and faster
- Training methods that will help increase your speed

Taking barefoot running to a higher level isn't easy, and running 30 minutes barefoot on a sidewalk is much different than attempting an ultra-marathon without shoes. This chapter offers you methods that can help you take your abilities to the next level.

Extending Your Barefoot Training

One way to plan for your first 12 to 18 months of barefoot running is to compare your plans against your past running accomplishments. If you have already run a few marathons in shoes, then working up to doing so barefoot in this time frame might be in the realm of possibility. However, if you have never even run a 5k (3.1 miles) event, then it will take you much longer to prepare for a barefoot marathon.

Only after you have established a solid barefoot running base should you consider working in longer and/or faster runs, and be forewarned that this may take several months to accomplish. You may already feel lighter, faster, and stronger, but you will have to work harder still.

You have already learned that when first starting out, barefoot running forces you to slow the pace and cut back on the mileage, as this is the only way your body can truly adjust. As your feet and body become stronger, you will be able to add more distance and speed to your running regimen. The slow development of the bodily systems (cardiovascular, neurological, and even glandular) allows runners to become endurance athletes. Time and incremental challenges will help you increase how far and fast you can run without shoes.

Assessing Readiness for Training

As a general guideline, you will need at least three months for the initial transition, followed by another three to six months of conditioning, before thinking about increasing your distance and speed. It might take several more months before you are truly able to go longer or faster in bare feet.

Before you begin training for distance or speed, ask yourself the following questions to assess if you are ready to take your barefoot running to a higher level. These questions will also apply to runners who have chosen to incorporate minimal-footwear running into their programs.

1. Can I run 45 minutes to one hour barefoot without pain?

2. Can I do so easily on a variety of surfaces at different temperatures (road, sidewalks, various trails, hot roads, or cold surfaces)?

3. Do my feet still ache two days after running barefoot on any of these surfaces?

4. Have I experienced any recurrent injuries since I began barefoot running?

5. Have I dedicated sufficient time to enhancing my barefoot running form?

6. Do I have the time to increase my barefoot running abilities before any events or races?

If you answered no to one or more of these questions, or you have any blisters, cracking, or abrasions, consider taking more time before implementing the training methods outlined in this chapter. Write down what you need to work on to begin increasing your distance. Continue your barefoot running program for another month or so while working on these specific objectives. Remember to adjust any events you might have scheduled so you do not push yourself beyond your limits. If you do decide to run in a race, consider wearing minimal shoes and use it as a training run.

Understanding Distance and Speed

To get better at a sport, you must practice *that* particular sport. You are not going to get better at swimming by spending all your time lifting weights. To swim better, you must spend time actually swimming in the water. It is the same for barefoot running. You are not going to run faster or farther without devoting time to it.

In the world of endurance athletics, three elements control how you can improve: frequency, duration, and intensity. Frequency deals with how often you run, duration refers to the time or distance covered, and intensity is how hard you push yourself. Two ways to measure these elements are with a watch or a heart-rate monitor. Carefully planning, implementing, and adjusting these elements will allow you to run farther or faster without injury. Because each person is different, it is important to learn about your own body so you know what training methods will work best for you.

When you apply these elements to barefoot running, you must consider how each affects the whole body, including the feet. Frequency and duration depend upon a slow buildup of ability. If you attempt to run five times this week for 5 miles each day without developing the base for doing so, then you will experience pain, or possibly even injury.

Increasing intensity is similar, but runners usually see results much faster. The main concern when running barefoot at an increased pace is the quick wearing away of the foot pads, along with an increased risk of injury if you push yourself too hard. That said, the ability to run short-distance races (such as a 5k race) at a more intense level is easier to achieve than running a marathon on the streets of New York.

Consider how much of a role frequency, duration, and intensity will play. Increasing frequency, for example, will help you increase your mileage base over time. This is often a consideration for recreational runners who simply enjoy getting out almost every day. Adding one day every two to three weeks is one safe way to begin extending the frequency with which you run.

Increasing duration will require you to take more days off in between for recovery, which lessens frequency, but can contribute to the goal of adding mileage. Beginners should avoid increasing frequency and duration at the same time. As one goes up, the other should come down. As a rule of thumb, increase distance only by 10 percent per week. If you run 20 miles total one week, you might go 22 miles the next.

Finally, runners wanting to increase intensity must first have a solid mileage base. When you begin going faster, you will have to decrease your mileage accordingly. If you begin doing hill workouts, for example, start slowly with only one or two. Then take an extra day off to recover fully. It might mean less mileage now, but it will result in faster times later.

When combined, these three elements equal the overall *workload* of a runner. In addition to workload, your ability to run farther or faster is also dependent upon your running background, age, goals, drive, and time allotted for training. Some might also throw genetics into the mix, but the real difference between serious and recreational athletes is the way they balance frequency, duration, and intensity in their routines.

DEFINITION

Workload is the total accumulation of frequency, duration, and intensity during training. Measurable on different levels, it is the combination of all three elements over time with sufficient recovery—rather than focusing on one singular facet—that will lead to enhanced, injury-free performance in the long run.

Only with time, careful training, and plenty of recovery can you optimize all three elements. Barefoot runners in particular must learn to listen very closely to their bodies. Planning and setting goals are wonderful ways to take your running to the next level, but let your feet guide you. Don't let your goals overshadow your ability. If you do a track workout and your feet begin burning after your second lap, strap on a pair of shoes or try finishing your run in the grass. Always be willing to adjust your training plan according to your moment-to-moment situation. Only by progressively and naturally building strengths will you develop the skills necessary to run longer or faster without shoes.

It's All About Recovery

Recovery is one of the most important determinants of how good a runner you can become. A large percentage of runners believe they must work hard day in and out to become the best runner possible. Many self-taught runners simply do not think about recovery time. Some are simply not aware of its importance. Others believe that they will not improve by taking time off to rest. Some might feel that rest should be reserved only before or after competition. Many young runners think they don't need time off because they lack soreness or fatigue.

TIP TOES

Although you may feel recovered after a workout, make sure you give yourself ample time to rest. Although the cardiovascular and muscular systems can overcome training stress quickly, the tendons and ligaments of the body cannot. Because there is less bloodflow to these areas, you need to increase recovery time, especially for the feet. Avoid back-to-back days of hard training, and always allow for one or more recovery days in between workouts. This will allow even the smallest changes in tissue to become stronger.

If you plan your periods of training and rest well, you can build upon your ability from one workout to the next to compete at a higher level later in the season. Only with recovery can your body enter into what many coaches call the *supercompensation phase*, when you can actually enhance performance and ability. If your body does not get enough rest, your abilities will not improve; however, if you allow too much time between hard workouts, you won't improve as well as you could!

One factor remains constant: time. Only time devoted to barefoot running is going to make you a better, stronger, more efficient runner. Only time will help you break through old barriers. Only time equals recovery.

Three types of changes occur to the body and feet after prolonged barefoot training: instantaneous, collective, and enduring.

Each and every barefoot run you do will have instantaneous effects on you and your feet. During a workout, the bottom skin of the feet can become drier and slightly tougher. By themselves, instantaneous changes will do nothing for you if you take too much time off between sessions. Your ability will never really progress if your barefoot runs are too infrequent. The compounding of these instantaneous changes is what eventually results in long-lasting benefits.

The combined effects of barefoot running over a long period of time are collective. At a basic level, this means that the work you have done in various terrains and temperatures (over various seasons) will last from one month or season to the next. This is when all the pieces of the barefoot running puzzle will slowly come together for you. All your work on strength, stamina, technique, and form will help you evolve into a proficient, well-rounded athlete able to attempt new challenges in distance and speed.

Enduring changes are the long-lasting effects of barefoot running. The strengthened tendons, ligaments, bones, and muscles of the lower legs and feet will remain surprisingly robust and flexible after you have dedicated several seasons to barefoot running.

If you experience an extended hiatus from barefoot activity, you will be able to more easily transition back into the sport when you return.

Advanced Conditioning for Barefoot Running

Now that you have undergone several months of barefoot activity—stretching, strengthening, walking, hiking, and running—conditioning the body even more will help you reach your goals. The fine-tuned muscle fibers, strong hips, engaged core, and rugged feet will help you reach the finish line.

The exercises in this chapter are slightly more advanced conditioning techniques designed to build upon those discussed in earlier chapters. The focus here is on the larger muscles of the upper leg, namely the quadriceps and hamstrings, along with the core and lower back. Stronger upper legs result in less stress on the whole body and give you more stamina to maintain proficient form on longer (or more difficult) runs. If you already do strengthening routines for the upper legs and core, continue doing them. Avoid heavy weightlifting, however, as that builds muscle bulk rather than muscle endurance.

For older, more mature athletes who wish to strengthen their bodies, exercising the upper legs and core can be beneficial. Exercises with a focus on these regions are often used to ward off arthritic pain, but talk with your doctor before you attempt anything here. A medical professional can offer insight into what regions of the body you need to specifically focus on. A physical therapist might also offer some alternative exercises more suitable to your individual needs.

The following exercises are good to start with if you do not work your upper legs often. Use these as warm-ups, or begin doing them for a few weeks to gain some initial strength and flexibility. Then move on to the next section to try out some more difficult routines with an exercise ball.

Stair Workouts

In running clinics provided by Barefoot Ted (www.barefootted.com), he will often discuss, demonstrate, and have participants attempt to jump up and down stairs. The goal is to promote better form (as you cannot land with straight legs or on the heel without pain) while allowing the body to land as lightly and gently as possible.

Jumping up and down stairs will help prepare and strengthen your muscles to absorb greater impact. You can also practice landing lightly and gracefully, which is beneficial for barefoot running.
(Photo by Fazia Farrook)

When first attempting Stair Workouts, go up and down one step at a time. Then increase it to two. As you jump, keep your arms relaxed, posture aligned, and knees bent, and allow the feet and legs to handle the impact. Feel free to incorporate other stair jumping or running drills into your conditioning. Start out with three sets of five jumps twice per week before increasing the number of sets.

TIP TOES

In the gym, use a stair-climbing machine to get a full-body workout that builds stability, balance, and strength—all characteristics of proficient barefoot running form. Maintain posture, keep your core engaged, and avoid twisting. Do not hold on with your hands, but instead move your arms naturally, while stepping at a brisk, steady pace. Start out doing only a few minutes per session until you get your body used to the motion.

Simple Leg Lifts

Lifting the leg in this manner is one way to build upper-leg strength isometrically, without using weights.
(Photo by Fazia Farrook)

In order to do Simple Leg Lifts, sit on the floor with your hands behind you. Bend one leg so that the foot rests comfortably on the floor while stretching the opposite leg straight out in front. Begin by lifting the straightened leg off the floor. Hold for five seconds before lowering the leg back down to the floor. Do two sets of three to five repetitions per leg. Alternatively, you can slowly lift the leg up and down five times per set.

This leg lift is similar to the previous exercise, except that this one focuses more directly on the outer hip.
(Photo by Fazia Farrook)

This variation is called the Simple Side Leg Lift. While lying on your side (preferably on a yoga mat), rest your head on one arm. You can place the other hand in front of your body to help with balance. Begin by lifting the straightened leg up to shoulder height. Hold for a count of three, and slowly release back down to the rested position. Do two sets of five repetitions per session.

Wall Glide

Rather than going to a weight room to use a squat machine, practice this exercise in your own home.
(Photo by Fazia Farrook)

In order to do the Wall Glide, stand with your back straight against a wall, feet slightly apart. Your heels do not have to touch the wall. While looking straight ahead, lower your back against the wall so that the knees bend to a 45-degree angle (be sure your knees do not go over your toes). Slide down, as if you are sitting in a chair, for a count of three seconds, hold for one second, and move up the wall slowly to return to a rested state. Do two sets of five repetitions twice per week.

Hip-Hop with an Exercise Ball

Not many of us have the luxury of a personal home gym. Luckily, an exercise ball is a cheap, fun, and versatile alternative that allows you to work out in your own home without having to drive anywhere, pay a membership fee, listen to blaring music, share workout stations, or sweat profusely in front of others. Available in various colors and diameters, exercise balls are also referred to as fitness balls, balance balls, stability balls, yoga balls, or even Swiss balls.

Using an exercise ball for your workouts is one way to hone your body's strengths more naturally than when using weights. The ball requires you to hold a stable position as you work out, making you engage the core muscles of the torso with each and every routine.

In these exercises, you are going to focus specifically on the quadriceps and hamstrings, commonly referred together as the thighs. Strong quadriceps and hamstrings move you through each running cycle, absorb shock, and keep minor changes in terrain from affecting your knees and lower back. For distance or speed, strong (but not bulky) upper legs are the key to prolonged movement. For most of the following exercises, a yoga or exercise mat is also a handy accompaniment.

TIP TOES

Choose and use your exercise ball wisely. First, be sure your ball is burst-resistant. Next, choose a diameter that suits your height. Most exercise balls are sold in metric sizes, namely 55, 65, and 75 centimeters. For individuals of 5' 5" or less, a ball of 55 cm will work well. For those up to 5' 10", a 65 cm ball is adequate. Taller individuals should consider a 75 cm version. Underinflating the ball slightly when you first begin using it will help you maintain control.

Warm up with the Bouncy Ball routine before attempting harder routines on your exercise ball; begin by sitting upright on top of it and gently bouncing up and down. This will give you a feel for the stability required just to balance on it. Placing your hands on the ball will help offer some support if you need it. Begin pushing off with your feet and trying to bounce progressively higher. As you do, you will begin feeling your upper legs at work. This is also a great way to get your heart pumping!

Carefully bouncing up and down on the ball is a great warm-up for the upper legs and core.

(Photo by Fazia Farrook)

This advanced routine places emphasis on the hamstrings and the core.

(Photo by Fazia Farrook)

To start doing the Hamstring Burn, sit down in front of the ball, and place your lower ankles (near the Achilles tendons) on top of it. Find a comfortable, stable point where the ball does not roll out from under you. Lie down and place your hands palm down and close to your buttocks, which will help provide support and stability. Raise your backside up into the air while pushing the pelvis toward the sky. When you are well balanced, roll the ball with your heels toward your body then roll it out again. Do this three to five times before bringing the buttocks back down to the floor to a resting position. Do only two to three sets twice per week when first starting this exercise.

Working the outer quadriceps will also help stretch the iliotibial band, which is a muscle extending from the gluteus to the knee. It is this region that can become tight during prolonged running.
(Photo by Fazia Farrook)

This Outer Leg Lift is similar to a plank exercise, but easy to do with an exercise ball. Begin by sitting to the side of the exercise ball with one arm rested on the top center of the ball. Push yourself on to the knee of the leg closest to the ball while placing the side of the torso on the ball. Your upper leg, the floor, and your kneeling leg will form a triangle. Begin by lifting the extended leg off the floor to a comfortable height, but don't strain your hip. With this routine, you can either hold your leg in place off the floor or do leg lifts. Other options include varying the height of each lift or rotating the foot in forward and backward circular motions. Move to the other side of the ball to work the other leg. Start out doing only two to three raises per leg twice per week to get a feel for the workout.

Working the inner thigh is also important for overall upper-leg fitness and flexibility.

(Photo by Fazia Farrook)

Begin this Inner Leg Lift by sitting next to the ball while raising one leg up on top of it. Rest the entire lower calf and ankle on it so that the leg is held straight to your body. Find a point of balance so the ball does not move out from underneath your leg. Lie down on your side and extend one arm so that your head rests comfortably on it without straining your neck. The leg on the floor should rest comfortably bent at 90 degrees on the floor. Begin the exercise by lifting the inside leg up slowly toward the raised leg. The lift should come from the hip on the floor. After five or six lifts, you should feel the workout on the inner quadricep. Don't forget to work each leg!

Gripping the ball with the lower legs will help to work your inner quadriceps; the outer quadriceps and hips work to lift the ball off the floor.

(Photo by Fazia Farrook)

Start the Full Leg Lift by sitting while placing one foot on each side of the exercise ball. Lie down and grip the ball between your ankles. Place your hands at your sides, palms down, to help with stability. Make sure your head is resting comfortably on the floor to prevent straining. Begin by lifting the ball slowly (count to three) above your body to a point where your knees are in line with your hips, keeping your knees bent during the entire exercise. Lower the ball back down toward the floor slowly (while counting to three). When the ball touches the floor, lift again. Start by doing two sets of five lifts twice per week before extending this workout. You will feel this one in your lower abdominals as well.

This exercise is a variation of the previous exercise but incorporates the arms into the movement. This provides a workout for the upper abdominals, abdominals, and back muscles.
(Photo by Fazia Farrook)

V-Ups are an abdominal workout that were first made popular before the introduction of the exercise ball, so you can practice without a ball first to perfect the movement. Begin as described in the aforementioned routine, but this time when the ball is at its peak above your hips, engage your upper torso (similar to an abdominal crunch), move toward the ball, and grab it with your hands. As you return your legs and upper body to the starting position, extend your arms above your head and tap the ball to the floor. Reverse the exercise by lifting your upper torso with the ball at the same time that you lift your feet from the floor. Place the ball back between your feet and return to your starting position. Do only a few of these lifts per week until you get used to it.

A One-Legged Squat works your upper legs in a motion similar to barefoot running form, where the quadricep is engaged throughout the cycle.
(Photo by Fazia Farrook)

To do a One-Legged Squat, stand with the exercise ball behind your body, and raise one leg behind so that it rests comfortably on the ball. (The top of your foot will be on top of the ball.) Keep the other foot flat on the floor. Begin by squatting down so that the leg on the floor bends to about 45 degrees before coming back up. The ball will roll slightly behind you as you bend up and down. Do two sets of 5 to 10 squats twice per week.

This exercise works the entire outer quadricep.
(Photo by Fazia Farrook)

To begin a Sideways Hip Extension, stand to the side of the exercise ball. Finding a stable balancing point for this workout can be tricky, so place one hand against a wall for stability if you need to. Bend your knees slightly. Then lift one leg on top of the ball, so that the side of your foot rests on it. Most of your weight will be on the grounded leg. Begin by slowly extending the leg on top of the ball sideways away from the body. When the leg is fully extended, roll the ball back toward your body. Complete two to three sets of five repetitions when first starting this exercise.

Benefits of Cross Training

Cross training is one of the best ways to keep your entire body fit, balanced, and free from injury. It is especially beneficial to barefoot runners who have adapted their technique in a way that engages most of the body in a forward motion. Following are the top five benefits of cross training for runners.

Balanced Muscles

Although barefoot running provides a workout for various muscle groups, certain regions are not engaged as much as others on each and every run. The adductor muscles (the muscles on the inside, upper legs) in particular are not used all that much during running. Strengthening and toning this part of the upper thigh (through exercise ball drills or even swimming) will help your legs absorb shock better, become sturdier, and look and feel great.

Cardiovascular Health

Improving your cardiovascular fitness will help your running, especially in the off-season. If you want to hit the ground running in the spring, doing supplementary aerobic activity in the winter, such as swimming or spin cycling classes, is one way to balance your slower outdoor runs with intense indoor workouts.

TIP TOES

If you are a regular swimmer, then you may notice increased sensitivity underfoot if you head out to run within an hour or so after a swimming session. After swimming, be sure to dry your feet well with a blow drier and rub down the bottoms of your feet (and between the toes) with isopropyl rubbing alcohol. Wear sandals to allow your feet to dry completely. If you are going to run immediately after swimming, walk for a few minutes on dry earth or pavement so your feet can dry completely.

Fewer Injuries

Because cross training helps to balance the body's muscle groups, you will actually decrease your chance of injury. Doing other aerobic routines gives your running muscles a break while still working your nonrunning, and slightly weaker, muscles. More balanced muscles also decrease your chances for overuse injuries; these can occur from doing the same movements day in and out.

Recovery from Injury

Being injured does not necessarily mean that you cannot stay active, and cross training is one way to help your body recover if you do end up with a running injury. Another activity, such as swimming, cycling, or rowing, can help you maintain cardiovascular health while allowing other parts of your body to recover from trauma.

Keeps You Inspired

Finally, cross training helps prevent the running doldrums from ruining your outings. Doing other activities besides running helps keep both your mind and body sharp. It is a way to make friends, hone different abilities, and work the mind and body differently. Although many runners enjoy hitting the course daily, doing other fun physical activities one or two days a week will help make running more desirable.

Finding Your Cross-Training Activity

Ideally, you will cross train with a sport that helps you reach your overall running goals. Avoid sports that might injure you rather than help you improve upon fitness, flexibility, and overall well-being. Jumping into that weekend game of football is probably not a wise move.

Search for routines that are low impact, or at least those that will not jar your body, joints, muscles, or bones. Playing football might be scratched from the list, but low-impact sports such as cycling, soccer, skating, swimming, dancing, yoga, and certain forms of strength training are all viable cross-training options.

Because barefoot running form requires an aligned body, avoid sports that may require you to maintain a misaligned stature. Find a sport that helps promote good posture instead. When cycling, attempt to keep your back as straight as possible without stressing your neck, and you might want to consider using a comfort or hybrid bike that will allow you to sit more upright. When swimming, learn to keep your head aligned and rotate the hips to breathe (rather than simply twisting the neck or torso).

Try an activity that might offer you the benefits of both *aerobic* and *anaerobic* activity. This might include soccer, which has periods of intense activity combined with times of slower play. Tennis, racquetball, and badminton are other sports that combine aerobic and anaerobic activities.

DEFINITION

Aerobic activity is an exercise of prolonged activity, such as running, swimming, or biking. One of the main goals is to improve the cardiovascular system and its ability to transport oxygen sufficiently to the muscles. **Anaerobic** activity includes those sports that focus more on strength, quickness, or agility. Football, soccer, basketball, tennis, and even golf might all be considered anaerobic.

Find a sport that allows you to enhance other skills, such as hand and eye coordination. Racquetball or handball might offer a rewarding experience, but if you would rather do something outside, consider ultimate Frisbee or rock climbing, which can build muscle stamina and strength. Moreover, such extracurricular activities help you learn to balance the body while moving in different directions. This can help you fine-tune your abilities for the challenges of barefoot running.

Try to become involved in something that will give you as much mental stimulation as it does physical. Team sports, which often require each individual to play a certain role for the group to be successful, are a good example. Games of strategy, teamwork, and planning provide a form of mental exercise.

Because cross training is not your main focus, participating in seasonal sports is an acceptable option. In-line skating, cross-country skiing, or even baseball can help develop certain strengths for your running program.

Remember that cross training does not mean that you have to learn an entirely new sport. Feel free to dabble in other recreational pursuits until you find one or more that you really enjoy during part of or throughout the entire year. This might include weight training, yoga, dance, or something as fun as laser tag. Regardless of what you choose, cross training and enjoying other pursuits will ultimately help your barefoot running goals by making you a more well-rounded, aware, and mindful athlete.

Exercising Naturally with MovNat

MovNat (www.movnat.com) is an athletic pursuit founded by Erwan Le Corre as a result of his knowledge of Methode Naturelle. At a young age, Le Corre's father frequently took him outdoors to enjoy the natural world where he would run, jump, crawl, and climb. When Le Corre was 19 and living in Paris, he was introduced to a program called "Combat Vital," or a system of mixed martial arts. He then spent the next seven years doing athletics using the local environment as a workout playhouse. Le Corre took to the idea of Parkour, or the "art of moving" through one's environment as efficiently and naturally as possible. At age 27, Le Corre began exploring other activities such as sailing, Olympic weightlifting, rock climbing, triathlon training, trail running, and Brazilian jiu-jitsu.

Six years later, Le Corre found many similarities in his newfound training techniques and those within the realm of Methode Naturelle, a training system created by Frenchman Georges Hébert in the early 1900s, based on natural movement. Soon after, he decided to adopt new ideas and begin training others to move more naturally. And thus MovNat was born.

MovNat is based on the mantra, "Explore Your True Nature," which relies on three main principles: respecting the laws of nature, trusting our primal heritage, and satisfying real world demands. In an interview with *Men's Health* magazine, Le Corre said, "I know guys who can run marathons but can't sprint to anyone's rescue unless they put their shoes on first. Lots of swimmers do laps every day but can't dive deep enough to save a friend, or know how to carry him over rocks and out of the surf."

MovNat workouts are created around 12 requisite movements. A few of these include walking and running barefoot, throwing objects (such as boulders), carrying loads (downed trees), lifting (other people), jumping (onto a tree), swimming (in the ocean), and defending oneself (using martial arts). It seems as though Le Corre has gotten something right—his nickname is the "World's Fittest Man." MovNat training workshops are currently available in the United States and promise to "reconnect, realign, and revitalize."

Barefoot Training for Distance

Initially, the main difference between speed and distance are the types of stress placed on the body's muscles. Running faster will eventually limit what distance you can cover, and running longer distances will lower your speed. Balancing both speed and distance is a big job for self-coached athletes, and doing so in bare feet adds a whole other dimension to the equation.

Running farther barefoot is possible through a gradual progression of the skill sets that you have already developed, with one extra element—the long, slow run, which occurs on the LSD (or long, slow day). Working longer runs into your existing running regimen can be the sole factor that makes or breaks your distance-running goals. Only LSDs can help you build endurance, and only endurance will help you reach the finish line.

TIP TOES

Try LSDs with a club or jogging partner. Doing so at scheduled intervals will give you something to look forward to and help the time go by faster. Camaraderie is all part of the fun, so if you cannot hold a conversation while running an LSD, then you are pushing yourself too hard.

Before heading out the door to run barefoot or in minimal footwear for an hour, be sure that you have worked your way up to the undertaking. If you have only been running 30 minutes three times a week, then going out for an hour, although possible, may not be the best course of action. You risk injury. Instead, add only 5 to 10 minutes to each LSD you do. In this case, you should run for 35 to 40 minutes at most. Barefoot runners can vary the terrain to ensure that the feet receive varied workouts.

Covering longer distances can increase bloodflow by promoting capillary growth, which will result in stronger feet capable of withstanding even more varied terrains and temperatures. More bloodflow also means stronger tissue (ligaments, tendons, and feet and calf muscles), which decreases recovery time. Finally, by covering longer distances barefoot, you build your confidence in your unshod abilities. Witnessing your own progression in the sport keeps it fun and interesting.

Running farther barefoot can also make you a faster runner. Without doing any speed training whatsoever, you will eventually have the capacity to run shorter distances faster as you spend more time running longer distances slower. The natural progression of speed is one of the benefits of increasing your mileage gradually, and it is over the long haul that faster speeds are naturally attained and maintained.

Run Farther by Running Less

Weekly long runs are the foundation of most runners' philosophies, whether they run barefoot or not. Time your LSDs carefully; when you are able to run longer distances, frequent long days will not enhance your endurance as much as you might think.

As a rule of thumb, for both long runs and races, take one easy day from distance sessions for each mile you covered. For example, if you ran an LSD of one hour on Sunday, covering 10 km (or 6.2 miles), you can do another long run the following Sunday. If, however, you ran 16 km (or about 10 miles) previously, you would not run another long, slow day for 10 days. Half-marathon runners may take two weeks between long-distance sessions, and marathon runners may complete only one significant long-distance run every three weeks to one month.

Watch the Watch, Not the Pedometer

Try to measure your outings in time rather than distance. Time is a more reliable way to record your trainings. Plus, it may help keep you from running too fast. Remember the mantra "spending time out and about is what it is all really about."

If you try to turn your longer runs into race-pace outings too early, you could potentially injure your body. LSDs are of great importance for your heart, muscles, and mind. Enjoy the journey without worrying about the destination.

Barefoot Training for Speed

Our bare feet are our lightest footwear. There is no other way to run as free and light, but doing so with increased speed and intensity is entirely different from a walk on the beach. The muscles, tendons, ligaments, bones, and skin of the foot must evolve even more if you want to introduce speed to your running program. If you have not devoted at least four to six months to barefoot running (running at least three times, or 10 to 30 miles, per week), then give yourself more time before introducing any intense workouts into your training program. And, like everything else in barefoot running, speed takes devotion, careful planning, and, most importantly, time.

By nature, distance runners usually want to run faster to beat personal records, place in races, or simply feel the wind rush by them. Sacrificing one, two, or even more seasons in the hopes of running faster barefoot may not be a practical option for many runners today, especially for the elite. Professional runners have too much at stake to chance that barefoot running will make them faster. Such runners might consider implementing more barefoot activity into their routines, but may not choose to race that way.

The first barrier to speed while barefoot running is the greater vertical impact force on the musculature of the entire body, but especially the foot. When first increasing speed, it can cause discomfort—even to those who have spent months running barefoot. It will take the feet at least another three months to become stronger, more elastic, more flexible, and used to pounding the ground.

Another barrier beyond that of impact is the way surfaces change when you begin running faster. That cement sidewalk can turn from creamy to craggy in no time. The ventral skin and foot padding must also adjust with time to become even more robust, tougher, and more resilient.

Finally, when you run faster, it is more difficult to maintain proper form. As you speed up, you will have to pay even closer attention to maintaining proper foot landing, a quick cadence, and an aligned posture. In no way should you sacrifice form to shave time off your runs. After your form begins to disintegrate, so will your body.

Runners who do not want to surrender their current competitive edge for hopeful future gains (in economy, technique, and injury prevention) should consider alternatives to barefoot running when speed training or racing. Although you must still acclimate the feet and body to running at higher speeds, doing so in minimal footwear can save your feet much wear and tear. Take note, however, that the risk of injury is heightened because minimal shoes may allow you to go much faster or farther than your body is capable. You may not feel pain in the feet or lower legs until it is too late. One option is to balance speed work in shoes with regular barefoot runs. Balancing the two can potentially help you work on increasing your speed while ensuring you don't injure your body.

Building Up to Speedwork

Biologically speaking, you must train the muscles to counteract the buildup of hydrogen ions (and lactic acid) at the cellular level. Certain levels of acid are normal (and even beneficial) during performance, but after the tissue becomes saturated, your muscles cannot contract efficiently and fatigue soon sets in. Over time, the body learns to deal with acid accumulation by shielding these ions from permeating the muscles. Your ability to maintain a faster pace over longer distances is directly related to how much *speedwork* you've completed.

DEFINITION

Speedwork is a form of training where the runner completes a workout at a faster pace than what is normally run. The pace can be based on past race splits or future goals. Speedwork can vary from one workout to the next, or within workouts.

Increasing your ability to run fast barefoot will take much more time than you might normally be used to devoting. It might take three or more times longer than a runner who wears regular shoes, mainly because a shod runner can skip over the conditioning of the feet nearly altogether.

Before starting any speedwork, be sure that you take your time getting your body used to the new endeavor. Do one speed session every 7 to 10 days, and ensure that the duration (distance or time) does not surpass 5 percent of your weekly mileage. After the first two months, increase this amount to 10 percent. After the three-month mark, introduce an additional speed workout every other week. Eventually, you can build up to two sessions of speedwork per week (but never more than three) that equal 15 percent of your total mileage. In any given week, speed sessions should not be of the same type, take place on the same terrain, or occur on consecutive days.

Avoid sprinting at full speed when first doing speedwork. Instead, adjust your pace to last throughout the entirety of the workout. Going all-out might debilitate or injure you. For the first several weeks, rate your speed or intensity on how you feel rather than with a clock or heart rate monitor. This will help you to control your pace using the sense of feel rather than worrying if you reached your goal time. Rest assured that increased speed will occur naturally with time.

After your feet have become more conditioned to running fast, you may wish to base your workout times on past race results. Average and then break down your most recent 5k or 10k race times. Because you are training in bare feet or minimalist shoes, add at least 30 percent (or even 50 percent) to this average to determine what splits you should be working toward.

To illustrate further, if you averaged 27 minutes for your last three 5k races while wearing shoes, then your average for 400 meters (or one full time around a regular track) is 2 minutes and 16 seconds. Running a certain distance more than once is referred to as repeats. Therefore, while doing a set of 200-meter repeats, your goal would be to average 68 seconds in shoes. Add 30 percent to this total to calculate the speed at which you can aim for while barefoot. The new total would now equal about 88 seconds per 200 meters. If all else fails, rely on your feet and form to guide you.

Before any speedwork, warm up by jogging easily for 5 to 10 minutes. Next, jump rope or do jumping jacks, followed by some light stretching. Striding out, or increasing your pace in short bursts, is another way to get your heart pumping and your blood flowing. Focus on staying upright, staying relaxed, and maintaining a high cadence. After any intense workout, cool down by running slowly for 5 to 10 minutes, followed by stretching.

Kinds of Speedwork

For some runners, simply going out to run without planning how fast you will go is part of the fun. Certain runners—including those who run mostly for recreation—are able to naturally pace their workouts. For most of us, however, having dedicated times set aside for barefoot speedwork is the best way to ensure that you fit it into your programs.

Running faster requires more energy output, which means you will run harder. That may not sound overly appealing, but varying your speed workouts is one way to keep things fun. After just a few weeks, you and your feet will begin feeling more fit. Remember to emphasize quality over quantity. Doing two repeats with solid form and feeling great is better than doing five, getting sloppy, and not feeling good about the workout.

Speedwork generally includes but is not limited to the following.

Fartleks

Fun to say and more fun to do, fartlek is a word meaning "speed play" in Swedish. Fartleks are workouts in which speed is varied throughout a run. Such workouts can be structured or left open for the athlete to put together. As an example, you might repeat intervals of running 4 minutes easily followed by 1 minute at a faster pace for 20 minutes total. Doing a few weeks worth of fartleks before jumping into more regimented speedwork is one way to get the body used to dealing with different speeds, boosting acid production, and readying the feet for their new gears. Doing fartleks barefoot on grass, dirt trails, or at the beach is a real kick!

Hills

One of the best workouts for both shod and unshod runners wanting to work on speed is hills. By and large, hills help to make runners stronger, less prone to injury, and well rounded. For barefoot runners, doing hills on a variety of surfaces will help to make the feet and legs much stronger and more flexible. Hills also offer more energy return (or elastic bounce) with each step.

Start off doing two to three hill repeats that last anywhere from 30 seconds to one minute. Jog slowly downhill after each, which will give you some time to recover. After a few weeks, begin increasing the number of repeats you do. Add one extra hill to your workout while increasing the time of each hill by 30 seconds every two weeks to slowly increase the workouts. Build up your ability to do hills of various grades for two to five minutes in length.

Tempo Runs

The best-kept secret in the arsenal of speedwork is tempo runs (a.k.a. tempos). If you want to run faster at any race distance, tempos are the answer. The benefit comes mostly from training the muscles to use oxygen more proficiently while keeping acid in check over a longer period of time.

Tempo runs tend to last anywhere from 2 to 12 minutes (known as tempo intervals) to more than an hour (known as lactate-threshold or simply "LT" or "threshold" runs), depending upon your fitness level and planned race distance. You can do shorter versions at varying distances, usually from 400 meters (a quarter mile) to 3,200 meters (about 2 miles).

Making tempos work for you is an art in balancing speed and distance, or intensity and duration. Worked into your peak weeks of intense training, tempos are one way to extend your running ability. If your goal is to cover a 5k race well, work up to doing 15- to 30-minute tempo runs. Those doing a 10k event might try aiming for 30 to 50 minutes. If you hope to complete a half-marathon, work slowly up to tempo runs of an hour or more. Marathoners need to gradually increase their tempo runs to cover at least one third of the race distance.

Figuring out your tempo pace can be tricky. Although knowing your 5k race splits is helpful, it is not necessary. Using a heart-rate monitor is an option for those who understand the finer points of heart-rate zones; a pace held in zone three to four will suffice. For the rest of us, a tempo run should be maintained at 70 to 80 percent perceived effort (where 100 percent is a pace you cannot maintain for more than a minute or two). Many runners—especially of the barefoot variety—judge this pace by comfort level. A tempo run should be paced at a few notches above comfortable, but not to the point of being uncomfortable. It is a pace where you recognize that you are working harder than usual and your mind is working hard to help foot placement, all while running at an increased intensity that you can maintain over the required distance.

Barefoot runners should start by doing tempo runs of two to five minutes on a safe surface. Doing workouts on harder, smoother surfaces will help you to monitor your landing and impact more easily. The grass on the inside edge of a track might also work well for some runners. Work up to one tempo run per week, adding one minute per session. Remember to always let your feet guide you, maintain sound form, and never push beyond your limit. If your feet feel like they are being put through the grinder, stop; throw on some shoes and head home. For the next run, lessen your expectations, try a different surface, and remain optimistic.

Intervals

After you have worked fartleks, hills, and even tempo runs into your barefoot routine, begin throwing in some intervals (a.k.a. repetitions or "reps"). During these workouts you might push yourself faster than race pace. Barefoot and minimal-shoe runners should proceed with caution to ensure that their feet and lower legs can handle the increased impact brought about through such intense workouts. Moreover, they should be astutely aware of form, cadence, posture, and arm positioning.

You can do intervals at any distance or for any amount of time, but they tend to fall between the 30-second and 10-minute mark. For example, a set of five 200-meter sprints with a one-minute break in between each could make up an interval workout, with rest times between reps varying. When you first introduce intervals into your regimen, rest for as long as it took you to run. Only then should you begin the next sprint.

Alternatively, as you progress, walk or jog lightly between reps. Advanced runners can even do pyramid workouts, where a workout escalates and descends in distance. One example would be the following workout set (with a one-minute jog between each): 200 m, 300 m, 400 m, 500 m, 400 m, 300 m, 200 m.

Ultimately, going longer and faster is no mystery. Increasing your distance gradually with speedwork will pay off handsomely for your running endeavors. A careful combination of distance and speed will help to balance your mind, body, and feet more than anything else in the world of running.

The Least You Need to Know

- Before pushing yourself farther or faster barefoot, assess if you are truly ready to do so.
- Recovery is one of the most important and least understood facets of long-distance running.

- Conditioning the body, especially the upper legs and core, through advanced exercise routines and cross training is one of the best ways to prepare for distance and speed.

- Long, slow days (LSDs) are essential to increasing the endurance of your heart, body, feet, and mind.

- Fartleks, hill repeats, tempo runs, and intervals are vital components of speed-work that will help you increase and maintain your pace over longer distances.

On Your Mark: Racing Barefoot

Chapter 15

In This Chapter

- What to know before you race barefoot
- How to decide if you should race in minimal footwear
- How to prepare for short-, mid-, and long-distance races
- What to do before, during, and after racing barefoot

Both shod and unshod runners enjoy the challenge of a race. You can attempt new heights in your running career, and at this point in the season, you might be ready to attempt a few races without shoes. The distance, speedwork, and time you have dedicated to barefoot running will pay off after the gun is fired.

Pros and Cons of Racing Barefoot

The dangers of running longer or faster without shoes are amplified due to the increased stress placed on the feet. They must absorb, counteract, and flex with the impact of landing even more than when you are jogging. For the underprepared, barefoot racing may result in injury and an early end to your running season.

For the well prepared, barefoot racing can be the high point of a running season. First-time barefoot racers should forget about matching old performances or placing well in their group. Leave the watch behind and focus on maintaining excellent form, enjoying the course, and being mindful of your body. As you become more skillful in barefoot racing, pushing yourself to match or beat old times becomes easier, more enjoyable, and less risky.

ON YOUR TOES

If you have not prepared yourself with longer runs and speedwork, avoid pushing yourself during a race. Even if you decide to run in a minimalist shoe or racing flat, hold back if you have not trained speedwork while wearing them. If the race takes place in temperatures or on terrain in which you have not had the chance to properly prepare, it is better to err on the side of caution by wearing some sort of foot protection.

You should decide whether to use shoes on race day long before stepping up to the start line. If you doubt your ability to finish, consider starting the race in bare feet and carry your shoes with you. Alternatively, have a friend or family member meet you at predetermined points on the course with shoes. If you are not in the top ranks, your chances of being disqualified are slim.

Running in shoes, even though you have completed adequate barefoot training, is also a choice. If you do decide early on that you prefer to race in footwear, then complete a high percentage of your more intense workouts and long, slow days in the shoes you will use to race. This will help you maintain your form and allow your feet to get used to them, ensuring that you do not end up with blisters during the race.

Racing Faster Barefoot

Barefoot runners will claim that they can run faster than when they run in shoes, which makes sense given the weight of most of today's mainstream footwear. Running and respiratory economy have been shown to improve after you take off your shoes, especially as distance increases. Over a long run, shoes can add lots of extra weight that your legs must lift and swing in front of the body.

Although barefoot running will help you immensely with form, injury prevention, and efficiency, it does not mean that you will necessarily break personal records in your first, second, or even third season. When first starting out, it simply takes the legs, feet, and body too long to adjust for you to expect to set a personal record right away. Nevertheless, you can't dismiss the idea that having stronger, more resilient, natural springs will make you faster. With enough training, time, and development, your barefoot racing abilities become limitless.

Get Ready to Rumble

If you are planning on signing up for a race in your first year of barefoot running, make sure you're ready to do so. Basic questions to ask yourself include …

- Have I trained properly for distance?

- Have I trained properly for speed?

- Are my feet accustomed to the climate/weather/terrain in which I will race?

If you are doubtful about any of the previous questions, study Chapter 14 about running longer and faster and give yourself more preparation time. Implement a plan of action that will get your feet, mind, and body ready for the event. Follow this advice: if you cannot do it at home in training, don't do it at a race.

The Duck, Duck (Save Your Feet) Plan

If you find yourself in a race or on any other run only to discover that you are just not ready for that particular event, have a predetermined exit strategy in mind. Both professional and amateur athletes alike use certain races as a test or building block of the training plan.

Essentially, a "Duck, Duck (Save Your Feet) Plan" can mean one of two scenarios. The first is that you show up to a race, go through the motions of getting your body and mind ready for the event, begin, and, at a certain point, "duck out." For example, if you were only able to run 3 miles barefoot at a 6-mile event, you would run only half of the race before stopping mid-performance.

The second option is to complete only the portion of the race you are ready for in bare feet and then finish the race in shoes (mainstream or minimalist, depending upon what you are used to wearing). Carrying your shoes with you during an event is an option, or having a friend or family member meet you at an agreed-upon point is also a possibility.

This tactic is useful because you will not feel like you did not accomplish a goal. Whether you decide to stop midway or to continue in shoes, the plan takes gumption and planning. Showing up to an event with a group of barefoot runners, or even one partner, can help with any initial angst. The more events you are able to attend (when you are prepared), the less uneasiness you will feel about being barefoot amongst shod-wearing runners.

Remember not to push yourself past your limit in regard to distance or speed. Duck out or put on shoes exactly as you have planned. If you can avoid wearing a watch and paying attention to time splits at a race, you will be able to focus on your form and pace without distractions. If you have not practiced running fast or for a long period of time, do not do it at an event.

Pre-Race Contemplations

Selecting a race to dedicate your time, sweat, and money toward can be a difficult task. If you have participated in running competitions before, then you might have a better idea of what distances to try in bare feet. Road races are the most common type of event in which both recreational and professional runners participate. One reason is because there are so many of them; in fact, road races outnumber off-road ones by nearly 10 to 1. Road races can vary in distance, but the most common types of races worldwide are 5k, 10k, half-marathon (21.1 km or 13.1 miles), and full marathon (42.195 km or 26.2 miles).

You might feel like pushing the limits of your training to attempt a longer-distance race sans shoes. However, tenderfoots should begin with short-distance events to get a feel for what barefoot racing is all about. Spending the first year or two participating in short- to middle-distance events is a great way to build up to longer ones.

Although doing a 5k race will not seem like much of an accomplishment to some distance fanatics, it is a worthwhile distance to begin barefoot racing. Without the undue pressure to finish a longer race than you're ready for, a 5k race gives you an idea of your current skill level, helps you ascertain if you are truly ready for longer races, and helps you build up to longer distances. Completing a handful of short events will also allow you to use what you have learned to generate, adjust, and better outline future training routines.

For runners with some shoeless racing experience, choosing future events might be slightly easier. You can consider doing a trail race, a 10k event, or a race of even greater distance. Completing a longer race is an admirable feat—the challenge combined with the training commitment makes the idea appealing to many endurance athletes. The skills required, especially for your feet, are tremendous but definitely reachable.

Event-Focused Barefoot Training

A certain amount of speed will come naturally to barefoot runners who begin increasing distance. For short events, devote more of your energy to speedwork. Fartleks are fun, but hills, tempo runs, and short intervals in particular are going to help you the most. If your foot pads begin to burn while you are running fast, slow down. Try moving to the grass or putting on minimal shoes or racing flats. Always take a day off (or run easily in minimal shoes) following an intense workout. If your feet begin to hurt in any way, refrain from training for an extra day or two. Stretch and massage your lower legs and feet. As you increase speedwork, maintain leg strength by completing some of the exercise ball routines described in the previous chapter. That will help you build up that extra bit of strength you need to finish strong.

Most runners live for middle-distance races. They are long enough to challenge, yet short enough to give it your all. The 10k race is the most popular distance in the United States, with the half-marathon coming in a close second. Finding a pace that you can maintain for such a span takes multiple trial workouts. As you participate in more races, your pace will come more naturally to you. Middle-distance athletes should not devote a large percentage of workout sessions to short, speedy intervals. If you are a middle-distance runner, spend more time honing your pace.

Marathons and ultra-marathons are often revered as the epitome of endurance races. For both shod and unshod runners, completing LSDs (long, slow days) is key. More advanced athletes can also work in periods of longer intervals with race-pace tempo runs. Throwing in regular bouts of speedwork will help you maintain your form, while core workouts will keep you feeling strong throughout the event.

Tapering Down for Race Day

One of the main components of preparing to race well is to taper, or reduce running duration and intensity, in the days or even weeks leading up to race day. For both barefoot and shod runners alike, tapering down properly is one of the key components to a strong performance at an event. At the basic level, tapering means figuring out how much you need to rest and how much you need to maintain before competition.

Tapering should be based on an individual formula, but it can be difficult to configure. You'll have an easier time when you've had some racing experience. Runners of short-distance events need to taper less than those completing a marathon, for example. The key is to not reduce your training to a point where you feel lethargic when the race begins. However, you do not want to do so much activity that you feel fatigued at the start of the race.

Barefoot runners must not only consider the tapering of their bodies, but specifically of their feet as well. Erring on the side of rest is advisable, but don't allow your feet to soften from underuse. Continue doing barefoot activity up until race day, but do less of it, less intensely. By the same token, giving your feet a killer workout on trails, sand, or road within a few days of the race will not do them any good either.

For short-distance events, such as a 5k race, begin tapering down 8 to 10 days before the event. If it's your first race of the season, reduce your mileage by 20 percent and do some short sprints and strides four to five days before. If you have a few races under your belt, reduce mileage by only 10 percent while maintaining 50 percent of your intense sessions. Run on comfortable surfaces and avoid any challenging terrain. Consider running on grass, which lessens impact but still gives your foot pads friction and stimulation.

For middle-distance events, such as a 10k race, begin your taper 10 to 12 days before the event. If it is your first race of the season, follow the same rules shown previously in regard to duration and intensity. For those who have completed at least two or three races, cover 80 percent of your race distance seven days before your race. For the last 20 percent of this run, practice your intended race pace. Four days before the event, run a set of three intervals at race pace for three minutes each. The day before the race, do some light stretching. Run gently for 10 minutes (or walk for 30 minutes in sandals or shoes) if you are feeling nervous about the next day's event.

For longer races, such as a half-marathon, taper down at least 12 days before the event. This would increase to 15 to 18 days for a marathon. If it is your first or second half-marathon of the season, reduce your overall mileage by 25 percent. Then follow the previous guidelines for a runner with a few 10k races behind them.

If you completed two or more longer-distance barefoot races, reduce your weekly mileage by 10 to 15 percent. For a half-marathon, 10 days before the event, complete a set of 8 repeats of 3 minutes at race pace. Between each one, take a one-minute break. Five days before the race, do 3 repeats of 8 minutes at 80 percent race pace. Take 2 minutes to recover between each. Three days before the race, complete 5 2-minute intervals at 90 percent race pace. Rest the next day or run 10 to 20 minutes in minimal shoes to loosen up. Stretch, hydrate, and eat well, but avoid over-fueling.

Following each day's run, stretch adequately and massage your lower legs and feet. If you are traveling to a race, take a tennis ball with you and use it to massage your feet in the car and at the hotel. Keep your feet as dry and rested as possible.

Talking with Officials

The USA Track & Field (USATF) governs track and field, long-distance running, and race walking in the United States. Most races tend to follow the rules, regulations, guidelines, and even recommendations outlined by this nonprofit group. Currently, the *USATF Competition Rules Book* does not cover barefoot running. As such, race directors and their board members can set their own rules and regulations about barefoot participation in their events.

ON YOUR TOES

You may not be banned for running shoeless, but you can be disqualified if you wear headphones while racing. Back in 2007, the USATF banned headphones for all runners in a controversial law known as Rule 144.3. Due to feedback and difficulty in enforcing the ban, the organization repealed the ruling. It is now at the discretion of the race director of each event. Currently, only runners taking part in the USA Championship may not wear headphones. Read the rules of the event you wish to run for specifics.

If you're not sure if you will be allowed to compete barefoot, contact the organization or race director in charge of the event. It might be as simple as asking for permission or clarification. If needed, give them time to do further research. Make yourself (and any other runners who may back the barefoot cause) available to discuss the matter in person. Most decisions for races are based on insurance-company stipulations, so race directors might not have true authority. Nonetheless, it is an opportunity to advocate for barefoot running, make the racing organization aware of the trend, and help spread the word.

If the organization/race director ultimately decides against allowing barefoot runners to participate, you may request a further meeting to raise public awareness. Ask if you might interview a member of the organization for your local paper. In the end, you may choose to run the race anyway without shoes (and potentially be disqualified) or simply wear minimalist shoes. Each one of us is a representative in the barefoot running community, so encourage acceptance through diplomacy in words and action.

A Barefoot Race-Day Kit

You may have the jitters as you prepare for your first barefoot race. To prep yourself, create a list of things you need to take with you to the event. Think of any supplies you might need before, during, or after the competition. During the race itself, you may want to have certain supplies stashed on your person. Here is a checklist to get you started:

- ❑ Watch (optional)
- ❑ Car key
- ❑ Small amount of toilet paper
- ❑ Snacks or gels
- ❑ Timing chip
- ❑ MP3 player (optional, if allowed)
- ❑ Cash
- ❑ Sports tape, bandages, moleskin
- ❑ Minimalist shoes

For first-time barefoot racers, consider not wearing a watch so that you focus on allowing your feet to guide you. If you have built up your ability and confidence and have learned how to pace naturally, it is appropriate to carry a watch. Barefoot runners should also consider leaving their music players at home. If you aren't plugged in and distracted, you will pay closer attention to your surroundings and be able to respond faster to messages from the feet and body if needed.

Stowing snacks or gels is easier if you safety pin them onto the band of your shorts or pants or carry a runner's pack. Wadding cash, toilet paper, and bandages into the key pocket of your attire is an option. Some women racers have revealed that they stuff such amenities packed into small, resealable plastic bags into their sports bras. Before the race, apply waterproof sunscreen, especially on your nose, lips, neck, ears, arms, legs, and the top of the feet and toes. Because most races start early in the morning, you might want to take along a cheap long-sleeve shirt that you do not mind tossing to the side when the race begins. Alternatively, many entrants wear garbage bags with a hole cut in the end for the head to fit through. Volunteers will usually collect and donate clothes or recycle plastic left behind.

Apply anti-chafing balm or petroleum jelly to your inner thighs, around and below the armpits, and around the neck. Some balm, such as Body Glide (www.bodyglide.com), also acts as sunscreen. For longer events, consider covering your nipples with round bandages or moleskin to prevent chafing. Barefoot runners might consider taking along (or adding a layer) of second skin (www.spenco.com) for their feet. Others even take superglue just in case. For both road and trail races, consider taking along minimal footwear. Certain socks, aqua shoes, slippers, or sandals might be worth carrying in case you run into any problems.

Race-Day Considerations

Barefoot racing is a dream come true for many first-timers, when all your hard barefoot work pays off. Before the starting line, during the race, and after the finish line, you will have to take certain steps to ensure that you are prepared, run well, and finish strong.

Before the actual race begins, make sure that you have certain logistical matters taken care of. Many races require you to pick up your event packet either the day before or in the morning before the race. Make sure you receive both your number bib and safety pins to attach it to your shirt. Most races require you to attach the bib to the front of your shirt so that it is visible at all times throughout the event. Make sure you pin all four corners of the bib so that it does not flap while you are running.

In addition to your race number, many events will have you wear a timing chip. This allows an automated clock to keep track of your splits at different intervals of the competition. Some throw-away chips are integrated into the bibs, but this is not yet commonplace. Most chips are tied or laced into your shoes. This poses more of a problem for both barefoot runners and minimal footwear athletes. Talk to a race official beforehand if you are concerned about the matter. Otherwise, fashion your own ankle strap to hold the chip in place. A leather string, duct tape, and scissors should help you get started. You might also consider tying it onto the drawstrings or storing it in the small pocket of your running pants or shorts. Before the race, ask the officials if you might step over the start mat to see if you trigger a beep from the system. If so, you are good to go.

Before the race, warm up adequately. For short events, run 10 or 15 minutes followed by some short sprints. For longer events, run for 15 to 30 minutes, and do some longer strides as well. Stretch lightly. If it is a chilly morning, consider wearing jogging pants and minimal shoes to keep your lower body warm, and then remove your shoes and pants a few minutes before the race begins. Allow your feet to get used to the terrain and dry completely. If the surface is wet and you haven't run much in soggy conditions, consider keeping your shoes on throughout the race. Wet, soft feet have a tendency to blister more easily if your form begins to lag.

As you approach the start line, stay to the side of the crowd. After the race begins, start cautiously until the mad rush dissipates. This is the only time of the race where you should keep your eyes focused on your feet. Your odds of getting stepped on are slim, but remain wary until you have plenty of space to see the ground in front of you. When you are free, shake your arms loose, adjust your posture, fix your eyes ahead of you, and move into second gear.

Throughout the run, maintain all the aspects of form that you have worked so hard to develop. Keep your arms tucked comfortably with your hands relaxed. Maintain a straight posture and extend your chest to help stretch your diaphragm, which will help you breathe freely. It also helps you to utilize gravity for forward motion. Keep your stride short and cadence high with your feet pitter-pattering on the ground. If you find that your feet are slapping down hard or that you are heel striking at all, slow down, readjust, and continue.

During the run, it is ideal if you skip the first water station. Most likely, you will not need it. If you pre-hydrated well enough, you may not need water at all if your race is less than a half-hour in length. Some runners will not drink if races are less than one hour long. If it is exceptionally hot outside, take a sponge to cool down or simply dump a cup of water over your body. If you decide to grab some water, slow down, find a clearing, take a few sips, and keep moving. Your feet will most likely get wet from all the water being tossed around. Continue out of the water stop, find some dry ground, and run slowly for a moment to allow your feet to dry.

Some shod runners will always be sure to run from one point to the next in a straight line to avoid adding extra distance onto their run. Barefoot runners, however, need to look for the smoothest, barefoot-friendly path they can find throughout the course, whether it is grass, dirt, or along the painted lines. This might add a few seconds to your overall time, but it will save your feet as the race continues. After you have run in more races, then taking the quickest route between point A and B might be feasible.

As you approach the finish, maintain your form, but push for a strong finish if you feel up to it. Smile like a champion! Then keep moving through the chute so that other runners do not collide with you. Hand over your timing chip, grab some fluids and snacks, and keep walking.

When you find your loved ones, give hugs, snap photos, and keep drinking fluids. If it is cold outside, change your clothes. Put on pants and shoes if necessary. If your feet hurt, get to a warm place, wash them with warm water, dry them completely, and then apply ice (covered in a thin cloth) to the bottom of your feet for 15 minutes. Grab some high-quality food, keep hydrating, and pat yourself on the feet for a barefoot race well run!

Post-Race Cogitations

Enjoying the rush from a race makes completing the event worthwhile. Even if your feet hurt, legs ache, and stomach is in knots, a finished race builds your self-confidence, prepares you for future events, and simply feels great. After you eat a hardy meal, if you feel like sleeping, hit the sack. Getting in a power nap or sleeping longer will help you recover much quicker than putting off the rest your body needs.

Depending on the length of the race, take the necessary days to recover. For short events, you might need one to three full days away from running. For middle-distance events, take two to five days off completely. For longer events, such as a marathon, taking five to seven days off will not hurt you in the least.

During this time off, feel free to work in some low-impact cross-training exercises. Walking in the woods (best in shoes) will help keep you calm and your muscles loose. If you have any blisters, abrasions, or other injuries on your feet, take even more time to recover. Avoid doing any hard barefoot activities beyond light stretching and massaging.

After your prescribed rest time, gradually begin running barefoot again. Regardless of the distance you ran, when you start running again, start with an easy 20-minute run on a hard, smooth, and flat surface. Stretch and massage your feet afterward. After another day of rest, run for 30 minutes on the same type of terrain. If you are still feeling well rested, do another 30- to 40-minute session within the next two days. Then begin adding in the barefoot form drills, strengthening exercises, and core workouts. Assess and document how you feel in your barefoot journal. Do some barefoot walking on trails if you want to maintain versatile foot pads, but wait until you have completed 5 to 10 recovery runs before carefully alternating terrains again.

Fully recovering to the point where you are ready to race again depends on the distance raced and your physical makeup. For 5k races, runners often begin adding more time, distance, and intensity to runs after seven days of recovery. Middle-distance runners should consider taking at least 10 days to recover before implementing full workouts back into their routine. Half- and full marathon runners should take it easy for 12 to 25 days, respectively, before slowly building back up to their previous training levels.

Avoid Post-Race Doldrums

As you work back up to race condition, continue nourishing your body, stretching daily, and getting plenty of sleep. Half- and full marathon runners in particular should get at least 9 to 10 hours of sleep per night for the first week following an event, and longer if possible. Adequate rest assists in healing the body and fighting off potential sickness. Keep hydrated through the night. Check your resting heart rate each morning to see how your recovery is coming along, and record these variables in your journal.

Remember that your recovery after the first race of the season does not need to be hurried. As you take some easy days running to recover, keep in mind that you have plenty of time and that you are trying not to overwork your feet. After you build up your training and complete an event, get adequate rest, then sign up for and resume training gradually for another. This will help keep your ambition high while you continue building your barefoot running abilities.

Short-distance racers can plan more events per season as they build up to longer runs. Those already running middle to longer distances should take adequate time to recover but can plan shorter events in between longer bouts. This will not only help you to gauge recovery, but will serve as helpful training for priority events. Alternating events of varying distances and terrains is a fun way to keep the season interesting. If your last race was on the road, try a fun and safe trail event. Variation in training and racing is the best way to keep your mind, body, and feet flexible, healthy, and ready for the next adventure.

Time for Some R&R

When your racing season is over, you and your body can enjoy some rest and recovery. Various theories exist about what recovery times are sufficient for athletes. Runners who have only run a few short races during the year can get away with a couple of weeks of downtime, while long-distance and professional runners will need more time off. During this time, feel free to maintain cross-training routines, but avoid running workouts. Take walks, stretch, and enjoy the time away from the sport.

As you begin running again, consider your plans for the next season. Doing so will get you excited about what is on the horizon. Consider traveling to a new region to compete. Jot down some new barefoot running goals. You might find some new events that really tickle your … feet!

The Least You Need to Know

- If you have not trained to run fast barefoot, do not attempt to do it in a race.
- Decide whether you will run a race in bare feet or minimal footwear well before stepping up to the start line.
- Tapering down, or lessening your mileage and speedwork, before an event can help you and your feet perform their best.
- Carry a barefoot kit with you during your race, and take foot attire in case something unexpected occurs.
- During your first race, do not worry about your finishing time. Focus on form and safety instead.

Food for the Sole

In This Chapter

- How to create a balanced diet for your body and feet
- How to fuel your body before, during, and after running
- Why eating healthy is better than taking supplements
- What supplements women and older athletes should consider using
- What vitamins, minerals, and nutrients are beneficial for barefoot runners

Our society neglects to recognize the importance of a balanced diet. Athletes tend to be slightly more conscious of what they put into their bodies, but not always. Eating a variety of high-quality, healthy foods is only one component to proper nutrition. Knowing how to properly fuel the body for running is another.

The minimalist philosophy behind barefoot running can also be applied to nutrition. Much like shoe-manufacturing giants, modern food producers are adding more junk to their products than you need. Rethinking the way you eat, the way you think about food, and how you fuel is an ever-changing element in the world of athletics and training that is as important as any other factor in your training.

Eating for Barefoot Running

Eating healthy food and properly fueling the body for athletic pursuits may not be a priority in your life. You live in a busy world, and thinking about the details of your diet is time-consuming. If you approach the dietary discussion with a new mindset, however, decisions about food can be fun, simple, and enjoyable, just like barefoot running.

Shoeless runners need to pay careful attention to the food they eat due to the demands that barefoot running places on the body. Essentially, barefoot running changes who you are as a runner. From the ground up, you are rebuilding yourself as a new, improved, stronger, and more efficient machine. The changes taking place internally to the mind, body, legs, and feet are substantial and should not be taken lightly. Knowing how to fuel the body as it becomes stronger is one way to better handle the demands of barefoot running.

ON YOUR TOES

Before you decide to change the way you eat, talk with your doctor. You might also seek the advice of a qualified nutritionist or registered dietician. Direction from professionals in the field may help you generate an individualized plan perfect for your own dietary needs.

The importance of food and proper fueling take on an even greater role when you start pushing your barefoot running abilities. You should only attempt to run faster or farther without shoes when you are healthy, and being properly fueled helps keep you that way. What you eat will affect how far or fast you can run. Moreover, eating properly decreases recovery time, allows the body to heal quicker, and gets you to the finish line feeling better.

Learning More About Eating

Begin learning about a balanced diet by studying the food guide pyramid (www. mypyramid.gov). This chart demonstrates the importance of grouping food into different categories and balancing the intake from each category. When it comes to counting calories, fats, and proteins, however, runners need to know more than the average person because they lead such drastically different and more active lifestyles.

One way for runners to ensure they are eating a healthy diet is to divide the daily plate by percentages. Many sources note the need to eat 50 percent vegetables and fruit, 25 percent protein, and 25 percent carbohydrates. These percentages will vary depending on your workout routine. Runners, in general, need more high-quality calories and protein for muscle maintenance and growth.

Several books on the market can help you learn more about nutrition, specifically for athletes. Some especially helpful ones are *The Athlete's Plate: Real Food for High Performance*, by Adam Kelinson; *The Athlete's Palate Cookbook*, by Yishane Lee; *Sports Nutrition for Endurance Athletes*, by Monique Ryan; and *Nancy Clark's Sports Nutrition*

Guidebook. No single source will tell you everything you may wish to know or apply to your own eating habits, but wrapping your toes around the basic theories will help you expand your understanding of athletic nutrition.

Lean, Mean Protein Machine

Protein is a big concern for athletes. In the weight room, you will see bodybuilder types pounding bottles of the stuff. But, according to well-known sports nutritionist Nancy Clark, most athletes eat either too much protein each day or not enough.

Protein is important for athletes because it helps repair muscle damage that occurs during training or racing. It is the only way that one day's hard work can build upon another. Protein also plays a vital role in maintaining a healthy immune system and is a catalyst to help your body burn fat. It also helps your body manage, balance, and create hormones. The disadvantage of protein is that it is not stored in the body but rather used or converted immediately.

In general, athletes should eat two to three servings (about 4 to 7 ounces or 115 to 180 grams) of protein-rich foods per day, depending upon their activity levels, body size, and other physical demands. As a basic rule, eat 1 gram of protein per day for each pound you weigh.

Chicken, tuna, and beef are great sources for protein, as are legumes and low-fat dairy products. Avoid fast-food burgers and instead opt for seafood, free range, and wild meats. Although more difficult, you can also get the essential protein your body needs to maintain itself through plants and other products. The best sources for protein besides meat are breads, cereals, and soy products such as tofu, brown rice, tomatoes, and beans.

Don't Go Hard on Carbs!

Admittedly, athletes need carbohydrates for energy and fuel and to help restore depleted reserves in muscles and organs following an intense workout session. Certain drinks or gels might help you get what you need if taken shortly following a hard workout or race. This will actually help your muscles recover more quickly.

For the last few decades, carbs were sold as the miracle food for athletes. Runners were told to eat carbs at every opportunity while evading fat, and they believed that eating a carb-loaded diet would help performance, weight, and mindset. We now know that a diet centered on carbohydrates is not all that healthy. Because of the way carbohydrates raise blood sugar levels, they are often digested quickly, burnt immediately, and leave you hungry for more. They generally cause an energy burst followed by a rapid fall in blood sugar, leaving athletes feeling moody, grouchy, or out of balance following a carb overload.

Eat carbs from high-quality, unrefined sources to benefit from slow-burning energy. Avoid snacking on refined packaged goods. Instead, grab a piece of fruit or whole-wheat toast and peanut butter to balance both protein and carbohydrate intake.

Fat Is Back

Fat has gotten a bad rap over the years. Runners attempting to manage or lose weight often avoid fat, but the truth is that fat is a necessary component of a proper and balanced diet, especially for athletes.

There are both good and bad fats. Good fats include the monounsaturated variety, which not only help keep cholesterol levels down, but also provide prolonged energy. Fish is one good source of healthy fats, one of which is omega-3, a fat that has been shown to improve immune, joint, heart, muscle, brain, and skin health. Nuts, avocados, olive oil, tuna, seeds, and certain game are also good sources for healthy fats.

Bad fats are saturated fats and are most often found in packaged foods. You can find these fats on food labels by looking for the word "hydrogenated." These fats cause weight gain, heart disease, clogged arteries, and many other health problems.

Fat is one of the essential keys to helping runners perform better. Eating more fat will actually teach your body to burn it—rather than carbs—when you exercise, which can help you lose weight. Studies have revealed that an increase in the fat in a runner's diet has a direct effect on increased endurance, cardiovascular efficiency, and VO_2 max—the body's ability to transport oxygen to the muscles—for long-distance events.

Fueling Before, During, and After Running

Athletes often disregard the importance of fueling the body properly before, during, and after running. Preparing the body, performing well, and recovering quickly are signs of a well-nourished runner.

If you need to change your eating habits, start out with small changes and work your way up to a fully balanced, nutritional diet. The body needs time to retrain itself to properly use the fuel you give it. Meal and snack planning that balances protein, fat, and carbs is a good place to start. Rather than eating a candy bar after work, eat an apple or trail mix on the way to your favorite running spot.

During this dietary transition, cut back slightly on your training. Give yourself plenty of rest and recuperation between workouts, and allow your feet plenty of downtime. A change in diet is like quitting a bad habit, and the body will resist change to some degree. You may be more moody, fatigued, or sore than normal. With time, however, you will begin feeling more refreshed, energized, and ready to run.

Early Bird to Evening Nutrition

If you start your day with a run, try to eat something at least 30 minutes to one hour before you head out. You will feel more relaxed, and scientific studies have proven that you will actually have more endurance. Try something simple at first, such as two handfuls of trail mix, a sports bar, or a small bowl of oatmeal. Try to ingest 200 calories for that extra energy boost. After your run, have a balanced breakfast made up of both carb and protein calories. This should tide you over until mid-morning or lunch.

FROM THE SOLE

Mom was right! Breakfast is the most important meal of the day. Eating in the morning gets your metabolism burning more calories, jumpstarts your brain, reduces stress, and helps you prepare for the day's activities. Barefoot runners need to be as alert as possible to be mindful of foot placement and form.

Do not forget the leftovers from the night before for a recovery breakfast—especially after a harder or longer workout. The calories from last night's pizza are just as useful in the morning. Leftover fish scrambled in eggs served with toast will help your muscles recover even more quickly.

An ideal balanced breakfast contains fiber, protein, and calcium, so cereal is a good choice. Look for cereals that have less than 10 grams of sugar, 3 to 4 grams of fat, and 5 or more grams of fiber. Cereal and a few pieces of fruit make a quick, nutritious meal for those on the go.

If you rush out to work following a run, you still have a plethora of breakfast choices. Add some granola to a cup of yogurt. A bagel with peanut butter, blended fruit smoothie, raisins and peanuts, graham crackers and milk, or pita bread stuffed with cottage cheese are all quick, easy, and nutritious ways to start your day. You can make instant oatmeal in a mug at home or at work. Breakfast drinks are liquid meals that also work as on-the-go nutrition.

Lunch-hour runners need to make sure they follow the same guidelines as pre-breakfast athletes; otherwise, hunger pangs may end your run at the nearest sandwich shop. As an alternative to a big breakfast, eat a mid-morning meal or energy bar for the fuel you need to complete a mid-day excursion. This is also a decent time to eat a carb-heavy snack instead of protein or fat. Save that as a power lunch following your workout.

Similarly, after-work athletes should not only have a nutritious breakfast, snack, and lunch, but also a quick bite before they head out for their evening run. You might consider having a second mini-lunch two to three hours before leaving work to run. Smoothies, energy bars, nuts, and toast and honey all make healthy afternoon treats.

Fueling During a Workout

Generally speaking, if you are working out for less than 60 minutes, you only need to drink water. If you will be running for more than an hour, consume enough calories to replace the ones you have lost while running. Generally, you will need 100 to 250 calories (in the form of quickly digestible carbohydrates) for each extra hour of training. Sports drinks provide both calories and carbs, and gels also work well with sufficient water intake. Other options are pretzels and energy bars.

TIP TOES

If you cramp up during a run, chances are the culprit is fuel related. Most of the time, it is a matter of hydration. Drink a bit of water and see how you feel. If you are running longer distances over an hour, a sodium imbalance can also cause cramping, and a potassium variance might cause certain athletes more trouble than others. Try drinking a sports drink, which should contain some amount of sodium and other minerals—called electrolytes—meant to help replenish the body. Eating too close to your workout time can also cause you to cramp.

This general formula will not work for everyone, as these variables depend on your weight and size and the intensity and duration of your run. Certain athletes may need to experiment with salt intake if they sweat a lot or work out in a particularly hot environment.

If your workout extends to two or three hours in length, you will have to practice nutrition. Triathletes, especially, will usually have to work out a plan of eating and drinking that carries them through an entire day of physical activity. Runners should do the same to learn and even teach the body how to handle longer workouts. You'll have to adjust some variables for weather or other circumstances, but you can use the same tactics of nutrition you have practiced at events. Teaching the body how to handle its fuel when you run is imperative in keeping you healthy and performing your best.

You don't have to buy expensive refueling foods. In fact, making your own trail mix or fruit bars doesn't take long, and it will save you money and requires fewer packaged goods. Additionally, you will know exactly what you are eating and where it came from. Similarly, consider reusing a safe drinking bottle that you refill with your own filtered tap water. Add your own powdered refueling drink. If it's a hot day, keep your bottle in the refrigerator while you are at work. Grab it before you head out to exercise. The incentives to thinking ahead are not only financial but also environmental.

Refueling for Recovery

The goal of eating and drinking soon after a workout is to spark recovery as quickly as possible. Always drink water and eat a light snack within 30 minutes of a hard or long workout, or at least one hour following a regular run, to replenish your body's losses adequately. This is a good time to ingest 300 to 600 calories of carbohydrates. Good choices include carb and protein shakes, bars, bananas, a peanut butter and jelly sandwich (on whole wheat bread), or chocolate milk. Continue to gradually fuel up on carbohydrates followed by protein until you are satiated. This might require a period of three to five hours of rehydrating and snacking for half- and full marathon runners. As a rule of thumb, refuel slowly for as long as you worked out or raced.

After restoring your carb levels, stop eating them and any processed foods. Focus on nutrient-rich produce, protein, and healthy fats that will help rebalance your body. Vegetables, fruit, salads, nuts, oils, fish, beans, and lean meats are all good options.

Special Dietary Considerations

The dietary recommendations outlined throughout this chapter are far from "one size fits all." The foods outlined are considered to be generally good for you and your body before, during, and after running. But some people might have allergic reactions, beliefs, or distastes that keep them from eating certain things.

One movement that is becoming increasingly popular and fits in with a back-to-basics approach to athletics, such as barefoot running, is discussed in *The Paleo Diet*, by Loren Cordain. Its premise is that eating like a caveman may be the best diet for the way we have evolved. This includes eating foods that were available from about 2,600,000 to 10,000 years ago. This excludes modern foods that are processed, agriculturally based, or sold from animals found in feedlots, for example. According to researchers, Paleolithic people did not suffer from the health issues found in modern society. Although threatened by environmental dangers, humans lived healthier lives free from cancer and diabetes. A paleo diet adapted for the modern endurance athlete is described best in *The Paleo Diet for Athletes*, co-authored by Loren Cordain and triathlete legend and coach Joe Friel.

Fish, shellfish, eggs, tree nuts, vegetables, roots, fruits, mushrooms, and wild game are included in the diet. Grains, dairy, beans and legumes, sugars, potatoes, and processed foods are excluded. A paleo regimen includes foods rich in soluble fiber, antioxidants, omega-3, and monounsaturated fats as well as foods low in *glycemic carbohydrates*.

DEFINITION

Glycemic carbohydrates are rated using the glycemic index, a method of categorizing carbohydrate-based foods on how they affect insulin levels. Originally, the index was developed for diabetics, but athletes can also better understand what foods are low or high on the glycemic index. Foods that make your blood sugar rise quickly are high and foods that do not raise insulin levels as much are low. Low glycemic foods, such as nuts, fruits, and lentils, are better for you.

The other key components of the paleo diet include eating fruit found naturally in the forest (such as berries), lean game, and oils from fruits and nuts (olives, avocados, almonds, or coconuts). Juices and coffees, agave nectar, salt, and sugars are excluded. A small amount of raw honey is a debatable component.

Such diets also recommend eating when you are hungry, not necessarily at set times throughout the day. The paleo diet has sparked a similar dietary and lifestyle movement called caveman living (www.hunter-gatherer.com). Not eating for a day or two before gorging on wild game cooked over a fire is commonplace.

When applied to modern endurance athletes, the key component is the need to return to a simpler, natural diet. Deciding to adhere to one movement or another would be a personal decision. What is most important is that you make changes gradually, eat when you are hungry, and keep your diet balanced, nutritious, and as devoid of processed, packaged food as possible.

Vegan and Vegetarian Runners

Vegan and vegetarian athletes can substitute certain foods for others to accommodate their needs. These runners need to be especially conscious of getting enough calories, iron, and other essential vitamins in their diets. Plant-based foods are usually not as high in calories as meat-based ones, so greater quantities of food must be consumed for the same amount of nutrients. Plant-eaters also need to ensure that their diet is still rich in quality carbohydrates.

TIP TOES

Vegetarian and vegan endurance athletes are often acutely aware of their dietary needs. If you are vegan or vegetarian and wish to learn more about sports nutrition, consider reading *Vegetarian Sports Nutrition,* by D. Enette Larson-Meyer, and *Thrive: The Vegan Nutrition Guide to Optimal Performance in Sports and Life,* by Brendan Brazier.

Iron deficiency is one of the leading causes of fatigue for both female and male athletes. The best way to avoid iron deficiency is to eat foods that are naturally high in iron, such as fortified cereal, enriched grains, leafy-green vegetables, dried fruits, legumes, nuts, and seeds. It is beneficial to consume iron with vitamin C, which aids iron absorption. Before considering an iron supplement, consult your doctor.

Vegetarians may also have problems getting all the vitamins runners need to perform well, most noticeably those of the B-complex variety, including thiamin, riboflavin, niacin, biotin, pantothenic acid, vitamin B_6, vitamin B_{12}, and folate. One solution may be a multivitamin. Some nutritionists recommend consuming multivitamins or supplements of organic origin and not those made chemically. If you want to get these vitamins and minerals from food-based sources, increase your intake of whole grains, leafy-green vegetables, and legumes.

Eating Disorders in Runners

Eating disorders are most common in female athletes but not uncommon in males. They can wreak havoc on your health, running goals, and livelihood. The Female Athlete Triad is an affliction coined by the American College of Sports Medicine that focuses mostly on the issues of amenorrhea, disordered eating, and osteoporosis in women. The condition is almost always associated with issues related to nutrition and exercise.

Amenorrhea involves the loss of menstruation for three or more months after several regular cycles. Amenorrhea is most often a direct result of an estrogen deficiency, which is a big problem because estrogen plays an important role in calcium absorption and ensures bone growth and maintenance. A lack of estrogen can lead to osteoporosis.

Disordered eating does not necessarily have to be extreme, such as starving oneself. It can also be an unhealthy preoccupation with body image that leads to restrictive eating habits. It is important for athletes to fuel their bodies correctly, not avoid calories to lose a few pounds. The low energy consumption and high energy output, if not halted, can lead to amenorrhea.

Osteoporosis occurs when one has a loss of bone density, which leads to more fragile bones and a higher likelihood for injury, overuse trauma, and stress fractures. In women, this can lead to a serious weakening of the hips or pelvis. Premature osteoporosis is especially dangerous because of potential permanent bone loss.

These issues pose a great problem to barefoot runners. Exerting more energy than you put into your body will eventually cause trouble. And, because of the foot's makeup of nearly 100 bones, 26 muscles, and tightly woven tendons and ligaments, not eating properly can result in several foot-related problems that would normally heal or be made stronger in well-nourished athletes. You have to eat healthy to keep your feet healthy.

Be sure to get enough calories, protein, fat, iron, and calcium to keep your body healthy and injury-free. If you struggle to balance nutrition and activity, sometimes only a slight modification in your training schedule or diet is necessary to get your body back on track. Do not be afraid to talk with a doctor or registered dietician about any of the problems you might be having.

For more information about eating disorders in athletes, check out the following:

- National Eating Disorders Association (www.nationaleatingdisorders.org): This site provides information about eating disorders and body image, as well as resources and a referral network.

- BodyPositive (www.bodypositive.com): Dedicated to boosting body image at any weight.

- Female Athlete Triad Coalition (www.femaleathletetriad.org): An organization dedicated to building awareness and preventing the Female Athlete Triad by promoting good health and well-being for all female athletes.

Nutrition for Senior Athletes

As you age, your body processes the food you ingest at a different rate. Both young and old athletes should be conscious of their own particular dietary needs and how their bodies handle certain foods. Mature athletes whose metabolisms have slowed will not require the same number of calories as athletes in their 20s, for example, but they still need to maintain a high-caloric intake that fuels their day-to-day activities.

Older athletes have the same dietary needs as younger ones, but they need to be especially mindful of fat consumption. Older athletes have a harder time burning off excess fat compared to younger runners. Older athletes also need to maintain high levels of protein that reflect their muscular recovery needs.

In addition, senior runners should monitor hydration more closely than younger ones. The runner's body can deal with dehydration much easier in its 30s in comparison to its 60s. Older runners should get plenty of water the night before, the day of, during, and after exercising.

Vitamins and Supplements for Runners

It can be difficult to take in all the right nutrients. Many people, whether they are runners or not, supplement their everyday diet with tablets, pills, or gel caps containing an assortment of vitamins, minerals, oils, or other animal, plant-based, or manufactured products. Ironically, sifting through aisles of supplements can actually take longer than shopping for high-quality foods in grocery stores or at farmers' markets.

If you have a choice, choose wholesome, organic, and natural foods over pills any day. This lets your body choose what it needs and doesn't need for tissue maintenance, repair, and growth. Neither well-informed personal trainers nor coaches recommend overdoing supplements. Being active and eating correctly allows you to understand how your body works. Adding to or supplementing your nutrient intake can throw off homeostasis, or the equilibrium of internal systems.

Nonetheless, certain supplements can help runners stay healthy, feel more energetic, and stay mobile. Getting sufficient vitamin C, E, and K seems to help athletes recover more quickly from the damage that running long distances or training intensely can cause. It also appears to help prevent sickness, especially in the respiratory system. Because eating large amounts of fruits, beans, and vegetables may still not be enough for some athletes, they can use supplements to round out a complete diet.

As mentioned previously, before you begin a regimen of vitamins or attempt to supplement your existing diet in any way, seek the advice of a qualified professional. Altering even one component of your diet can cause adverse reactions in the body. Fatigue, altered mood, skin rash, and problems with the liver, heart, lungs, and brain can occur. Although not as heavily regulated as prescription drugs, the power of supplements should be taken seriously.

Multiple Benefits of Multivitamins

Multivitamins are a common nutritional supplement. In one dose, the body is supplied with the major vitamins and minerals needed to maintain a healthy body. Some multivitamins also contain antioxidants along with herbal blends. New Chapter (www.newchapter.com) offers organic supplements of high-quality ingredients. Their Every Woman line, for example, consists of whole-food based supplements that add hormonal, immune, and herbal blends specific to women's needs.

Look for a multivitamin that has around 100 percent of the daily value of most of the vitamins listed. Too much of one can affect absorption of another, so you may not need 500 percent of any one nutrient. To optimize absorption with a multivitamin, take the supplement with or after a meal. Keep in mind that multivitamins generally do not contain very much iron or calcium, so some people may need to take an additional supplement. Seek the advice of your doctor in all cases.

Other Supplements to Consider

Many athletes swear by glucosamine, chondroitin, and MSM (methylsulfonylmethane) for their joints. Glucosamine is a building block of joint tissue, while chondroitin helps fight the breakdown of tissue and cartilage in the body. These are usually paired together. Products with and without added MSM are also available. MSM provides naturally occurring sulfur that helps in the production of collagen, which is important for cushioning the joints. Such supplements are available in nearly all general health-food stores, grocery stores, pharmacies, or online.

Fish oil may also benefit runners. Though eating fresh, cold-water fish is the best source of fish oil, supplements are also available that contain doses of omega-3 rich in EPA (eicosapentaenoic acid) and DHA (docosahexaenoic acid), which fight joint-damaging enzymes and reduce joint inflammation. Omega-3 is often paired with omega-6, which is a plant-based oil similar to omega-3.

Vitamins for the Feet

Overly dry skin on your feet can lead to cracks, splits, and nasty infections, none of which are conducive to healthy barefoot running. The most important thing you can do to keep your feet healthy is to stay hydrated, which is not only good for the inside of your body, but for the skin on the top and bottom of the feet, the toenails, and all the muscles, tendons, ligaments, and bones that make up your feet.

Moisturizing the feet can also keep them looking and performing healthily. Use vitamins A, D, and E enriched ointments or balms. Treat the tops of the feet and toes, while using such products sparingly on the bottoms of the feet. Avoid any creams that will cause your foot pads to soften or retain moisture.

Vitamin C is an antioxidant that your body requires for tissue growth and repair. It also strengthens the immune system. Bioflavonoids (or citrin), which are found in fruits such as lemons, grapes, plums, grapefruits, and apricots, also help with tissue repair by strengthening the capillaries, which results in better bloodflow and tissue maintenance for the barefoot runner. They can also be used for anti-inflammatory purposes. Finally, vitamin C benefits the feet greatly as they contain more than half of the body's bones. Keep your bones healthy, and your feet will remain strong, healthy, and happy.

Ch-Ch-Ch-Chia Seeds

Those popular chia figurines (www.chiapet.com) of the 1990s are not only fun to watch sprout but the seeds are good for you, too! Known as "running food," chia seeds are a high-energy endurance food that was even used by the Aztecs!

Chia seeds contain soluble fiber, which helps to slow down the conversion of carbohydrates into sugar. This prolongs the rate at which sugar enters the bloodstream, which provides more long-lasting energy. Additionally, chia seeds absorb several times their weight in water. In your body, chia seeds act as small water and electrolyte reservoirs that help keep you hydrated over a longer period of time during exercise.

Chia seeds are also rich in omega-3, the same beneficial oil found in fish. Moreover, these small seeds pack a protein punch. One does not need to combine them with any other protein source to get the necessary nutrients that would usually come from meat-based products. Chia seeds also contain calcium and iron, along with the full range of B vitamins, making them nearly a perfect food for vegetarians. Have some before or after working out, or as a crunchy snack throughout the day to reap the benefits of the nutrient-packed seed.

These seeds are versatile in how they can be used. When sprinkled into salad, stir-fry, or granola, they are difficult to taste. Some people soak them in their favorite juice or drop them into their fruit salad to help absorb fluids. Dissolved in water, chia seeds turn into a gel that can be eaten by the spoonful or added to pudding or your favorite smoothie recipe.

The Least You Need to Know

- Creating a balanced diet is important for fueling your body, staying healthy, and avoiding injuries.
- It is important to consider what you put in your body before, during, and after a run.
- Some groups of athletes, such as vegetarians, women, and older runners, need to pay close attention to their diets to be sure they are getting all the nutrients they need.
- Glucosamine, chondroitin, MSM, fish oil, chia seeds, and vitamin C can be beneficial supplements for barefoot runners.

Glossary

aerobic activity An exercise of prolonged activity, such as running, swimming, or biking, to improve the cardiovascular system and its ability to transport oxygen sufficiently to the muscles.

anaerobic activity Sports that focus more on strength, quickness, agility, or technique. Football, soccer, basketball, tennis, and even golf might all be considered anaerobic activities.

barefoot running sandals Sandals designed for running with a minimalist approach.

biomechanics The study of the mechanics of living things. It examines what movements occur and the forces that make them happen. Footwear biomechanists study how shoes alter the way you walk and run.

corticosteroids A group of medications that simulate the actions of cortisol, a naturally occurring hormone in the body. In contrast to the muscle-building anabolic steroids, corticosteroids are primarily used for their anti-inflammatory effects.

distance running For the purposes in this book, distance running involves distances of more than 5 km (3.1 miles).

endurance running Involves running at a pace that is sustainable over a longer period of time. Endurance events include extreme events, such as a marathon or ultra-marathon over various terrains.

exertional hyponatremia A disorder that can occur in athletes who drink too much during exercise.

glycemic carbohydrates Carbohydrates that are rated using the glycemic index. Foods that make your blood sugar rise quickly are high on the index, while foods that do not raise insulin levels as much are considered low on the scale.

hip flexor   Skeletal muscles that help you to fully move the femur bone up toward your pelvis. This is a common place for pain or injury in runners, and lightly stretching the hip flexor after you have warmed up (and before a workout) is one way to avoid stiffness later.

lactic acid concentration   Produced and used during exercise, lactate (measured as lactic acid concentration) was once thought to cause soreness and muscle fatigue when produced. Runners who reach their max performance are said to have reached their lactate (or anaerobic) threshold.

lymphatic vessels   Small vessels that drain excess fluid in the tissues and return it to the bloodstream. These lymph vessels pass through lymph nodes where large clusters of white blood cells examine the fluid to determine whether any infection is present.

mid-foot strike   Describes landing flat on the foot in a shoe with a contoured footbed where the forefoot, mid-foot, and heel bear the weight of the landing simultaneously.

molding   The process where the feet slowly change their shape over many years. They will often take on the shape of footwear.

motor skills   Skills that require coordinated movement. Running is an advanced motor skill that is not achieved in childhood until crawling and then walking have been progressively achieved.

OSHA (Occupational and Safety Health Administration)   A division of the U.S. Department of Labor. OSHA regulations are to protect the employers and the employees only, and therefore do not apply to customers or clients who may wish to go barefoot.

periodization   The process of breaking up a training season into specific periods of time. Classic periodization is a pre-planned manner to build up the body, increase intensity, taper down, and control when you will peak, or perform your best.

Pilates   A workout system that focuses on strengthening the core, or torso, of the body and spine. Similar to yoga, Pilates works on the connection of mind and body to promote the exertion of the muscles through graceful movement and breathing.

randomized controlled trial (RCT)   A trial controlled by professionals where half of the study's participants are chosen at random to test a certain variable.

sensory perception   The body's ability to understand the world around it using the sense of touch. This information is collected by nerves, sent with neurons, and processed by the brain. The process is how we "feel" what is around us.

speedwork   A form of training where the runner completes a workout at a faster pace than what is normally run. The pace can be based on past race splits or future goals. Speedwork can vary from one workout to the next, or within workouts.

stress fractures   Hairline cracks that tend to occur over a period of time, also known as fatigue or overuse fractures. They result from too much, unusual, or frequent pressure on a part of the body's frame.

talus bone   A bone found in the tarsus region of the foot that helps to form the lower region of the ankle.

tenderfoot   In the barefoot running world, someone who has yet to get used to running without shoes.

tendons and ligaments   Fibrous connective tissues, which connect bones together. Tendons attach each end of a muscle to the point where it inserts into a bone. They also allow contracting muscles to move two bones closer together. A single ligament will connect two bones together directly. Tendons and ligaments therefore limit how far bones can separate when you move. Then, they elastically return the bones to their resting position when the tension is removed.

topographical map   A representation of an area of the earth drawn to a certain scale that shows contour lines that relate to surface and altitude of a location. They also often relate information about the location of rivers, woods, and areas where people reside.

ventral skin   Barefoot walking (and barefoot hiking) will toughen the foot's ventral skin, or the skin located on the bottom of the foot. Over time, this skin will become used to the elements and will not be as tender.

workload   The total accumulation of frequency, duration, and intensity during training. Measurable on different levels, it is the combination of all three elements over time with sufficient recovery—rather than a focus on one singular facet—that will lead to enhanced, injury-free performance in the long run.

Resources for Barefoot Living

Though you might toss your shoes aside every so often, the majority of people will continue to live in a mostly shod world. A certain percentage, however, will choose to take barefooting to a whole new level by experimenting with the "barefoot lifestyle." This appendix takes a look at what being barefoot a majority of the time is like, provides you with resources to explore the matter further, and helps you connect with other barefooters in the world.

Going Barefoot in Western Culture

"No shirt, no shoes, no service" is a common mantra throughout the Western world. Our society has been led to believe that going barefoot is dangerous and unsanitary. We teach children to wash their hands to keep germs at bay, but we don't tell them to always wear gloves. Asking someone to wear gloves in a store, or staring at someone because their hands are not covered, sounds silly.

More people are learning about the benefits of going barefoot in their daily lives. Some full-time barefooters came to their current realization after discovering the simple joy of going without shoes in other parts of their lives (walking outside, gardening, or going to the beach). Some were tired of suffering recurring foot problems, so they chucked their shoes to alleviate injury, aches, or pain caused by constricting footwear. And a growing percentage of people are becoming barefoot as a result of the barefoot running movement.

Interviews with Barefoot Pioneers

The goal of barefoot living is not to convert the masses to go without shoes full time. It's just to raise public awareness of the benefits of increased barefoot activity. Because it's fun, friendly, and refreshing, barefooters believe it's just another way for society to connect with their surroundings and each other.

In the next few years, going barefoot will hopefully become more accepted in modern society. Pioneers of the shoeless lifestyle have dedicated themselves to teaching others about the benefits of freeing the feet. Here are their stories.

The Primalfoot Alliance

The Primalfoot Alliance (www.primalfootalliance.org) is an organization formed to help raise worldwide awareness and promote a conversation about going barefoot in modern society, whether at work or play. The following interview is with Barefoot Michael Buttgen, founder and president of the organization.

Q: How long have you been living a barefoot lifestyle?

A: I have been a barefooter since the spring of 2005. I first started out driving barefoot in the summers, but then found I liked doing more and more things without shoes. By early 2009, I was a full-time barefooter.

Q: What is your favorite part about being barefoot?

A: I thoroughly enjoy the comfort of letting my feet be free. It really bothers me when I wear shoes, knowing that my feet are caught inside footwear. I am always reminded that they are hot and sweaty. Even wearing sandals is less comfortable than barefoot because I don't have a direct connection to the ground.

Q: What are some challenges you have experienced along the way?

A: The main challenges in going barefoot have come from other people. I have seen a lot of discrimination just because I want to let my feet live free of shoes. There are *so many* people who believe that feet are inherently disgusting, sweaty, and fragile. For many business managers, bare feet are simply a liability and they are convinced that I am going to hurt myself if I do not wear something. Because of that, I have often been asked to put on shoes or leave.

A much lesser challenge has been breaking through my own perceptions of what feet are capable of [doing]. I will admit that there have been times I have said to myself, "I'm not sure *that's* okay to do barefoot." Time after time I find out I was wrong.

Q: How have you handled these challenges?

A: It is important that people be well educated about the benefits of going barefoot while also addressing their concerns. When it comes to discrimination against bare feet, I have always tried to be courteous—but also straightforward and confident. Whenever questioned by management, I have clearly explained why going barefoot is not a risk worth being concerned about. Most of the time this still does not work, but hopefully they will walk away from the situation and reconsider their thoughts on the matter.

I have handled the challenge of my own perceived limitations by pushing myself to try new things and trusting my body to be resilient. I have done things barefoot I never would have thought possible. As time goes on I will do even more. Believing you can do something is often the main factor in actually doing it.

Q: You are the founder and president of the Primalfoot Alliance. What is the organization's mission?

A: The Primalfoot Alliance was founded to create unity behind the cause of advocating against discrimination. I saw that when barefooters made individual pleas for going barefoot, those pleas fell on deaf ears. There is strength in numbers, and that is what we hope to provide. We want to be able to say to these businesses, "Look, there are lots of people who are okay with this; they all believe that what you are doing is wrong and this is why."

Q: How do you think the Primalfoot Alliance is going to change the barefoot (and shod) world?

A: We are going to educate and advocate. We intend to talk with businesses, schools, libraries, public transportation, and other organizations that have been known to discriminate against people who go barefoot. We will show them that the risks associated with going barefoot are very low and the benefits are high.

Our society has promoted shoes as the answer for so long that nobody remembers a time when bare feet or minimal footwear was the norm. If the Primalfoot Alliance can begin to turn the tide and remind people that feet are not meant to just hold footwear onto the ends of our legs, we will really get somewhere. The ultimate goal is not necessarily to convert everyone to go barefoot, but just to make it an acceptable practice; people will be able to go barefoot generally where and when they would like to without the risk of being discriminated against.

Q: Where do you recommend someone who is interested in the barefoot lifestyle start?

A: Start slow. It is crucially important for people who have spent most of their lives in shoes to remember that it will take some time to take their feet back. Feet are magnificent at healing themselves, but as the old saying goes, "Rome wasn't built in a day." I always tell people to start with one step more than they are used to. I know people who never go barefoot inside their own home except to shower and sleep … maybe! To them, I say to take off their socks and shoes, sit on the couch, and just feel the floor. Ball up their toes a few times and then wiggle them around. Do that for a few minutes. This begins reclaiming flexibility and sensation. Eventually they can actually get up and start walking around their house. This begins to reclaim foot strength. If someone is comfortable with all that, they can move outside. Stand barefoot on the sidewalk, deck, or grass and feel it with their soles. The overall point is to slowly and systematically introduce the feet to new things and help feet remember how to be feet.

The final thing I would say is that it is important for everyone to maintain his or her feet and toenails with regular grooming. Ladies should wear nail polish without formaldehyde, DBP, and Toluene and use removers without acetone to prevent nails from drying out, cracking, and being more susceptible to fungus. Actively clean your feet when you bathe and fully dry them off afterward by using a towel and then walking barefoot for a while. If you are already dealing with a fungal infection, consult a health-care provider about the best way to clear it up.

Barefoot in Canada

One might think that going barefoot in Canada would be ill-advised due to long winters. The following is an interview with Barefoot Moe (aka Mauricio Morales), barefoot pioneer, diplomat, and webmaster of Barefoot Canada (www.barefootcanada. org) who has spent the last couple of decades proving Canadians (and the world) otherwise.

Q: How long have you been living the barefoot lifestyle?

A: I have been living predominantly barefooted over the last 15 years. However, I got seriously interested in the barefoot lifestyle about 20 years ago, after I moved from El Salvador to Canada and discovered the online barefooters' associations.

Q: Where do you go barefoot?

A: Pretty much everywhere. I try to incorporate barefooting in my daily routine as much as I can. Unfortunately, there are always social and environmental obstacles that impede me from being barefoot 100 percent of the time. However, I think I manage to be barefooted around 90 percent of my time, year-round. This includes work.

Q: What is your favorite part about being barefoot?

A: I love being truly independent and free of social preconceptions about footwear and feet. I also like getting tough, dirty soles. They are my personal recognition for my chosen lifestyle.

Q: What are some challenges you have experienced along the way?

A: Aside from living in a country where I have to deal with a long and cold winter, all other challenges I face have to do with social stigmas, ignorance, and complete disregard for the benefits of letting one's feet be and develop the way nature intended.

Q: How have you handled these challenges?

A: I can't do much about the winter, so I do the sensible thing and wear protection on my feet when it gets too cold for comfort—the same way I protect other areas of my body during that time.

When it comes to people, I tend to react depending on the situation. If at all possible, I will engage in a dialogue to share some of the knowledge I have acquired over my years as a barefooter. Otherwise, I try to deflect and/or ignore negativity as much as possible, since I don't have the time or the energy to convince people who are completely closed to the idea that going barefoot has any kind of benefit.

Q: How can barefooters best advocate for the lifestyle?

A: I believe that what the barefooting community is lacking all over the world—and especially in the Western Hemisphere—is actual visibility. People can write and share valuable information about our lifestyle in numerous ways but barefooting will always be regarded as a "theory" until we become a common sight in our communities. It is only then that we will get the acceptance we all need in order to truly incorporate our lifestyle in today's society.

Therefore, I think the best way to advocate for the lifestyle is to get out there and just go barefoot, be proud of it, not make any excuses for it, and share the information with anyone who shows interest. It is then that we will truly see the ripple effect we all desire.

Q: Where do you recommend someone who is interested in the barefoot lifestyle start?

A: Getting familiar with the information that all barefooters share through our sites, associations, and publications is a great place to start and get informed.

Personally, I have written a section for barefoot beginners on my site; it can be accessed directly by visiting http://barefootcanada.org/tips-for-beginners.

I also have a good collection of links to other sites that will be of interest to anyone who wants to learn more about barefooting. It can be found at http://barefootcanada.org/links.

Going Barefoot and the Law

One of the major reasons people do not spend more time barefoot in public places is that they believe it is illegal. Businesses can post their own dress codes, but it turns out that what many of us thought were laws against going without shoes are actually recommendations and not written laws.

Driving Without Shoes

There have been no conclusive studies on the dangers of barefoot driving, but some argue that the soles of your feet have less traction than rubber on a shoe. It is therefore surmised that it can be more dangerous to drive without footwear. If you wish to have a better feel for the pedal while barefoot, look into various gas pedal covers, such as the Barefoot Gas Pedal Cover (www.speedwaymotors.com). Although the company that sells these does not endorse barefoot driving, its covers do increase the surface area of the pedal, making it potentially safer for barefoot motorists.

In the United States, each state can stipulate whether barefoot driving is against the law or not. Some states, such as Alabama and Ohio, allow it, while California does not. Most often, it is recommended that you wear shoes for safety. A police officer could, in any state, give you a ticket for reckless or negligent driving if he decides to. If you get a ticket for barefoot driving and the law is on your side, be cordial to the officer, then challenge the ticket in court.

The benefits of driving barefoot are similar to those that you receive elsewhere, namely an increased sensitivity and the possibility of swifter reaction times. Some barefoot drivers claim to get better gas mileage due to their ability to control speeds more precisely—even better than cruise control, which can vary motor speeds too rapidly when going up and down hills. Driving barefoot also allows your feet to breathe. Not only is this healthy, but it also helps keep you cooler. Cooler feet might make you feel cooler all over, which may prevent you from using the air conditioner (another gas waster).

Shoeless Shopping and Dining

As stated before, it is the right of the owner of each business establishment to create his or her dress code, which should be posted clearly in a public place. Many proprietors are not fully aware of the actual regulations regarding people entering without shoes, so they err on the side of caution. To date, no OSHA (Occupational and Safety

Health Administration) regulations or state laws ban shopping or dining without shoes. Furthermore, it has never been shown to be a liability to a business owner. To be certain if you can shop or dine barefoot in your area, contact your local department of health for confirmation.

Many people believe that it is not sanitary to dine without shoes in a restaurant. In reality, it is no less sanitary than walking around in shoes. You probably wash your feet more often than your shoes, right? While we hope this is the case, it is ultimately the proprietor's decision, so if they continue to push the issue, simply take your business to a more barefoot-friendly establishment!

The owners and managers of some shops and restaurants do deserve some credit. After perusing barefoot lifestyle forums and talking to other barefooters, numerous stores (including major department stores and local businesses) do not mind if you enter sans shoes. If the posted regulations do not prohibit it, then go right in. If you are stopped, then it is an opportunity for you to advocate for the barefoot lifestyle and possibly enlighten someone about the actual laws and regulations. In the end, if store owners and managers know that they are not liable and it is not against the law, doors welcoming barefoot enthusiasts might open up across the United States.

Dealing with Shoddy Treatment

Going barefoot in society is still perceived as strange, uncouth, and unhygienic. When one decides to go barefoot in public, some may stare, whisper, point, or comment. Most will simply ignore it.

Because barefooters are currently the minority, it is important to remain steadfast when an incident arises. A premise of the movement is to educate people about the benefits of strong, resistant, and healthy feet, and if you choose to go barefoot in public places, you are choosing to be an ambassador of the movement. The few people who do talk with you will hopefully digest what you have to say and read and research for themselves. They might even free their feet someday! Here are some fun ways to respond to the quick reactions of bystanders.

The *Look*

A prolonged stare as if you are an alien from another planet, the *look* is one of the most common reactions that barefooters receive. When passersby stare, seem shocked, or point at your bare feet, you can respond if you wish. One of the best reactions is to simply acknowledge that you are being unconventional by offering a friendly thumbs-up.

"Where are your shoes?"

If someone asks you where your shoes are, you could tell them that you choose to live a barefoot lifestyle—your feet are happier for it.

"Don't your feet hurt?"

One of our favorite responses to this question is from Barefoot Ken Bob Saxton who states, "Not since I stopped wearing shoes!"

"What if you step on something?"

Tell them that most barefooters have a wonderful set of tools to navigate terrain—their eyes! This might also be a good time to seriously explain that you began walking and running barefoot, your reaction time has increased, your soles have become tougher, and you avoid minor hazards just like you would if you were wearing shoes. Besides, nails and chewing gum pose a certain threat with or without shoes.

Keep Your Feet on the Ground

All in all, it is best to avoid reacting negatively when possible. If you wish to go barefoot but want to avoid confrontation, the best tactic might be to simply enter an establishment wearing shoes or sandals and ask for a quick meeting with the manager or owner. If it is a local operation and you frequent it often, let the manager know that you are a valued customer and would like to discuss entering without shoes.

The person may not give you a direct answer right away; she might have to contact the health board, talk with lawyers, and look further into your cause. Be willing to come back (still wearing shoes) to discuss the issue further. This might give you time to do a little research yourself. Visiting in person is better than discussing the issue on the phone—you will want your sincerity to show.

Another tactic is to enter an establishment with sandals and then simply remove them when you are walking amongst the shelves. You can carry them in hand (soles facing each other to prevent dirt from getting on your hands) or toss them in your tote bag. If someone stops you, talk to him or her openly about the situation. If a store clerk asks you to put on your footwear, you might ask politely to speak with the manager. If you make no headway, simply put your sandals back on. Avoid sneaking into a place without shoes that explicitly does not allow the practice. Doing so might add to the already substandard treatment that many barefooters receive.

One of the best places to get used to going shoeless is to frequent businesses near the beach, if you live near the coast or are on vacation. However, as mentioned, places are more likely to post signs to the contrary. While away from home, you might find it easier to work through some of your barefoot barriers while in public. However, doing so where you live might be better as you can become an advocate for your community, which is where real change begins.

Another place to practice going barefoot is your local mall. Join the mall walkers in the morning to help spread the word. In the wintertime, this is also a nice place to jog to keep your feet used to the harder surfaces. If you are asked about not wearing shoes, mentioning that you are a barefoot enthusiast might be more beneficial to your cause. If you are not inside any stores, you should have the right to go barefoot in public corridors. Talking to the mall manager before going barefoot might be a good idea. Explain that you represent a barefoot club (if this is the case) and your group would love to share the public space, just as other groups do, free from discrimination.

If you are traveling to other countries, then going shoeless may or may not be seen as acceptable. If possible, learn to recognize signs in the local language that prohibit entering barefoot. Explaining the barefoot lifestyle in another language might spark an interesting conversation, but try to avoid confrontations and always wear a smile.

Adding to Barefoot Michael Buttgen's advice, enter an establishment with confidence, in suitable dress, with your feet properly groomed. If approached, speak calmly when confronted by clerks, security guards, or managers. Not many of us have feet suitable for modeling, but keeping them looking their best will help to educate the public and business owners that going barefoot is safe, natural, and beautiful.

Top 10 Barefoot Quotes

If you are looking for a barefoot slogan or quote to share and possibly live by, here are a few of our favorites:

1. "Set your feet free, and your mind will follow."
   —*Society for Barefoot Living*

2. "Shoes? I don't need no stinkin' shoes!"
—*Barefoot Ken Bob Saxton*

3. "Changing the running world one odd look at a time."
—*Barefoot Runners Society*

4. "Run, naturally."
—*www.Barefoot-Running.us*

5. "The human foot is a masterpiece of engineering and a work of art."
—*Leonardo da Vinci*

6. "A grown man, barefoot, walking on mousetraps, just to get an audience to laugh. It's sad in a way."
—*Colin Mochrie*

7. "If I had my life to live over, I would start barefoot earlier in the spring and stay that way later in the fall."
—*Nadine Stair*

8. "He that goes barefoot must not plant thorns."
—*English Proverb*

9. "The shoemaker's son always goes barefoot."
—*Ancient Proverb*

10. "I saw nothing out of the ordinary in running barefoot, although it seemed to startle the rest of the athletics world."
—*Zola Budd*

Be a Barefoot Diplomat

Numerous individuals and groups are currently promoting the barefoot lifestyle. You don't have to alter who you are or even add the title "Barefoot" before your name to be a *real* barefooter—although it is fun to see how it sounds. You do not even have to be a part of any organization to be an advocate. No matter where barefooting takes you, however, you should strive to be a barefoot diplomat.

Learn to deal with various scenarios, questions, and reactions from others. While making a joke is fun, choose your conversations carefully. Barefoot Moe's tactic is to take his time to advocate his perspective, but only to those who ask sincere questions. When he encounters people who are sarcastic, close-minded, or not really interested, he carries on without paying much attention. Being able to keep your cool, smile, and talk with others sensibly is an art that becomes easier over time.

Start out slow and find your own way in the barefoot world. Join a group if you would like to learn more or meet other barefooters, and keep reading, researching, and trying new things. If you are approached by someone who asks you a question, it is important to be honest and tell him that running or simply going barefoot is something you have heard a lot about and you are giving it a try. Hopefully the individual takes off his shoes and joins you for a few minutes. Being a barefoot diplomat is simple but something for which you should plan ahead. Introduce your feet to a variety of areas over time, and enjoy the world up close and personally.

Resolving to go barefoot does not have to be for any one purpose, such as running, walking, or challenging society. It does not mean that you have to go without shoes forever, or even all the time. It can be for the pursuit of a healthier you or to shed daily stress. Ultimately, taking off your shoes is a collective expression of your ability, willingness, and desire to connect with others and the earth at a point where nature and humanity find common ground.

The Future of Going Barefoot

The future of barefoot activity for the masses is bright. Barefoot running, which was viewed as a passing fad, is becoming an accepted way of exercising more naturally. Though it was considered uncivilized to walk in public places without shoes, going barefoot is, in fact, gaining acceptance. A society that once believed feet to be unsanitary, dirty, and unpleasant will continue to see and hear about the benefits of allowing the feet to strengthen, move freely, and reconnect with the earth.

The idea of spending more time barefoot in your daily life is catching steam. Open-minded medical professionals are approaching the barefoot movement with their own ideas, and the experts who have dedicated their lives to learning all they can about the human body recognize the masterpiece that is the bare foot. Because of this, small companies are paving the way to barefoot-friendly apparel.

Unfortunately, only a handful of shoe manufacturers are listening. Larger corporations are following an older model in design, manufacturing, and marketing. Their products will still flood the market, but their firm grip on the consumer may fade over time. Those who hear of the barefoot movement may begin searching for alternatives to their regular, mainstream brands. No longer do societal fears or shoe companies have the liberty to control both our bodies and minds. The future of barefoot living lies in promoting education, growth, and choice.

Those who have embraced the barefoot movement are doing a wonderful job of spreading the word. Websites run by doctors, runners, hikers, and other barefoot types are detailing their own anecdotes and findings about how going barefoot is healthy. The progress may be slow, but it is definitely steady, especially with the advent of online and in-person social networking. People are hearing, thinking, reading, researching, and trying theories out for themselves. The future of going barefoot depends upon individuals willing to share what they have learned.

Barefoot Parks

One interesting way that the joy of barefoot activity is being spread is through private or community-funded barefoot parks (or, on a lesser scale, reflexology paths). Common in a handful of European countries, barefoot parks are places where both kids and adults can get together to enjoy, explore, and learn about the world around them using their feet. One outstanding source is Barfuss Park (www.barfusspark. info/en), which lists "theme parks for healthy, free feet." The site also has a section dedicated to design methods for constructing your own barefoot park or "foot sensation trails" that you can build for local events and easily dismantle following the festivities.

Barefoot Children

The barefoot movement also targets parents to teach them the benefits of increased barefoot activity for their children. When your kids are beginning to walk, the last thing you should do is strap restrictive shoes on their growing feet. If children spent more time barefoot, even up until high school, they would suffer less potential trauma later in life. For starters, their feet would not mold to constrictive footwear, staving off bunions, unnatural bending of the toe joints (which affects the toes, causing "hammer toes"), or muscle, ligament, and tendon atrophy.

Podiatrist Ray McClanahan emphasizes the importance of properly aligned toes in keeping feet healthy. His research indicates that most shoes on the market today cause the wearer to over-pronate, inducing foot problems later. That's one major reason kids need to go barefoot now. Growing up barefoot allows children's feet to develop naturally and support the movements of their bodies. Additionally, you must not hinder babies' nerves from sensing the ground, which aids in the development of their balance and control. As they continue to mature, while the need for certain protection is obvious, you need to choose shoes that allow their feet to feel, expand, and flex with the ground.

Parents for Barefoot Children (www.unshod.org/pfbc) is dedicated to parents who want to learn more about the benefits of allowing their kids to go barefoot. This site is rich with research, photos, solid advice, and information. Not just for parents, this is a definite must-read for everyone interested in barefooting!

Finding Fellow Barefooters

Learning more about the barefoot lifestyle and connecting with other barefooters has been made easier with the advent of websites and on-the-ground organizations dedicated to bringing people together. Certain places in the United States, such as Boulder, Colorado, and various spots in California, are hot spots for barefooters. If you find a local barefoot running or lifestyle community, contact them for more information. Other resources include the following:

The Society for Barefoot Living (www.barefooters.org), a group of people who are committed to going barefoot pretty much everywhere. The site is designed as a forum for the barefoot community to support one another and as a place to meet other members. The group's mission is to promote barefoot acceptance worldwide.

The Barefoot Runners Society (http://barefootrunners.org). The website connects barefoot runners based on location so that they can run and socialize together.

Meetup.com (www.meetup.com) is a popular spot to find groups of people interested in various activities. The idea behind the site is to connect online and then meet up in real life to do activities together. It is easy to locate and join barefoot running and lifestyle groups.

Barefoot Clinics and Workshops

Barefoot running clinics and workshops are springing up across the country. Many local running groups host barefoot workshops, and, ironically, even some running stores (perhaps interested in selling minimal footwear) are beginning to sponsor barefoot runs for their clients. Here is a listing of sites offering more information about where to find a session near you.

Barefoot Running (www.barefoot-running.us) is a barefoot running and minimal footwear platform full of quality articles, videos, and information aimed at educating and promoting barefoot activities for everyone.

Barefoot Running University (www.barefootrunninguniversity.com), started by ultra runner Jason Robillard, offers workshops to those wanting to learn more about barefoot running, training, and living. He also published a helpful booklet available on the site.

RunBare Running Clinics (www.runbare.com), led by well-known barefoot runner Michael Sandler, is based in Colorado where Michael coaches the Boulder Running Club. He has led clinics across the United States, so check out his website for more information. He also recently published his own book about barefoot running.

Barefoot Ken Bob (http://barefootkenbob.com) went barefoot long before the barefoot running or lifestyle movement came along. He has been featured in numerous running glossies, radio shows, and TV stations. Throughout his career as a barefoot runner, he has posted some of the best tips, advice, and commonsense methods on his website. Ken lives in Huntington Beach, California, and offers year-round clinics in the area, but he also offers workshops in other areas of the United States. Check his event calendar for dates and locations.

Other Barefoot Resources

America's Podiatrist (www.americaspodiatrist.com)
Based in the Heartland of the United States, Dr. Michael Nirenberg is one of the leading podiatrists in the nation backing the benefits of increased barefoot activity. His blog posts make for interesting, eye-opening reading.

Barefoot Running Shoes (www.barefootrunningshoes.org)
Reviewing all the exciting new barefoot running shoes available, this is a good place to find some discounts on any minimal footwear you might like to try.

Barefoot Ted McDonald (www.barefootted.com)
A personality and leader in the barefoot running movement, Barefoot Ted has several adventures worth following!

BarefootRunner (www.barefootrunner.com)
A great website with minimal footwear reviews and more information on running more naturally and healthy living.

Birthday Shoes (www.birthdayshoes.com)
One of the most popular minimalist footwear sites online, you will find reviews of shoes, along with useful guides about different models being released.

Living Barefoot (www.livingbarefoot.info)
One of the best barefoot living sites out there, one of the best features here is "The Living Barefoot Show." Conducting radio-style interviews with well-known names in the barefoot world, you will learn more than ever about barefoot activity in all facets of life.

Minimalist Running Group (groups.google.com/group/huaraches)
Founded by Barefoot Ted, the forum is gathering more members daily offering practical advice for those running in bare feet or minimalist footwear.

Running Barefoot (www.barefootrunning.fas.harvard.edu)
A study led by Dr. Daniel Lieberman at Harvard University, his work has opened the floodgates to theories surrounding the pros (and possible cons) of barefoot running.

Running Quest (www.runningquest.net)
A great all-around running site, this site will teach you about natural running form and barefoot running.

Barefoot Journal and Event Log

Weekly Barefoot Journal

	Monday	Tuesday	Wednesday	Thursday	Friday	Saturday	Sunday
Date							
Weather							
Activity							
Route							
Distance							
Physical							
Mental							
Notes							

*Physical and mental score 1–5; a score of 1 being excellent and a score of 5 being extremely sore/fatigued/stressed.

Week of:

Planned Time/Distance:
Actual Time/Distance:
Planned Terrains:

Barefoot Objectives:
1.
2.
3.

Overview:
Weekly Barefoot Time:
YTD Barefoot Time:
Total Physical Score:
Total Mental Score:

Other Notes:

Barefoot Event Log

Event Name	
Event Date	
Event Location	
Distance of Event	
Weather	
Main Objectives	
Physical Notes	
Emotional Notes	
Positive Points	
What to Improve	
Other Notes	

Index